W9-BYK-068

THE YANKEE COMANDANTE

ALSO BY MICHAEL SALLAH AND MITCH WEISS
Tiger Force: A True Story of Men and War

ALSO BY MITCH WEISS (AS COAUTHOR)
Hunting Che: How a US Special Forces Team Helped Capture the World's Most Famous Revolutionary
No Way Out: A Story of Valor in the Mountains of Afghanistan

THE YANKEE COMANDANTE
The Untold Story of Courage, Passion, and One American's Fight to Liberate Cuba

MICHAEL SALLAH AND MITCH WEISS

LYONS PRESS
Guilford, Connecticut
Helena, Montana
An imprint of Rowman & Littlefield

Lyons Press is an imprint of Rowman & Littlefield

Distributed by NATIONAL BOOK NETWORK

Copyright © 2015 by Michael Sallah and Mitch Weiss

Map: Alena Joy Pearce © Rowman & Littlefield

British Library Cataloguing-in-Publication information available

Library of Congress Cataloging-in-Publication data available

ISBN 978-0-7627-9287-0 (hardcover)

∞™ The paper used in this publication meets the minimum requirements of American National Standard for Information Sciences—Permanence of Paper for Printed Library Materials, ANSI/ NISO Z39.48-1992.

To our wives and children

God may save all, but human rescue is only for a few.
—SAUL BELLOW

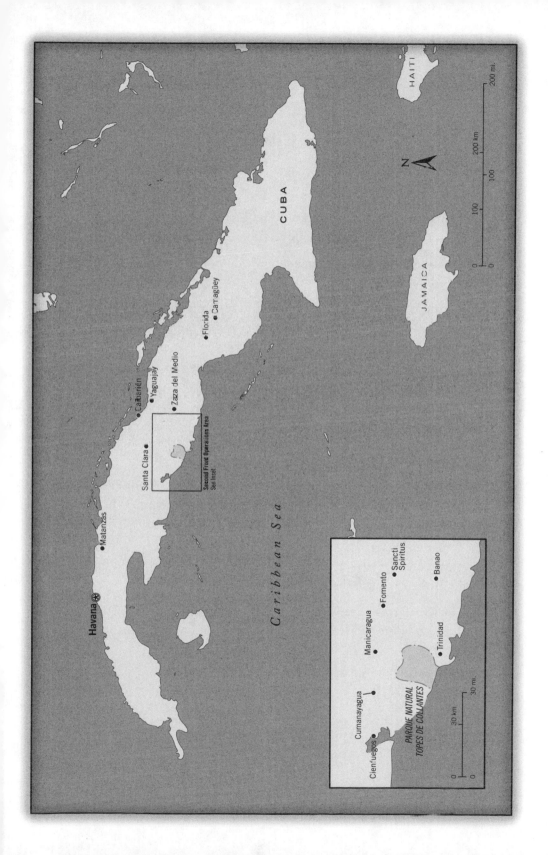

Cast of Characters

Morgan later wrote about Lorenzo's bravery in a letter published by the *New York Times*.

William Morgan: leading figure of the Cuban revolution and the only American to achieve the rank of comandante, the highest command level in the rebel forces. Known as the *Yanqui comandante*, he later organized a movement against the new revolutionary government after Fidel Castro began forging ties with the Soviet Union.

Domingo Ortega Gomez: captain whose rebel team intercepted enemy soldiers during the final days of the fighting and stopped them from escaping.

Pedro Ossorio Franco: former member of Castro's intelligence unit sent to spy on Morgan, but who eventually sided with Morgan and threw his allegiance to the Second Front. He was also later charged with trying to overthrow the government and sentenced to thirty years in prison.

Roger Redondo Gonzalez: captain and intelligence officer who warned Morgan in 1960 that Soviet military advisers were arriving in Cuba.

Olga Rodriguez Farinas: popular student leader and protester forced to flee to the central mountains during the revolution. Morgan's second wife, she spent eleven years in prison, leading hunger strikes and spending much of her time in solitary confinement. After her release, she moved to Morgan's hometown of Toledo, Ohio, in 1981, where she waged a campaign to restore Morgan's citizenship and return his remains to America for reburial.

Roger Rodriguez: rebel fighter and medical doctor who escorted Morgan to the mountains to fight for the Second Front.

26TH OF JULY MOVEMENT

Fidel Castro Ruz: charismatic founder of the Cuban revolution who led the fighting from his base in the Sierra Maestra mountains in 1958. Known as the "Maximum Leader," Castro served as prime minister and president until illness forced him from office in 2008. A virulent anti-American, he was leery of Morgan's growing popularity with the Cuban people and tried to bounce Morgan from the post-revolutionary forces.

Raúl Castro Ruz: younger brother of Fidel, who became one of the most important figures in Cuba's leadership. An avowed Communist since the early days of the revolution, he bitterly opposed any recognition of the Second Front, calling for the entire unit to disband. As of 2008, he is president of Cuba.

Ernesto "Che" Guevara de la Serna: Argentinian physician and avowed Marxist who joined the Castro brothers to help lead the revolution. During the fighting, he tried unsuccessfully to take over the Second Front before the final campaign that drove Batista from power. He later clashed with the Second Front leaders over their pro-Democratic stance and tried to strip them of their ranks.

OTHER REBELS

Faure Chomón Mediavilla: leading student rebel and Second Front supporter who broke with the unit over its decision to wage war in the mountains rather than taking the fight to Havana. After the revolution, Castro appointed him ambassador to the Soviet Union.

TARGETS OF THE REVOLUTION

Fulgencio Batista y Zaldívar: Cuban leader who seized control of the government in two separate military coups, the first in 1933 and the second in 1952. A populist leader in his early years, he later forged ties with US businessmen and mobsters, reaping millions in kickbacks while cracking down on his opposition through torture and imprisonment. He fled the country on January 1, 1959, after the rebels took control of Santa Clara and the Escambray mountains. He died in exile in Spain in 1973.

Manuel Benítez: corrupt chief of Cuba's national police under Batista, who fled to Miami and later became a key informant for the FBI.

Antonio Regueira: Batista army lieutenant whose prolonged shootout with Morgan in the battle of Charco Azul underscored the tenacity of both sides in the early months of the revolution.

Ángel Sánchez Mosquera: tenacious Cuban army colonel who fought numerous battles with the rebels in the Sierra Maestra mountains before being sent to the Escambray mountains to stem the rebel incursion.

Francisco Tabernilla Dolz: Cuban general and army chief under Batista whose demoralized forces struggled against the rebels, prompting him to declare that the war was lost well before the final surrender.

THE TRUJILLO CONSPIRACY

Augusto Ferrando: Dominican consul in Miami and bagman for Trujillo who helped the dictator devise the plan to overthrow the Castro government with Morgan's help.

Rafael Trujillo Molina: longtime dictator of the Dominican Republic who hatched a plot to overthrow the Castro government in 1959 with the help of Morgan. Trujillo put a $100,000 bounty on Morgan's head after discovering that the American had served as a double agent for Castro.

Ricardo Velazco Ordóñez: Spanish priest and Trujillo operative who helped the dictator plan the conspiracy against Castro and convinced Trujillo the plot would succeed.

AMERICANS

Dominick Bartone: Cleveland organized-crime figure who supplied guns and a plane to Trujillo in the plot to overthrow Castro.

Ellen Mae "Terri" Bethel: Morgan's first wife, whom he met while working in a Florida circus in the 1950s. She filed for divorce in 1958, three months after he left for Cuba. They had two children: Anna and William Jr.

Philip Bonsal: career US diplomat and last American ambassador to Cuba, who fed information to the FBI about Morgan's activities in Cuba.

Frank Emmick: CIA operative from Ohio who helped finance Morgan's venture to breed fish and frogs in Cuba for sale to American restaurants.

J. Edgar Hoover: director of the FBI, who became obsessed with Fidel Castro's rise and Morgan's role in helping Castro stay in power.

Alexander Morgan: father of William Morgan, who agonized over his son's decision to fight in the Cuban revolution.

Loretta Morgan: mother of William Morgan, who tried to stop his execution and later pushed to restore his US citizenship and to return his remains to America for reburial.

Frank Nelson: CIA and mob operative who first approached Morgan about carrying out an assassination of Castro for one million dollars.

Leman Stafford Jr.: veteran FBI agent ordered to track Morgan's movements between Miami and Havana in 1959 and 1960.

Introduction

Darkness had enveloped La Cabaña, the ancient prison fortress near Havana Bay. Most of the inmates had been ordered to their bunks, and most of the death sentences had been carried out without a hitch. But the commanding officers instructed the guards to remain alert. The firing squad stood gathered at the craggy, bloodstained wall outside, waiting. No one from the chapel area—God's waiting room—would see morning.

William Alexander Morgan, his thick arms bound by handcuffs, walked down the long, dark hall, past the cells of inmates huddled in their own filth. At his side, the priest hurried to keep up. They passed the chapel where Morgan had knelt in darkness the night before and whispered his prayers. At the guard station, uniformed men gathered to watch the prisoner and the priest. The guards would make sure that Morgan didn't see dawn. They had swung open the exit door. There, his escorts were waiting to whisk him away.

The stone-walled hallway narrowed between the chapel and the center of the prison and then opened to the inner courtyard and the dark sky. As they passed the next station, Morgan and the priest were met by more guards eyeballing them. Rarely had a prisoner captured so much attention in Fidel Castro's prison, where more than 597 men had been hauled to their deaths since the revolution ended two years before. But rarely had the prison housed anyone like Morgan. Even the guards stepped back as the muscular, six-foot-tall prisoner walked by, oblivious to those around him.

He was the *Yanqui comandante.*

Two years earlier, he had been a hero of the revolution. He had won the hearts of millions of Cubans by helping to liberate them from a brutal dictator. Not since Theodore Roosevelt charged up San Juan Hill had an American captured the imagination of the country like this. He had come to Cuba for adventure, but he wound up leading a ragtag band of rebels to a series of stunning victories that forced military dictator Fulgencio Batista y Zaldívar from power.

Morgan's image—wild beard, blond hair, powerful build—splashed across magazines and newspapers, joining Castro and Che Guevara as icons of a revolution celebrated around the world.

Young boys kept trading cards of him, women begged for his autograph, movie producers tried to track him down, and writers wanted to tell his life story. In America, he verged on celebrity. But William Morgan was more than a celebrity.

No one—not the guards, not the priest, not the prisoners who bunked with him in the hot, cramped dorm known as Gallery 13—knew how much lay at stake beyond these eighteenth-century prison walls. Castro was forging alliances with the Soviet Union, and America was about to lead a secret invasion to oust him from power. The plan was in place, the strike just five weeks away. While US-backed forces landed on the southern coast, Morgan and others would lead an insurrection in the central mountains.

Morgan already had stashed hundreds of rifles, hand grenades, and machine guns in safe houses. Soon he would hand them out to a small army of rebels who had been hiding in the mountains for months. During those months, he had been drilling them: push-ups, sit-ups, jumping jacks, target practice. The plan was risky—treacherous to some of the planners—but with Morgan and other rebel leaders in the Escambray mountains to fight Castro's forces, it stood a chance. If the plan succeeded, it would remove the threat of a Communist nation just ninety miles from America's shores.

The Kennedy White House had been monitoring Morgan's trial. So had J. Edgar Hoover, whose FBI agents had been tracking the Americano's movements inside La Cabaña. The CIA had sent its own agents to Havana to keep watch.

At the end of the hall, the door slammed behind him and the priest. If the rebel forces could spring him, if Tony Chao and the others could reach La Cabaña in time . . .

In the distance glittered the lights of Havana, a city on the brink.

Olga Morgan leaned down, pulled her two little girls close, and held them tightly. This was going to be difficult. It could be days—weeks, even—before she would see them again. But she had to get out.

She gazed for a moment at Loretta and Olguita and then walked past the fountain and sweeping arches of the embassy to the car. The driver had popped the trunk. Without hesitating, she raised one leg over the side, then the other, rolling onto the floor of the trunk. As planned, she turned on her side, curled into a ball, and nodded. The door slammed shut.

Darkness.

She could hear the driver's door close. The engine started. *Prisa, por favor.*

Hurry.

The messenger had just left the embassy and told her that she needed to leave. Morgan was going to escape. She needed to reach the safe house in Camagüey, where he would meet her. There wasn't much time. If everything went as planned, her husband would be free and on his way to the mountains. The Brazilian ambassador had warned her not to leave the embassy. She could be arrested, beaten, or worse by the G2, Castro's secret police.

But Morgan had always come through for her. He would come through again. No one could separate them.

She had wanted him to leave after the revolution so they could raise their two daughters in peace, even if that meant moving to America. But he wouldn't do it.

"I can't leave my boys," he said of the men who served with him in the revolution. Thousands of rebels were waiting in the Escambray, poised for another upheaval, this one more brutal than the last.

Her heart pounded as the car sped through the streets, turning corners, bouncing her back and forth.

The last time she saw him, she held his hand in the prison waiting room.

"I love you," he had said.

If she could survive for fifty more miles, she'd see him again. She had mustered the strength before, and she would do it again.

1

JOSE PAULA WAS WIPING DOWN THE COUNTER OF HIS DOWNTOWN
Miami diner when he spotted the grizzled stranger slip inside. Paula
knew just about all of his regular customers, but he had never seen this
guy before.

Rumpled and unshaven, William Morgan ordered a coffee, ambled
over to a square table with a white tablecloth, and plopped down. It was
not a good time.

In just minutes, people would be gathering inside the hot, stuffy eatery, pulling up chairs, inching up close to one another, echoing a word
that few Americans had ever heard: *revolución*. The restaurant, a recruiting station for the rebel cause, would soon be filled with bearded men in
stained, sweaty fatigues ready to convince young Cubans to return to their
country to fight.

Some of the men were running guns; others were on the streets collecting wads of cash. Paula needed someone to get the Americano out.
FBI agents were crawling all over Miami, looking for any signs of subversive activities.

With the island nation just ninety miles from the shores of the United
States, no country had more of a stake in the outcome. America's national
security was at risk. So was the entire hemisphere's.

Just days earlier, customs agents in Miami had nabbed two men and
seized a cache of weapons—five hundred rifles and fifty thousand rounds
of ammo—bound for Cuba. Trucks were pulling up to marinas at night,
unloading crates stuffed with vintage guns on the backs of the vessels.

Miami had become two places: the shiny postcard image with swanky
hotels, palm-shrouded beaches, and cruise ships, and an ethnic staging
ground for a revolution that was about to explode. Two worlds on a col-
lision course.

Motioning to two young men sitting at the counter, Paula told them
to see what they could do to get rid of the *Yanqui*. As far as Paula knew,
the guy cupping his coffee and dragging on a cigarette could be a US spy.

Edmundo Amado Consuegra, a thin sixteen-year-old with deep-set eyes, walked over to Morgan, nodded, and then sat down. After an awkward moment, he began to ask Morgan questions in broken English, but Morgan just shrugged.

A buddy of Amado's came over to the table and sat down. Tony Chao Flores, a tough sixteen-year-old with a temper, was more direct. He looked Morgan up and down, and then asked: "What are you doing in here?"

Morgan glanced up at Chao, and then looked across the room, where all the customers were staring at him. Any other time, he would have told the kid it was none of his business. If it meant a fight, then so be it.

But it had taken a long time to get here, and at this point, he wasn't going to leave. He didn't give a damn what anyone said. Just days earlier, he had walked out of his family home in Toledo, Ohio. It had been the day after Christmas 1957, and his sixty-two-year-old mother pleaded with him not to leave his wife and kids.

He had walked past the lights still glowing on the Christmas tree and the gift wrappings still strewn on the floor. He had walked past his father reading in his library and his two little kids, Annie and Billy, tucked in their beds. He couldn't explain to his wife, Terri, why he was leaving. All it would do was cause a fight in front of everyone.

It was hard enough living in his parents' home with his wife and children. But he couldn't tell them why he was splitting. Upstairs in his room was his last rejection letter from the army, a clear statement that he was not going to be reinstated.

It had been ten years since he was dishonorably discharged and sentenced to prison for going AWOL. Ten years since he was shipped to Milan, a forlorn prison in the frozen cornfields of southeastern Michigan. Ten years since he got out of the joint without a job or any prospect of a future.

He had tried to get back into the army even while he was locked up, but his first effort was turned down. Then he got the second letter in March 1957, telling him that unless they made a legal mistake during the court martial, he was a goner. *Damn it, doesn't anyone understand?* he would say.

Little Billy Morgan in 1934 at age six, playing Cowboys and Indians COURTESY OF
MORGAN FAMILY COLLECTION

The only one who ever understood was his mother, Loretta. Whenever everyone else ignored him in prison, she stuck by him. Even when it drove everyone else crazy in the Morgan household, especially his father, Alexander.

A brilliant engineer and ardent Republican who set up his family nicely in their gabled home in Toledo's fashionable Old West End, Alexander Morgan never understood why his wife gave the boy so many chances. In a neighborhood that included some of the wealthiest families in America—inventors of the spark plug, commercial scale, and Jeep—Billy Morgan was a train wreck.

By the time he was a junior in high school, he had been booted out of two schools and twice ran away from home after getting into scraps. "He liked to pick fights," said his only sibling, Carroll. He was eventually picked up by the cops for carjacking a man and going for a joyride with the guy gagged and bound in the backseat.

Maybe it was the blue marks left on his temples after he was born at the hospital in Cleveland in 1928—the doctor squeezing the forceps too tightly. He was like a blasting cap, ready to explode.

He would spend hours playing his favorite game—army, with make-believe guns and real knives. His mother once stopped him from jumping off the roof of their home with a homemade parachute strapped to his back.

So it came as no surprise when he called her from Arizona with the news shortly after his eighteenth birthday: He had joined the army. On the one hand, it was the sense of adventure, but on the other, he was about to take on responsibilities that went far beyond anything he was prepared to handle.

Loretta had expected him to phone her when he arrived at camp in California, but he had another surprise: He was married. On the way to camp, he met a twenty-one-year-old woman on the train and spent the next twenty-four hours wooing her. When the train stopped in Reno, they hailed a cab at night, woke up a justice of the peace, and spent the next two days in a motel room. "It was such a romantic thing," recalled Darlene Edgerton, who was engaged to another man. "Neither one of us took time to think of the long-term consequences." After they arrived in California, he was sent to Japan and she stayed behind. By the time he settled into his new army life, the marriage was over.

Loretta wasn't happy about the union, but she was more concerned about her son adapting to a military regimen. "I was in for trouble," she recalled. Months later, her fears came true when she got a call from the army's Company B of the Thirty-Fifth Infantry Regiment: Bill had been caught going AWOL and had escaped in dramatic fashion—overpowering a guard, stealing his .45, and forcing him to strip off his clothes so Morgan could disguise himself.

He later told a military court he was trying to help a girlfriend he had met shortly after arriving in Japan. She had become suicidal, he explained. But it didn't matter to the judge.

Morgan was sentenced to five years, first to Camp Cooke in California and later Milan federal prison in Michigan. Unable to adjust, he was labeled a troublemaker. "He is irresponsible, impulsive and untrustworthy," said a disciplinary report. "Does not deserve parole."

Morgan would later tell army psychologists his problems had nothing to do with any childhood issues, but rather a deep sense of boredom. "I was never satisfied with the sameness of anything," he said.

By the time he was released two years later, Edgerton had gotten an annulment and Morgan returned to his parents' home. On the outside, he acted tough, but on the inside, the dishonorable discharge—a black mark in the patriotic 1950s—cut deeply. No one knew his pain more than his mother. She would watch him as he left her home each day to search for work and see the look on his face when he'd return. His prison record kept coming back to haunt him.

For days after his release, he walked the streets. His mother pleaded with the monsignor to give him a job as a janitor at Our Lady, Queen of the Holy Rosary Cathedral, but weeks later, he chucked the broom and went on a bender, drinking with his old street buddies and violating his parole.

He eventually decided to leave Toledo and found his way to Florida, where he landed a stint in the circus. He became a fire-eater, devouring flames in front of heckling audiences during tent shows in the Deep South.

There he met Ellen May Bethel, known as Terri, a petite brunette who played the snake charmer—a favorite in front of drunken crowds. They married in Miami in 1954, and a year later, their daughter, Anne Marie, was born.

Needing a more stable job, Morgan and his family moved into an apartment in downtown Miami, where he landed a job as a bouncer and escort at Zissen's Bowery comedy nightclub. He would dress up as a clown and meet patrons at the curb while occasionally breaking up fights in the bar.

Patrons soon discovered the new bouncer was quick with his hands. Charlie Zissen was working behind the bar one night when three drunks came in and demanded to be served. When the owner refused, one of the men whipped out a knife and was about to plunge it into the old man's back. Suddenly, out of nowhere, Morgan jumped up, slammed the man to the floor, and took away his knife. The three then ran out. "I don't know how he did it," Zissen recalled. "He saved my life."

The Bowery was a hangout for the underground of Miami: gamblers and gun runners. And Morgan soon got to know many of them. One night, a shadowy figure came into the bar to offer Morgan a deal: Help him move guns to the Upper Keys and earn some cash. When Morgan showed up at the designated spot with the weapons, he was met by young Cubans in a boat.

It was his first exposure to a network of men who were joining a fledgling underground movement in their country. Riding in small boats, the men would come up to shore, pile the weapons under tarps and inside oil drums, and then vanish into the night. Their destination: the rebel camps in the mountains of Cuba.

One of the rebels was Roger Rodriguez, a young medical student who had put everything in his life on hold. Sickened by the poverty of his country—people in the mountains suffering from cases of malnutrition and leprosy—Rodriguez had joined the movement spreading across the island. The rebels needed money and they needed guns to fight the soldiers of Cuban dictator Fulgencio Batista y Zaldívar.

Morgan sat in silence, listening to the young intern talk about the desperation of his country. Some of the gun runners would make it to the hills, while others would get caught, never to be seen again. But it didn't stop them.

Morgan couldn't shake the image of the young men on the rickety boats pulling up to the shore under the moonlight. And as he spent more time at the Bowery, his marriage began to unravel. He and Terri were arguing at night. A second baby was on the way.

Both decided it would be better to pack their bags and head to Ohio to try to salvage what was left. But once again, Morgan struggled to find a job. He began venturing alone into the bars along the riverfront, where Toledo's gambling figures cavorted.

After a night of heavy drinking, he woke up and discovered he had nearly beaten a man to death. He swore he would never drink again, but his reputation as a tough guy was growing. He eventually caught the attention of Leonard "Chalky Red" Yaranowsky and Anthony "Whitey" Besase, local mob bosses.

At the time, Toledo—which once hosted the largest casino in the United States—was a mecca for illegal gambling. Gamblers from as far away as Chicago and New York would drop thousands on the crap tables at the Devon Club.

What separated Toledo from other mobbed-up towns was that it was a safe haven for wiseguys to hide out when the heat was on in Detroit and Chicago. Gambling was virtually in the open, with sawdust joints in every ethnic neighborhood and cops who took their share.

Morgan started as a bouncer in the clubs and quickly earned the criminal element's trust. Whenever there was trouble, he would jump in. It wasn't long before he became the muscle, collecting debts for the bosses.

With money in his pocket, he began dressing in suits and carried .38s in each shoulder holster, earning the street name Two-Gun Morgan. He could be intimidating, but also charming—a prankster who would quietly sneak up behind his street buddies and poke a gun barrel in their ribs. "I could have killed you right now," he would say, laughing.

Things were looking up for Morgan until a team of federal agents began to focus on illegal gambling across the country. One of their targets: Toledo. During a nationally televised hearing of a US Senate committee investigating organized crime, a Toledo mobster took the stand and admitted to everything: the clubs, the players, the cops. His confession spurred a massive crackdown, and by 1957, the gaming halls had shut down.

For Morgan, there was nothing left. If he continued to work for the local kingpins, it was just a matter of time before he'd be hauled in by the feds.

One day, he showed up at his parents' door, his wife and kids in tow. "Just for a few days," he said. His mother could never say no. He and Terri moved into his old bedroom down the hall, but nothing went right. The two bickered and on some days didn't even talk.

Morgan would storm out of the house and walk the neighborhood, past the old Victorian mansions and the manicured lawns where he grew up. He would walk by the Ryans and the Rosenblatts, but his buddies who once lived in those homes had moved away, graduating from college and working for the city's Fortune 500 companies.

When Morgan finally walked out of the house the day after Christmas 1957, he had few places to go. He knew he could always return to Miami, where he could crash in an apartment above the Bowery. His old friend Charlie Zissen would never turn him away.

There was something else drawing him back to Miami, something that he couldn't seem to shake. He had never forgotten the young Cubans who had come to shore to pick up guns, and then vanish over the horizon.

News reports of the unrest in Cuba were heating up on television, with footage of demonstrations in the streets of Havana. Morgan didn't know much about the politics in Cuba, but he remembered the look on Roger Rodriguez's face and the passion in his voice when he talked about the struggle to free his country. The young intern could have embarked on a medical career, and yet he was donning fatigues and fighting a war he had little chance of winning.

After arriving in Miami, Morgan walked around the block of the Paula Restaurant several times before venturing inside. He had made his decision.

He knew he would stand out. He had always been impetuous, acting on gut instinct. But this was his only chance of drawing the attention of people who could get him to Havana. All he needed was to get by Tony Chao.

The baby-faced kid with freckles stared across the table at Morgan, demanding to know why he had intruded into their world. If it meant squaring off with him inside the restaurant, Chao was ready. So was Amado.

Morgan could see that it was getting tense. He inched closer to the teenagers. If he could just show that he was on their side, he might be able to get them to listen.

Morgan knew all about the revolution and even helped deliver weapons to the rebels. The more he heard about their struggles, the more he wanted to join their cause, he said.

If they wanted to throw him out after he made his pitch, then so be it. But he had come too far to just walk. He told them that he had served in the army and had gone through combat training. He could fire an M1 with crack precision and take on anyone with his hands and feet. What he didn't tell them was that he was booted from the army before his first year, but no one needed to know.

Amado looked at Chao. First, no one knew this Americano. That was even less of a reason to trust him. From across the counter, old man Paula was still glaring at the table and looking at his watch.

Neither one of the teenagers could afford to make a mistake.

Amado may have already been under watch by FBI agents. He had gone to revolution rallies in Miami that had been attended by undercover agents. At sixteen, a photograph of him at an anti-Batista rally had just appeared in the *Miami News*. He had dropped out of Miami's Robert E. Lee Jr. High School and was working two jobs to save enough money to return to his country and join the barbudos.

Chao had already joined the revolutionary cause, running guns in Havana months earlier until the cops put him on their wanted list. If not for a sergeant who took pity on him and sent him back to Miami, he'd probably be dead. Chao was now itching to return.

While most teenagers in Miami were heading to sock hops, surfing, and dancing to Elvis, Amado and Chao were angry young men in a world where they didn't belong.

Morgan looked up and could see that he wasn't getting anywhere. If he left the restaurant now, there was probably less of a chance he'd be able to connect to the rebels. Then, he would really have nowhere to go.

Like so many other times in his life, he had to think fast. He had better come up with a good one. He had to show them that he had a real reason to throw himself into their fight.

He decided to spin a tale—one that he knew would capture the attention of the teenagers across the table. He said he wanted to go to Cuba to avenge the death of an old army buddy.

It happened during an uprising in March, he said, when a band of rebels stormed the presidential palace. At the time, his friend was standing on a hotel balcony watching the mayhem unfold when he was shot by one of Batista's soldiers. "He wasn't doing anything," Morgan told them.

Morgan said he was devastated by the shooting. His buddy was not just a friend—he had actually saved Morgan's life during combat in

Korea. Morgan had never forgotten. He needed to go to Cuba as much as anyone.

For a moment, everyone at the table was quiet. The teenagers looked at each other, not knowing what to say.

Even as a young man, Amado could see Morgan was hurting. Maybe—just maybe—there was a way they could help. They both excused themselves and walked over to Paula. For several minutes, they talked in the old man's ear and then came back to the table.

The teenagers told Morgan they were getting ready to leave for Cuba, Amado the next day and Chao a week later. Both had saved their money to return to their country and join the revolution.

They might be able to take Morgan with them. But even if they managed to get him to Havana without drawing attention, there was no guarantee they could deliver him to the mountains. And even if they could, he might not be accepted by the guerrillas.

But if this Americano was intent on fighting, they'd find a way to get him there.

2

THE SUN CRESTED OVER THE ROOFTOPS OF SANTA CLARA AS OLGA Rodriguez scurried up the steps of the crowded bus. Clutching the bag to her side, she moved to the back row, head down, and slumped in a seat.

The bus was just seventeen miles from Manicaragua, but she still had to pass by government sentries and roadblocks. She just needed to get the supplies to the rebels—medicine, food, and letters. Then she'd be able to turn around and come back.

Please, God, just get me there, she whispered.

If the Cuban government agents boarded the bus and searched the passengers, she would be yanked off the vehicle, beaten, and more than likely executed. She peeked out the window as the bus began to roll slowly out of the station. Outside, the streets, normally bustling with cars and pedestrians, were now filled with soldiers and guns.

Her friends at the Normal Teachers School in Santa Clara begged her not to do this. But with every passing day, she had been getting pulled deeper into a movement that was burrowing its way into the heart of Cuba.

She had led protests on the steps of the teachers school, where she was elected student government president in 1956. Months later, she was leading walkouts during classes.

The area surrounding Santa Clara had always been a center of political unrest, but in early 1958, it was nasty. For months, fellow students from the Student Directorio had been going missing and turning up dead, their butchered bodies found in ditches. Just weeks earlier, a seventeen-year-old friend of Olga had been tortured so badly by Batista's secret police that his heart gave out.

She found herself roaming to places like Leoncio Vidal Caro Park, spending hours listening to people rail against the government and the leader who had been in place since Olga was born: *Batista.*

What a betrayal.

His name alone was enough to inflame passion among the young students who saw him as a corrupt dictator beholden to US business owners and mobsters. In his quest for power, Fulgencio Batista had cut secret deals with companies like International Telephone and Telegraph and organized crime figures like Lucky Luciano, taking kickbacks and leaving most rural Cubans to wallow in their own misery.

But Olga was oblivious to the companies or the names of American mobsters. All she knew was that Batista was basking in the glory of opulent hotels and gaming houses while just a few hundred miles away, her own people were steeped in poverty without enough medical clinics or schools.

Their biggest disappointment was that Batista had once been one of their own. A mulatto born in 1901 to a poor farming family in Banes—a town dominated by United Fruit Company—Batista knew what it meant to be exploited. And in his first term as president in 1940, he kept his promises to the poor to build schools and hospitals.

To the simple, fun-loving guajiros, Batista was like Benito Juárez—the legendary Mexican president of the nineteenth century who overthrew a corrupt regime and helped rebuild the country to its earlier glory. Batista launched massive public works projects, except none of the wealth he created trickled down to the poor, who watched as the hotels and casinos lit up the Havana skyline.

Though he was defeated for reelection, Batista wasn't going to give up. From his palatial Florida estate, he plotted his return. In 1948, he won election as a senator, and in 1952, he led a coup to take back the presidency. This time, he returned with a vengeance, suspending the Constitution, banning labor strikes, and shutting down press freedoms. He prowled Havana "like a panther," chewing up his adversaries.

He would unleash the dreaded SIM, his secret police, on political opponents and anyone else who mocked his authority. Tired of the abuse, the poor people and students struck back. They began forging underground alliances to rescue their country.

For Olga, her own beginnings in the movement began in her cramped, cinder-block home when her mother would cry in the darkness because she didn't have enough to feed her five children. To Olga, her family was poor and nothing was ever going to change. As a little girl, she would watch as her parents headed to the tobacco shacks, where they would spend hours tying bundles of green leaves, barely earning enough to survive.

But it wasn't the hunger pangs that pushed Olga to the edge of desperation. It was her little brother, Roberto, who haunted her dreams and shattered her soul. When he was just nine, he stepped on a rusty nail while trying to rescue a cat trapped under a bridge during a rainstorm. Three days later, he shook uncontrollably from an infection raging through his body. Olga's parents managed to find someone to donate a tetanus antidote, but days later, they discovered the medicine had long expired.

As he lay in pain in bed at San Juan de Dios Hospital on December 11, 1948, Olga gave him her favorite shirt—slipping it over his shriveled body—before he took his last breath.

She remembered him being laid out in a coffin in her family's home, her mother and sisters sobbing. Then the long walk to the cemetery—seven blocks away—and the procession of people. The entire day, she refused to cry. "When I hurt inside, I can't cry," she recalled.

She tried to act as though she could move on, but the pain was overwhelming, waking her up in the middle of the night. *Roberto, why did you have to die?*

She already knew the answer: Her people were dirt poor, living in a shack with no running water or toilet. They should have been able to buy him the proper medicine to keep him alive.

By the time Olga returned to school, she was angry. No longer was she the little girl who skipped along Calle Independencia, playing with the other children. She became withdrawn—and alone.

She began spending more time talking to dissident teachers about subjects that had never before interested her: politics and war. She knew that Fidel Castro Ruz and his 26th of July Movement were already in the Sierra Maestra mountains, four hundred miles away, leading the cause. But in Las Villas Province, in the heart of the Escambray mountains, this is where the revolution would be won.

Batista's men, who vastly outnumbered the barbudos—the bearded revolutionaries—had armored cars, submachine guns, grenades, and even

B-26 bombers, all courtesy of the American government. If the rebels didn't get more supplies, more weapons, and soon, Batista's men would chase them into the swamps and all would be lost.

They needed a volunteer, someone who could slip in without being caught. Olga had nothing to lose. Her brother was dead. Her family was poor. She wasn't going to finish school. She agreed to board the bus.

She told everyone at the school that she wasn't afraid. But she was terrified. In Havana, police attacked one protester by stripping off her clothes, holding her legs apart, and thrusting a metal rod into her vagina, nearly killing her. When SIM officers barged into her hospital room, nearly a dozen nuns gathered around her bed to protect her. Around the same time, police tortured a young man by tearing off an ear, smashing his foot, and crushing his testicles.

As Olga stared out the bus window, she could see another checkpoint in the distance. The bus began to slow down.

Just look straight ahead, she thought. She counted the seconds. They needed to keep moving. They needed to make it to Manicaragua.

3

WILLIAM MORGAN WAS ABOUT TO HEAD INTO A FOREIGN COUNTRY THAT was sliding into a revolution. He didn't know a soul. He didn't speak the language. He knew nothing about the rebels or the dictator.

And yet, he would soon be boarding an airplane for Havana with everything he owned clenched in his hand.

As he walked into the concourse of Miami International Airport, he looked over and spotted Chao and some others gathered at the gate, all waiting to board the same flight.

For Chao, it was risky to bring Morgan. If he turned out to be a government agent, they could all be in danger. But if Morgan was truthful, he could bring much to the conflict. At twenty-nine, he was older than most of the rebels in the mountains, and with his army training, he could be invaluable.

God knows, they needed some military knowledge.

The young people heading to the mountains knew nothing about combat and even less about guerrilla warfare. *Nada.* And that's what the war in Cuba was about. They had never fired M1s. Or lived in the brush for days on end. Most of them had never killed a man. They did not know what it was like to watch someone's head explode from rapid fire or their guts spill out from a .12-gauge shotgun blast.

It was just a matter of time.

Their generation was like so many others in Cuba that had spawned revolutions over the past hundred years. It happened during the war of independence, when thousands of young Cubans took up arms against the Spanish at the dawn of the twentieth century. No one inspired the youth more than the legendary José Martí, the poet warrior who died in the conflict.

Then there was the revolt against President Gerardo Machado three decades later—eventually leading to the bloodless coup that brought in Batista. The cult of the pistolero would become a rite of passage, a kind of machismo that inspired each generation to rub out the last.

Morgan had only known Chao a few days, but already he could see the blond-haired, blue-eyed Cuban had taken up the torch. Chao and his friends could have been doing anything—going to the beach, getting an education, getting laid—but instead were restless to go home.

Chao's mother moved to Miami to get her brood away from the political turmoil of their country—the classic immigrant story—but the young Cubans weren't interested in blending into the American tapestry. They wanted to move back.

Chao stood next to the others at the gate, the veins bulging in his neck as he jabbed a finger in the air to make another point. As Morgan watched the young Cubano, he saw glimpses of himself as a younger man. "The Americanito," as Chao was called, was like a jitterbug ready to throw himself into the fire.

Maybe, just maybe, Morgan could recover what he had lost. He could reclaim what had slipped away. He gripped his suitcase as he walked to the tarmac. It was late December, 1957. Morgan had no idea at that point whether he'd ever come back. He was about to bolt into the sky with thirteen young men to fight an entrenched army that was hell-bent on wiping out every last one of them.

4

Unaware of much of the bloodshed, William Morgan could still feel the tension when he stepped into José Marti Airport. Cop cars were lined up along the terminal building, and men roamed the sidewalk with billy clubs and submachine guns.

With a white suit, white shirt, and dress shoes, Morgan looked like a tourist from Kansas on his way to the Nacional for a round of roulette and a daiquiri. His companions, however, had more to worry about.

They were young, Cuban, just the kind of travelers who were attracting the attention of Batista's guards. The government had been keeping lists of revolutionary activists in Miami, and anyone in the entourage could have been stopped.

Batista had assured the public the revolution was a joke and that he would stamp out the rebels like cockroaches, but the truth was that he had been quietly fretting about the impact they were having on his country.

He ordered police to patrol the Havana neighborhoods where activists had been holding demonstrations, and he had his dreaded secret police infiltrate the student groups at the University of Havana. He tried publicly to downplay the attack in March on the presidential palace, but the brazen daytime assault had come within a floor of the dictator's office before it was finally repelled. Some forty-five rebels died in the bloody mess, leaving Batista shaken and angry over the embarrassing near miss.

A month later, he got his revenge when his secret police raided an apartment in Havana and killed four of the conspirators.

Shortly after Chao and Morgan and the others passed through customs, they waived down a driver at the curb. With no more checkpoints, they just needed to get to the safe house.

Havana looked more or less the same, except for the new hotels piercing the skyline. The Riviera loomed high above them, an architectural wonder that had just opened with a gaudy party and Hollywood celebrities. Just beyond the Riviera, the Hilton, another monstrous symbol of opulence and prosperity, stood just two months from opening.

But beneath the glitz was a city on the edge, one that had become a magnet for raging young men looking to topple it all.

Amado had cleared the way for them with the other rebels, but Morgan didn't have to speak Spanish to know, as soon as they stepped into the safe house, that they were in trouble. The place was under surveillance, and no one knew when the secret police would knock on the door. Amado's contacts were supposed to show up days ago, but something had happened. No one was coming.

This wasn't good. Morgan and Chao now had to scramble to find someone in Castro's underground network to help them. The problem was that not only had Batista killed some of the urban organizers helping Castro, but the SIM had infiltrated key rebel groups. Make one wrong move—one bad contact—and they were walking into a trap. Morgan's mind churned as he looked out the window.

He had an idea, which he floated to the group through Chao. The Cuban students were the most likely suspects, so why not let an American make some of the contacts? By reaching out to some of the rebel groups, Morgan might be able to hit the right cell without drawing attention. They had to do *something*.

A pay phone stood just beyond the stores outside their window. Morgan could take the names and numbers and start calling. Many spoke some English, and if not, they would know someone in the group who did.

After the sun slid into the harbor, Morgan quietly slipped out and made his way to the phone booth. Despite the recent shootouts between the guerrillas and soldiers, the streets still thronged with tourists streaming into Havana. For all of Batista's blunders, he still controlled the mainstream media and effectively suppressed news of revolutionary successes.

Not far from the phone booth, Morgan saw a figure emerge from the darkness. At first, he didn't know what to expect, but as the man came closer, Morgan began to make out his face.

They both froze.

It couldn't be.

But it was.

In front of Morgan stood Roger Rodriguez, the former medical student who was steeped in the underground movement in Miami and had frequented the Bowery, the club where Morgan had worked.

"William," he said, walking over to hug Morgan. Many a night at the bar, Rodriguez had talked to Morgan about the problems in his country, and now their paths had crossed again.

Morgan remembered the young, idealistic student who always pledged to someday return. None of the young people liked Batista, especially Rodriguez. Maybe Morgan could get the help he needed. He knew he was taking a chance, but he opened up. Morgan needed to make contacts. He and his friends wanted to go to the Sierra Maestra.

"You *want* to go?" Rodriguez asked, puzzled. Morgan wasn't Cuban. He had no ties to the island.

But Morgan didn't have time to explain. He reached into his pocket and took out a list.

Rodriguez looked at the piece of paper under the streetlight. "My friend," he said, holding up the paper, "you've been deceived. These guys are with the forces of Batista."

Rodriguez, now a doctor, had been entrenched in the revolution for more than a year. He knew which groups had been infiltrated. The police would show up at the nightly underground meetings to break up the gatherings and threaten everyone. Then they would make arrests. Morgan needed to get out.

"You've got to go back," Rodriguez said. "You are going to return to the United States." It was too dangerous for an Americano. Morgan didn't speak Spanish. He didn't understand the politics of Havana, where so many people were turning on one another.

"I only got twenty dollars in my pocket," Morgan said. "I am going to the Sierra Maestra."

Rodriguez could tell that Morgan wasn't going to relent. If Rodriguez left him on the streets, he could easily be set up. It was a difficult position. He thought for a moment and offered an alternative: If Morgan could wait, Rodriguez would put him in touch with another rebel group. It wouldn't be easy, but he could direct Morgan to an entirely different stretch of the country. Castro's militia already had hundreds of guerrillas.

But this group needed help. They were young, inexperienced, desperate for reinforcements, and holed up in a dangerous area. Batista's soldiers were moving in, and the rebels needed weapons, ammunition, and other critical supplies.

When Morgan returned to the safe house, he and Chao said good-bye. They had grown close, but Chao had come to Cuba to head to the Sierra Maestra, not the other mountain chain. It was better that they separate for now. Someday, if they survived the fighting, they'd see each other again.

Now, all Morgan had to do was wait for Rodriguez. The tension had mounted in Havana as more rebels were rounded up. Protesters hauled in for questioning grimly went missing.

Esteban Ventura Novo, the dreaded police captain who dressed in all white, had been arresting the very people who were supposed to be helping Morgan and the others. It was no wonder that no one had showed up to escort them to the mountains.

By the time Rodriguez finally arrived with another rebel to drive, he had found out that Ventura's men were watching the very house they were occupying. There was little time to spare. Rodriguez served as guide, and Morgan sat tight and held his passport in case they were stopped.

Rodriguez knew the routes to take to avoid the checkpoints, but still, he couldn't take any chances. The police were getting wise to the movements.

As they sped along a back road out of the city, the driver pointed to the police stopping cars along La Rampa, the main drag. It had become so dangerous that they would soon be forced to find new routes out of the city. If they could make it to Las Villas Province, they stood a better chance of making it to their destination—in one hundred more miles.

If they kept moving, they could stay alive.

5

As the car approached Sancti Spiritus, the landscape rolled into gentle foothills. For hours, Morgan had been watching the vast expanse of plantations leading to the center of the country. It was hard to believe this serene land with palm trees rising into the blue sky was about to turn into a war zone.

Men rode on horses across grassy fields that seemed to stretch in every direction. In the distance, the tops of the mountains rose into the clouds.

As planned, the driver rose up a hill and entered the town, turning down a maze of streets until they pulled in front of a drugstore. Moments later, Reinol Gonzalez bounded out and held out his hand. For months, the pharmacy owner had been helping the cause, moving medicine, gauze, syringes, and other supplies to the rebels.

"You are the Americano," he said, nodding to Morgan.

Gonzalez formed a critical link in the underground movement, offering his store as a way station for young men on their way to join the cause.

Roger Rodriguez needed to get back to Havana, but he would leave Morgan that much closer to his destination. Somehow their encounter at dusk at the phone booth had been more than a coincidence.

For Morgan, it would be a long time before he could thank his old friend. For the first time since arriving in Cuba, Morgan was on his own.

Gonzalez escorted him inside, where they waited.

Morgan learned the underground movement was far more than what he saw in his brief stay in Havana. Runners went from town to town on horseback, collecting guns and clothes for the rebels. In every town, messengers ran critical information to the mountains, including army troop movements. The patchwork of people was a lifesaver for the rebels.

By morning, two dark men in fatigues came inside and greeted Gonzalez. Faustino Echemendia and Efren Mur had been going back and forth between the pharmacy and the mountains for days, helping volunteers reach the rebel camp. Both were farmers who had grown up on the land. They knew the mule trails and winding, narrow paths that snaked like arteries into the lower mountains. Wiry and tough, Echemendia resembled the street kids whom Morgan hung out with in Toledo. Any mention of Batista made his eyes narrow and he cursed under his breath.

What struck Morgan was that Echemendia wasn't afraid. He was good at slipping through army checkpoints, meeting with the rebels at dawn to deliver the young, skinny kids from Havana showing up to fight.

Still dressed in the same white suit, now flecked with dirt, Morgan jumped in a Jeep with the two guides. For the first hour, they headed south, watching as the land grew steeper, covered in thick brush and palms that grew taller and darker the more they drove. Soon the sun barely flickered through the trees. Morgan had been all through Florida—his version of the tropics—but he had never seen anything like the Escambray. Wild parrots flitted from tree to tree and occasionally a dark, furry animal darted across the path.

When they passed a row of hamlets, the Jeep came to a halt. They had reached the end of the road. Even a four-wheeler couldn't make it up these steep hills with so many jagged rocks. Rustling up their water jugs and other supplies, the two men jumped out, expecting Morgan to follow. .

As they burrowed their way up, they found themselves at the mercy of a path choked by prickly bushes and tangled vines that wrapped around thick mahogany trees. At first, Morgan kept up with his escorts, but after a while, he began dragging his feet. Echemendia and Mur had no problem navigating the trails, but Morgan hadn't even caught his breath. The sun arched high above the mountains, glaring down on the three men as they inched slowly into an open expanse. Much of the area had been cut back, and hammocks hung between trees.

These were the central mountains, where few people tread. It was off bounds for American tourists. It was off bounds even for the native urban population. But in many ways, it was the heart of Cuba. Not only did it contain some of the richest soil in the Caribbean, but also the most rugged people. Fiercely independent, they cared about two things: family and land.

No sooner did the men step into the open than Echemendia stopped hard in his tracks. He put a finger to his lips. There was something ahead.

In the distance, through the trees, were the sky and an open field. There could be soldiers ahead . . . or nothing.

Echemendia signaled for quiet. At first, it sounded like a soft cooing. As it faded, Echemendia mimicked the noise, almost like a dove.

The men heard rustling through the trees and then looked up to see a bearded, jut-jawed barbudo step out from the bushes and glare at them with steely eyes.

"Ayu Acama," he said, pointing his rifle at their heads.

Echemendia nodded. "Ayu Acama."

The man lowered his rifle and immediately walked toward them, smiling. It was

Ramiro Lorenzo Vega, one of the Second Front rebels, credited Morgan with saving his life. COURTESY OF RAMIRO LORENZO

Ramiro Lorenzo Vega, one of the rebels standing sentry at the edge of camp.

Lorenzo, a feisty twenty-year-old who fled to the mountains after Batista's police began cracking down on revolutionaries in Havana, had joined the unit weeks earlier.

As Lorenzo reached the two men and Morgan, more rustling preceded more men, who stepped out from the brush in olive fatigues clutching rifles. In seconds, they surrounded Morgan and his two escorts. Some of them had beards and sallow, dark eyes; others were dirty-faced kids holding M1s. The men recognized Echemendia and Mur, but they stared at Morgan in his stained and sweat-soaked suit and fancy shoes.

Echemendia raised his voice in Spanish. "*Está bien.*" He's OK.

Roger Rodriguez had vouched for him in Sancti Spiritus. The American could be a good fighter, but clearly the men weren't convinced. One of the rebels, a wiry barbudo with thick glasses, stepped out from the others.

Eloy Gutiérrez Menoyo had formed the rebel unit just two months earlier. He knew more than anyone how precarious it was for strangers to know the rebels' whereabouts. They lay just a stone's throw from Batista and his thugs compared to the rebels in the Sierra Maestra, hundreds of miles away.

"Who are you?" he asked.

With the help of a translator, Menoyo asked why Morgan was in the mountains and who had sent him.

For the first time, Morgan didn't know what to say. He never expected this kind of questioning. He needed to say something to put them at ease; otherwise, he was done. It was like being back at the Paula Restaurant, except this time he was in the wild, with barbudos carrying guns. He thought for a moment and then let it out. He had come to the mountains to avenge the death of a friend. Morgan told them the same story he had told Chao and Amado: Batista's soldiers had shot an old army buddy while he stood on a hotel balcony during the palace attack.

Menoyo stared into Morgan's eyes, listening. He had no way of knowing whether the visitor was telling the truth, but the rebel commander had a way of sizing up people quickly, and if Morgan was a spy, he was dead.

Morgan told him that he had served in the US Army. He could strap and shoot an M1, and he could throw a knife.

Morgan could see the rebels were trying to process what he was saying, but they were still suspicious. They had risked too much already. "They were afraid the police were sending him," recalled Roger Redondo Gonzalez.

Ultimately, the decision fell to Menoyo. Either the commander was going to let him in or they would escort Morgan to the edge of camp and ultimately back to a place where he didn't want to go.

⟁

The sun rose over the peaks of the Escambray, casting shadows over the camp as Morgan was rousted from his sleep. He was told to be up at dawn.

The men jumped from their hammocks, strung several feet above the ground between unruly banyan trees. Like most mornings, they lined up for a hot cup of *cortadito* and then gathered in the center of the camp.

Menoyo still hadn't decided what to do with him. It was only a matter of time before Batista's soldiers crept into the area. The rebels were far from ready. Most were farmers, students, or workers—poor people who had trekked into the mountains with nothing but the clothes on their backs. Some brought their own guns and knives, but otherwise they had no experience in guerrilla fighting.

For years, they had watched as the larger cities, especially Havana, grew in wealth and power while they still wallowed in a sharecropper existence. They had waited for roads to be built and for schools and hospitals to be established. They waited, but none of that happened.

Menoyo had formed the Second Front on November 10, 1957, planning to grow the unit with several hundred rebels to control the Escambray. The mountains were far more important strategically to the revolution than the Sierra Maestra mountains, where Castro had staked his claim, for one simple reason: They were much closer to the capital. For all intents and purposes, the Escambray formed the last line of defense between the presidential palace and the fiercely independent provinces where much of the discord brewed. No one knew that more than Menoyo. If he and his men could drive the soldiers out of the highlands—a tall order—then they could clear a path to Havana.

He had amassed just thirty men so far and was waiting for reinforcements and weapons. With the movement growing more popular, he was sure more peasants would come.

As the men were about to go out for drills, one of the camp leaders offered an idea: Take the gringo with them. He said he had served in the American army? Fine. They would run him like never before. Lázaro Artola Ordaz, a tough-as-nails camp leader, had helped Menoyo form the Second Front and had been fearless during the unit's brief confrontations with Batista's soldiers. Artola motioned for Morgan to join them. Dark patches of thick jungle and the dangerous *chichicaste* plant surrounded the camp. A cousin to poison ivy, the wicked shrub has prickly stems, but the natives had developed an immunity to its stings.

"We'll see what he's made of," Artola announced.

First, he started by ordering the men to line up along the bottom of the incline. The drill he had in mind not only tested their footing but also their endurance. Then, he raised his hand and ordered them to move. One by one, the men began climbing, some slipping on the rocks, breathing deeply as they reached the top.

Next, Artola ordered them back down. No sooner did they reach the bottom than he ordered them back up.

The others were taking quick, stutter steps, which they had learned to help master the terrain. Morgan kept up with the pack for the first cycle, but now he was struggling. His legs were tightening, his arms heavy, and he was starting to get dizzy.

Keep moving, Artola barked.

After another round, the men took a break. Artola glanced at the Yankee, whose white shirt was soaked in sweat and spotted in dirt. Soon Morgan would be begging to quit.

Artola ordered them back up the hill and back down again. After a few minutes, he put them on a new drill: walking the area's steep trail. For the rest of the day, the men trudged along the long, winding path, stopping occasionally for water but never for long.

Morgan's eyes glazed over, and he was close to passing out.

As they returned to camp, Menoyo and the others smiled as they caught sight of the Americano, his shirt stripped off, his face and arms badly sunburned. Tiny red welts from the chichicaste covered much of his body. Redondo had just come back from a food run when he saw Morgan limp into camp. "He was looking very bad," Redondo recalled.

Ignoring everyone around him, Morgan lay down in his hammock, exhausted.

This punishing training regimen continued. Each day, Menoyo and the others predicted that Morgan would quit. At the end of each day, Morgan stalwartly dragged himself back into camp, limping and covered in sores. He wasn't going to make this decision easy for Menoyo.

At one point, Artola pushed Morgan to the brink of collapse. He was exhausted, seething, his feet covered with blisters. Artola shouted at him to move. Finally, Morgan had enough.

Turning around and facing the team leader, Morgan lashed back: "I am not a mule."

For a moment, Artola was taken aback. He had been pushing Morgan for days without a word. But every man has a breaking point.

When they returned to camp, Artola walked over to talk to Menoyo privately. As the two men huddled off to the side, the other rebels stared curiously at Morgan, wondering whether he would be allowed to stay.

After several minutes, Menoyo shook his head. The Americano had stood his ground. He had followed orders even when he was about to drop. He was accepted into the Second Front. He could carry a rifle; he would fight for their cause. But make no mistake: He would obey orders. Menoyo was their leader. If Morgan had other ideas, he was dead wrong.

Again, some of the rebels angrily disagreed with Menoyo's decision. Morgan didn't belong with them, and they didn't trust him. He wasn't Cuban. He didn't speak their language. He came from the country that had supported Batista with planes, guns, and ammo.

Morgan could sense the resentment, but there was nothing he could do. For the first time since his army days, he had been given a rifle, olive fatigues, and a place to lay his head.

During maneuvers the next day, Morgan lifted his rifle and walked to the middle of camp, making sure the other men were watching. Leaning back, he squared his shoulders, took aim at a tree about five hundred feet from him, and, squinting one eye, squeezed the trigger.

The rebels were speechless. He hit the very center. Not even the unit leaders had shown that kind of precision.

The following day, he had another chance to show what he could do. Morgan took a turn standing sentry, keeping an eye on the camp's outskirts. Through a cluster of trees, he saw what appeared to be soldiers marching down a trail. He immediately turned and ran back to camp.

"They're here," Morgan warned Menoyo.

Menoyo quickly summoned his men to his side. They needed to set up an ambush. For Menoyo, the number one goal was getting weapons. If they could surround the soldiers and force them to surrender, he could lay hands on their guns and ammo.

Don't fire, Menoyo told the men. Repeat: Don't fire. They were to take the prisoners alive. If there were six men in their midst, an entire company could be nearby. There was no way they could take on that many soldiers now.

The rebels moved slowly to the top of the hill and stopped, waiting for the soldiers below. Morgan clutched his rifle, peering down until he spotted the men in their dark uniforms. Holding steady, he aimed and fired.

The soldiers dived to the ground and scurried for cover. Within seconds, they began firing back. The entire area erupted in gunfire.

Morgan stood and slowly walked toward Batista's soldiers, continuing to fire his rifle, while the other rebels stayed on the ground. The startled men kept watching as Morgan pressed forward.

Menoyo could see that two of the soldiers were injured—one struck in the shoulder—but the rest had jumped for cover and fled. Menoyo yelled for the men to cease-fire.

On the ground, the two soldiers were bleeding from the gunshots. Menoyo was furious. Normally unflappable, he couldn't contain himself as he approached Morgan.

"I told you not to fire!" he screamed in Spanish.

Morgan was stunned. He thought he was setting up an ambush—a basic field tactic. He didn't know he wasn't supposed to shoot. No one had told him in English.

Menoyo didn't have time to explain to Morgan through a translator why he didn't want to fire on the troops. Now he had a bigger problem: They had to get the hell out. The soldiers who escaped would tell their commanders, and soon Batista's soldiers would be crawling all over the hills.

For weeks, they had managed to build their small unit under the cover of trees in the foothills near Banao. From the day he arrived in the Escambray with just a few men, Menoyo's strategy had been to recruit men, gather weapons, and strike from calculated positions of strength. Now he had to scramble.

6

THE REBELS HAD TO FIND A HIDING PLACE FOR THEIR WEAPONS: FORTY-seven Italian 6.5 mm Carcano carbine rifles. Redondo and others volunteered to drag the guns down a trail so that they could stash them in one of the underground caves.

The other group, led by Menoyo, had to move quickly to a trail that stretched west into the next ring of hills.

They knew the wide sweeping terrain, and they knew the guajiros who had given them food and even their rusty old shotguns and knives. The rebels needed to stay out of the line of fire—and out of sight of Batista's men—until they could reach safety.

Menoyo's group scurried along the trail, stopping every few hundred yards to make sure no aircraft were soaring overhead. As soon as they found tree cover, they would wait until night to move again. For Morgan, it was a rough start. They had to flee because he had screwed up. This is what he got for not knowing the language. He wasn't going to be able to survive without learning it.

Menoyo was still angry at him for blowing their cover. But what really concerned him was that the Second Front wasn't ready for a serious confrontation with the enemy, and the soldiers were going to catch up with them.

No one in the Second Front understood the importance of experience and military training as much as Menoyo. Growing up in Spain in the 1930s, he watched as his family took up arms to protect themselves from Francisco Franco's soldiers during the Spanish Civil War. One of his older brothers, José, was killed at age sixteen during the conflict.

Not long after, another member of the family, Carlos, decided he was going to leave home to fight for freedom but against a new enemy: the Nazis. He joined the forces of Jacques-Philippe Leclerc in the liberation of Paris, and twice the French government decorated him.

Like his brothers, Menoyo was expected to take his place at the revolutionary table, even after the family moved to Havana after the war. Menoyo's father, a physician, was passionate about his political beliefs, condemning all forms of dictatorship. Even in his newly adopted country, he never wavered. After Batista seized power in 1952, the family aligned itself with the growing underground movement against the dictator.

The eldest brother, Carlos, quickly gained a following among the young student radicals. Smart and charismatic, he desperately had wanted to leave a mark on the growing rebellion. In March 1957, he led the attack on the presidential palace, but he wouldn't let his little brother, Eloy, join the assault. The family couldn't afford to lose two more sons if the plan failed.

Carlos led the commandos into the palace, tossing hand grenades as they made their way inside. Unable to find Batista, Carlos and his men bolted to a set of stairs but were quickly met by guards, who gunned them down. Eloy was devastated. Nothing was going to stop him from throwing himself into the revolution.

Where Carlos had been fiery, Eloy was quieter and reserved. Frail with thick, dark glasses, Eloy Gutiérrez Menoyo looked more like a college professor than a guerrilla leader. But when anger rose up inside him, he cast a cold, steely stare. He had large shoes to fill and not a lot of time to prove himself. This was a critical juncture in his command.

For two days, the men kept to the trail, walking mostly at night to avoid being spotted. They talked little, fearing that their voices would carry on the wind. They weren't allowed to smoke, and they stopped only to fill their canteens. They were exhausted.

Hours passed before they could sleep, making it harder to cut through the thick shrubs. Slowing each man was a knapsack stuffed with clothes, blankets, bandages, cans of condensed milk, ammunition, a hammock, and a nylon sheet to shield against the rain. Everyone pushed on until in the distance Menoyo finally saw the familiar row of sabal palms along the creek leading to Finca Diana. The farm set high in the foothills of the Escambray should have served as a welcome sight. But for the rebels, it was a painful memory.

Months earlier, Batista's soldiers had surrounded the fledgling rebel unit, which was lucky enough to escape into a nearby jungle, losing just one man. Not long after, the soldiers hunted down the rebels near the farm, this time killing six—a quarter of the entire unit—on Christmas

Day. Some of the rebels were close to giving up, but Menoyo refused to let them return to their homes. If they had even a shred of a chance of overthrowing Batista, it was here in the mountains, the hinterland, not the cities and certainly not Havana. They needed to stick it out until they had gathered enough men and weapons.

Menoyo had learned after watching his brother die in the disastrous attack on the presidential palace that the rebels needed to pull Batista and his men from their comfort zone—like Castro had done—into the mountains. They had to engage in guerrilla warfare.

~

The sun was rising over the mountains and Menoyo and his men were about to set up camp when word came from one of their scouts: The soldiers were in view.

He couldn't count them all, but at least a dozen were moving down a deer trail toward their position. Menoyo ordered the rebels to take cover with a clear view of the trail below and to wait for his orders.

This time, Morgan was ready, clutching his rifle. He was determined not to mess up.

With the rebels lined up on both sides, the soldiers came into view. Menoyo waited. *Tres . . . dos . . . uno . . .*

Finally, Menoyo motioned for the rebels to fire. Gunshots cracked from the ridge above. The surprised soldiers jumped for cover. Morgan stood up over the other rebels, gripping his rifle, as his rounds sliced through the brush, hitting the trees and ground below. The others stayed down and in place, but Morgan stood up and kept moving forward.

Some of the soldiers took position and fired back, but it was impossible to get clear shots by aiming upward. In just twenty minutes, the soldiers realized they were going to have to retreat or get pinned down and die. One by one, they stopped firing and retreated. For the first time, Menoyo and his men had repelled the enemy without running.

It was calm for now, but Menoyo knew the soldiers would return with more men and firepower.

~

A half mile from the skirmish, he could see the rocks jutting out from high above the pass. As the men neared the farm, Menoyo spotted the ridge. If they could reach that point, they could set up camp, wait for the soldiers to return, and launch another ambush.

Menoyo knew the soldiers would be bringing an entire company—and they'd be angry. If they, a ragtag band of rebel farmers, beat them twice, the soldiers would be humiliated before their superiors.

As they trudged up the steep hill, Menoyo decided to pull out their most formidable weapon: a Czech sub-

Jesús Carreras Zayas, one of the comandantes of the Second Front COURTESY OF MORGAN FAMILY COLLECTION

machine gun they kept for just this reason. A light model made just after World War II, the weapon was capable of spitting out 650 rounds per minute. It was all they had.

The man carrying the Czech gun, Jesús Carreras Zayas, had been with him from the beginning. The quiet, brooding rebel had left his job as a lab technician in the southern coastal town of Trinidad. Tough and ornery, Carreras drank and got into scrapes, bragging that he wasn't afraid of anyone. Most of the time, that was true. During the early days of the anti-Batista movement, Carreras was set up by an undercover agent working for the government. Rather than risk arrest, he jumped in a Jeep, shot the agent, and took off, taking a bullet in the shoulder in the process but managing to escape. Menoyo ordered Carreras to set up the machine gun, picking a spot with just enough range to spray the entire trail with bullets.

After taking time to scout the area, Menoyo directed some of the men to take positions along the high ground—one here, another there, others far to the right and left. Then he counted out more men and moved them to the rear. This way, the rebels could conceal their own numbers so the soldiers had no idea the size of the force they were fighting.

Menoyo dragged his knapsack and his M3 submachine gun to a point above the trail, sat down, and waited. The sun beat down on the men as they clutched their weapons.

Any faint sound—the snapping of branches, the flutter of birds scurrying from a nest—would be their sign. By three o'clock, one of the scouts rushed back. "*Vienen*," he whispered. They're coming—two hundred, maybe more, on the trail.

Menoyo was right. They were coming back with more men. Once again, Morgan gripped his rifle and took aim. As the first few soldiers appeared on the trail, Menoyo waited. Not yet. The more soldiers on the trail, the more they could surprise them, and the more casualties they could inflict.

Wait. *Wait.*

Menoyo gave the signal. Carreras opened up, unleashing a barrage that ripped into the earth. Some of the soldiers fell down, struck by bullets; others ran for cover.

Pinned down, the soldiers began firing back to stop the attack. "There was no place they could pass," Redondo recalled.

The soldiers were in chaos. Some were screaming on the ground. Others were trying to get away. As the two sides came closer, two of the rebels were hit.

Once again, Morgan rose above the fray, clutching his rifle, and now—standing up—began firing on the enemy in a frenzy. While the others looked on, Morgan continued moving forward, bullets flying on both sides, shooting round after round. The enemy slowly fell back, some retreating down the path by which they had come, others scrambling into the brush.

After several more minutes, it was over. Except for the dozen soldiers dead on the ground, the company had disappeared. The rebels waited several minutes, no one moving. Then, one by one, they walked down from the ledge.

They had done it. They had repelled at least two hundred soldiers in the same place where the army once had run them into the hills. The younger men stared at Morgan. They had never seen anyone stand up in battle and fire, refusing to take cover. "*Está loco*," they said. He's crazy.

Even Menoyo stopped for a moment and looked at his Americano guerrilla. He saw something in Morgan that he hadn't seen in the others. When the bullets were flying, the Americano didn't retreat. In a revolution that was about to get nasty, Menoyo was going to need him.

— ◆ —

No one had expected this, not the military leadership and certainly not the farmers who waited until dawn to venture to the ridge. More than a dozen men in uniforms—Batista soldiers—lay sprawled on the ground, their bodies riddled with bullets. The farmers were stunned. They knew about the battle, but they thought they would be burying rebels, not soldiers.

They couldn't leave the cadavers rotting in the sun, so they lifted them up and threw them on the backs of their horses. One by one, the horses moved down the path, the bodies tied to their backs. At El Pinto, the local store, the locals whispered among themselves about what had happened. Months earlier, they had watched as the guerrillas retreated. Now they were seeing something far different.

"It was important for the whole area," recalled Armando Fleites Diaz, one of the rebels. "We made a stand."

Word spread to nearby towns.

Redondo, the rebel who had split from the unit days earlier to hide the guns, heard about the rebel victory miles away in another town. By then, the stories had grown. "They were talking about the bearded, six-foot guerrillas," he recalled. But it was clear the victory at Finca Diana was having an impact on recruiting new members in the Escambray. Scores of farmers began showing up in the mountains, asking to join the Second Front.

MENOYO HELD UP THE MAP. "HERE," HE SAID, JABBING A FINGER ON THE crumbled, folded paper.

The other rebels peered over his shoulder and stared at the spot: Guanayara. To most of the men, it was no-man's-land, a remote area deep in the Escambray.

Everyone knew that Batista's army would return with everything it had: aircraft, mortars, more men. The Second Front needed to get out. If they could get to the mountain outpost, they could send word to the towns—their loyal networks—and dig in, build new positions. Every rebel force needed its own base. But this wasn't going to be easy. It meant crossing an uphill area covered by thick, wild brush with a couple dozen men and few supplies.

The only rebel to object was Faure Chomón Mediavilla, one of the leaders of the group who had long pushed for another strategy: waging war in the city, not the mountains. Now was as good a time as any to return to Havana.

Menoyo and Chomón had been quarrelling for days, and both men were beginning to show little regard for the other. Chomón didn't care that the rebels had just scored a victory. The rebels depended on the support of teachers and union workers in the cities, like Havana and Santa Clara. They needed to go back to the capital, hit at the top. Why risk the lives of these men on coffee plantations, Chomón asked, his voice rising.

But Menoyo dug in. He wasn't going to be told how to run the unit. He had decided long ago the way to win the revolution was by striking Batista where he was most vulnerable: in the mountains. Batista had no real presence in the countryside. His soldiers had never engaged in bush fighting. Menoyo had just shown that with the right training and tactics they could beat the army and then take their .50-caliber machine guns. If they could score enough victories in the hills, they would demoralize the enemy, which would surrender elsewhere. Like a picador in a bullfight, wear down the beast with the lance, one cut at a time.

By now, both men were yelling at each other.

In front of the other men, Chomón turned around and began packing. His time in the mountains was over. He and the men loyal to him would take some of the weapons and trek to Fomento, then Havana. Menoyo and others would push deeper into the mountains.

Chomón stormed off. It was done.

The two leaders would forge their own paths, but it was still a setback for the Second Front. Menoyo had lost more men and weapons. Weeks might pass before he could rebuild the unit to that same point. The guerrillas needed to leave the province and embark on a dangerous trek across treacherous terrain with no guarantees that they'd make it.

The wind howled through the pine trees, scattering birds into the night air. No one wanted to move. The rebels had been cutting through the thick brush leading into the highlands. Their bodies ached. The deeper they trudged into the badlands, the darker and more foreboding it became. Only a couple of the men had ever been this far in the mountains. It was hard to see even fifteen feet ahead, but the best time to move was at night.

Morgan had been dragging along the dark trail and was starting to feel dizzy. He had been shivering earlier in the day, and now his face, covered with grime, was turning red. Something was wrong.

But Menoyo couldn't wait. He had to keep pace in order to reach Guanayara in time. New recruits were going to meet the unit there, hopefully with badly needed supplies.

"Get moving," Menoyo told the men.

Some tossed down their hats, others threw up their hands, but all knew that they needed to follow orders. They rose, grabbed their knapsacks and rifles, and filtered back onto the trail.

Armando Fleites, the only physician in the Second Front, could tell that some of the younger recruits were leery of their new surroundings, so he took them aside. They needed to trust in Menoyo and the leaders, he said. They were all taking risks, but that's why they were in the mountains.

Like Menoyo, Fleites, a tall imposing barbudo with piercing eyes, was deeply influenced by his father, a doctor who took to the mountains thirty years earlier during a revolution against then-president Gerardo Muchado.

When Fleites decided to join the fight against Batista, his father gave him a handgun and hugged him. "It's your duty," the elder man told him. His mother gave him a cross.

As the men began climbing onto a trail, they noticed that both Morgan and Lorenzo were gone. Menoyo swung around and descended the trail, cursing under his breath. After passing a clump of trees, he came upon the two men, still on the ground.

"Get up," Menoyo ordered them.

Morgan looked up but didn't budge. "I need time to rest," he said. He had a bad case of the runs, and it was clear he was dehydrated.

But to Menoyo, it didn't matter. He needed to keep his men alive. Leaving them was not negotiable. He leaned over and looked Morgan in the eyes. Menoyo had made it clear from the outset that he was in charge, he said. If Morgan ever needed to dig down deep, he needed to do it now. If he ever needed to muster the strength to move forward, he needed to do it now.

Damn it, do it now.

Even in his fog, Morgan was surprised. It had been years since anyone had talked to him like this. But Menoyo had made it clear: The Second Front needed him, and Menoyo wasn't going to leave him in the bush.

Morgan rose to his knees and then stood. He immediately got behind twenty-year-old Lorenzo, who had torn the ligaments in his foot days earlier, and slowly helped him up. Then, Morgan took a rope out of Lorenzo's knapsack and tied it around the young man's waist. Taking the other end, Morgan tied it around his waist. Moments later, the rebels watched as Morgan, propping up Lorenzo, moved slowly toward them, one step at a time. Just weeks after Morgan's rocky start with the rebels, he was becoming one of them.

⌖

The rebels broke through the trees and threw down their packs. Soaked in sweat and covered in dirt, they fell to the ground. Everyone was hurting.

Lorenzo needed to be in a clinic, mending. Others had deep cuts from brush and thorns, and their feet were cracked and bleeding.

But now, almost to Guanayara, the rebels finally figured out why Menoyo had brought them here. The terrain was rough and steep, making it nearly impassable for Jeeps and trucks. The trees were some of the tallest in the mountains. The soldiers would have to come by foot. Menoyo was leveling the playing field. He gave the order to set up camp in a place known as Charco Azul.

Some of the rebels headed to a nearby farmhouse to talk to the guajiros, seeking their help. Before anything else, the men needed food and water. For days, their diet had consisted of coconuts and malanga, a dark, starchy root they boiled for a main course. Most of the men were fighting stomach or intestinal flare-ups, largely from dehydration and heatstroke. At least now they could crawl under the cover of mahogany trees to rest.

Exhausted, Morgan walked to the edge of camp and found a tree. It had taken all the strength he could muster to carry Lorenzo. He thought about his family, his children. It would be a long time before he would see them again, if ever. He had come close to passing out in the hot sun and being left behind. If he died here, no one would know why he was even in Cuba.

If he could just write it down, put it on paper, maybe he could explain to the people he left behind. He figured it was his only chance.

He walked over to the center of camp and asked one of the rebels for a piece of paper and a pencil. The young barbudo looked puzzled, but he handed Morgan a rolled-up piece. Morgan inched back into the shade. Leaning over, he scribbled down his thoughts. Even if no one ever read them, at least he could put them down in words.

"Why I am here? Why did I come here far from my home and family? I am here because I believe the most important thing for free men to do is to protect the freedom of others."

It wasn't about adventure or money or fame. It was about fighting against the "forces that want to take the rights of people away."

He reflected on his experience with Lorenzo. As a youngster, Lorenzo worked in a store in Havana and watched as Batista's soldiers shook down the owner for free food, while the poor could barely scrape together enough to buy scraps of bread.

Even after injuring his foot in the mountains, Lorenzo refused to lie down, said Morgan. "Here, the impossible happens every day. Where a boy of 19 can march 12 hours with a broken foot over a country comparable to the American Rockies without complaint."

Morgan folded the paper and walked over to Menoyo. He wanted to get it to the people supporting the Second Front in Havana. If anything happened to him, at least others would know why he was here.

8

THE REBELS GATHERED WITH THEIR RIFLES. SOME WERE TEENAGERS who had dropped out of school; others were in their forties, right out of the fields. One by one, they stepped to the line.

"*Listos!*" came the first command. "*Aspunten!*" And finally: "*Fuego!*"

With every order, they followed the three steps. Ready, aim, fire. Some of the shots splintered the tree, others barely grazed the branches. Most of the men had no weapons training, and the rifle's kickback was throwing them off.

Standing in the rear of the camp, Morgan could see the frustration on Menoyo's face. The Second Front didn't have enough weapons, and most of the new volunteers were inexperienced fighters.

Morgan set down the gun he was cleaning and strode to the firing line. He was supposed to wait his turn, like everyone else, but he couldn't help himself.

"*Mira*," he said. Look.

Taking an M1 from one of the rebels, he held the rifle in front of him and yanked on the sling to make sure everyone saw his grip. Wrapping the strap around his shoulder, he lined up the rear and front sights. Squinting, he took aim, and then—bracing his hold with the sling—squeezed the trigger. The bullet struck the tree dead center. No one said a word. Some had seen what he had done in the skirmishes at Finca Diana, the crazy Americano walking toward the gunfire.

Most of the rebels nodded with approval, but one stood in the rear, glaring over the other rebels' shoulders. Regino Camacho Santos—a Spaniard from the Canary Islands—grew up among people whose distrust of Americans had run deep since the Spanish-American War. He wanted nothing to do with them. It was difficult enough for him to watch Morgan wearing the fatigues of the Second Front, but the *Yanqui* was butting in where he didn't belong. Camacho, a veteran of the Spanish Civil War, was supposed to be the training officer, and he was being upstaged by a foreigner. As Morgan coaxed the rebels to the firing line, the Spaniard made a snide comment loud enough for others to hear.

Menoyo watched but didn't say anything—for now. The men needed time to accept Morgan, who was more than capable of helping them. The American may not have been one of the training officers, but he knew how to fire a weapon. This revolution was more than student protests. It was a war, and they desperately needed to learn how to fight.

One of the young rebels stepped to the line. Morgan adjusted the boy's rifle strap to make sure it was taut. The tighter the strap, the more support and the less kickback. "No look at me," Morgan told him, pointing to the tree.

The young man held the rifle and then fired. The bullet glanced a small branch.

"*Bueno*," Morgan said, smiling.

Camacho made another comment loud enough for everyone to hear and stormed off. It wasn't over between the two men, but the rebels were starting to warm up to the Americano.

Later that night, the men gathered around the camp. Sometimes, they told stories, sharing a rolled cigarette. Other times, they passed around an orange that someone picked off a tree. This time, they wanted to wrestle, squaring off to see who could pin whom. As Morgan watched the men size each other up to see who wanted to tussle, Camacho came over to him.

"*Vamos a luchar*," he said, pointing to the center of the camp. Let's fight.

Morgan smiled. Did he really want to wrestle? In front of everyone? Camacho didn't know that in Ohio Morgan had spent hours wrestling under the porch lights on summer nights. For a street kid, he was tough and knew every basic move, from sweeps and takedowns to full nelsons. He was bigger than Camacho and, in his own estimation, stronger.

Morgan didn't say anything, but Camacho wasn't going to leave it alone. Raising his voice, he made sure everyone in the camp heard him. "*Vamos a luchar!*" he said.

Morgan was blending into the unit, and he didn't want to upset anyone, but this crazy training officer, a hotheaded Spaniard with a chip on his shoulder, was goading him openly.

Everyone was looking now. Morgan had to defend his honor. He walked into the center of the camp where the others were standing and slowly unbuttoned his shirt. No sooner had he tossed it to the ground than Camacho snorted and lunged at him, trying to knock him over. Morgan stepped aside and let the Spaniard fly by and fall to the ground.

Some of the rebels laughed as Camacho, red faced, rose and ran at Morgan again, determined to bowl him over. Morgan again stepped to the side, but this time, he caught Camacho as he ran by, turned him around, and wrapped his arms around him in a bear hug. Morgan's face turned red, squeezing Camacho until his face, too, turned bright red. For a moment, no one said anything as Camacho began gasping for breath, unable to talk. After a few seconds, Morgan flung Camacho around and slammed him to the ground, dropping a karate chop that stopped just inches from his head.

The rebels were speechless. Camacho, the tough guy of the unit—a demolitions expert who had fought against Franco's soldiers—lay on his back. Morgan rose from his stance over Camacho, brushed the dirt from his fatigues, and stepped back. He wasn't going to gloat. As far as he was concerned, it was over.

"William didn't want to embarrass him," Redondo recalled.

Camacho didn't know it, but he had just been replaced.

Morgan and Menoyo both heard the gunshots. They knew right away they had to bolt back to camp.

The two men had walked off in the early morning to talk about Morgan's emerging role in the Second Front, but now they had to turn around. Grabbing their rifles, they took off down the trail, the gunfire cracking louder as they neared Charco Azul.

In the distance, they saw that dozens of soldiers had sprinted toward the thicket of trees where the rebels had set up camp. The rebels were firing from behind the trees, but at least a hundred soldiers were lining up around them. Two trucks circled the perimeter with .30- and .50-caliber machine guns tied to the rooftops. The rebels were trapped.

Instead of stopping to size up the situation, Menoyo and Morgan rushed toward an opening, firing rapidly into the line of soldiers. With a British Sten submachine gun, Morgan sprayed the path in front of him as he bolted toward the camp. For a moment, neither man was sure that the other was going to make it, but within seconds, they broke through the perimeter.

The rebels saw the two men moving toward them, firing at the soldiers from behind trees. By the time Menoyo reached his men, they were pinned down. They awaited his orders. But Menoyo didn't know how many soldiers had surrounded them. Worse, Batista's men had brought mortars. From the size of the units forming around the camp, the rebels figured they were fighting an entire battalion.

"The army locked us in," Redondo recalled.

The rebels had acquired new weapons and ammunition since arriving at Guanayara, so they could hold out for a while, but the mortar explosives were falling down on them. The enemy lines were closing in from every side.

In all of their encounters, the Second Front had never been in this kind of danger. This was payback for Finca Diana. More troubling was how the army knew the rebels' exact position. The attack was too calculated, too coordinated. Most of the farmers and townspeople supported the *revolución* or at least stayed neutral, but some civilians may not have liked the guerrillas for one reason or another. Menoyo and the other leaders had warned the rebels about treating the locals with respect, but ultimately the Second Front was treading on their land.

Some of the rebels found shelter behind a large stone wall at the camp and set up a firing position. The soldiers came ready and loaded. They could sustain a continuous assault on the rebels until they wiped them out. There was no way that Menoyo and the men pinned down in the camp could simply fight their way out of it.

But they had two wildcards: Artola and Carreras. It had just dawned on Menoyo that neither man was around. They had left in the morning on separate reconnaissance patrols. Artola had fifteen men with him, and Carreras more than a dozen. They'd come back, and when they did, they were both smart enough to figure out what had happened and jump in.

As long as Menoyo and the others could keep moving within the camp, they could buy more time.

Carreras had heard the gunfire and turned around, but he stopped short when he saw the soldiers forming their lines. Instead of attacking from ground level, Carreras and his men took to the high ground—a ledge above the camp—and set up their position there. After everyone was in place, Carreras took out his binoculars to scope out the enemy line. Then he gave the order.

At the same time, Artola and his men were approaching the camp from the opposite side. An experienced fighter, Artola noticed that the army was attacking from a traditional position, infantry in front and commanders in back. He and his men quickly took their place two hundred yards behind the officers' position. With everyone ready, Artola ordered his men to open up.

With Carreras firing from the high ground and Artola and his men shooting from the rear, the soldiers were totally confused. They were supposed to be fighting only a few dozen guerrillas, not a whole battalion.

Menoyo saw his chance to escape. He ordered his men to gather around him. This was it. If they were going to die, they would do so singing the Cuban national anthem and charging the lines. He raised his hand and pointed forward. The rebels followed, firing their rifles.

There was just one problem. Morgan couldn't parse the Spanish and didn't understand the order. He and several others stayed back and continued firing. Likewise, a smaller unit of government soldiers remained and returned fire. As he had done before, Morgan stood in place, gripping his Sten, shooting from a standing position.

One of the army officers decided that he, too, was going to fight back from a standing position. Soon, the two men—Morgan and Lt. Antonio Regueira Luaces—were making a stand like cowboys in a Wild West gunfight, each refusing to give in.

Morgan wanted "to slug it out with him," Redondo recalled.

Both men took turns diving for cover and then standing to return fire. Neither one was going to back down.

In the distance, Menoyo and the other rebels watched as the *Yanqui* continued to fire, stubbornly refusing to run. After several more minutes,

Menoyo finally ordered the other rebels to fire at the Batista lieutenant to break up the showdown. Most of the other soldiers had already long since retreated to the hills.

In the end, five rebels died, compared to thirty government soldiers. Neither side could claim a clear victory, but the rebels had escaped certain annihilation. Batista's army had dispatched five hundred men to avenge the loss at Finca Diana, and they had nothing to show for it.

On that day, April 3, 1958, the *New York Times* published a story about the emergence of a new rebel unit in Cuba: the Segundo Frente. Reporter Herbert Matthews chronicled the unit's brief history and its emerging role in the revolution, but he also included something else: Morgan's letter about why he was fighting in Cuba. Camp messengers had delivered the note to rebel supporters, who then put it into the reporter's hands. Now the outside world knew of the Second Front and William Morgan.

9

THE TRUCK JOLTED INTO GEAR AND SPED DOWN THE STREET. OLGA Rodriguez gripped the rails, her hair flying in the breeze. Batista's secret police had been running investigations of all the major revolutionaries helping the rebels. And someone had given them her name.

No one had expected this. The dark, pretty student government leader had been quiet about her anti-government activities to protect her family. For most of her student life, she had kept it that way. She had volunteered to smuggle medical supplies to the rebels only because no one suspected her as a rebel herself.

As the truck made its way toward the safe house, the driver begged her to keep down. SIM officers already had been to Olga's school. Soon they would target her parents' home on Calle Independencia. Olga thought about her parents, her sisters, and her cousin Gilberto, who lived with her family in the cramped little cinder-block house. She had put them all in danger.

Batista had been trying to root out the network in Santa Clara supporting the Second Front. In a new tactic, the cops were staking out the family and friends of suspects and then breaking them down through intimidation. It had never been this bad.

The truck pulled up to a house on the edge of the Central University of Las Villas in Santa Clara. The driver escorted Olga inside. For now, it would be her hiding place, but she had no guarantees about how long it would last. The cops were on a mission to hunt her down.

It wasn't a secret that Olga was president of the student government at the teachers college, a radical school with a long history of social protest. But many people didn't know how deeply she had delved into the cause. Not even her parents knew, nor her siblings. With every death, every missing person, Olga went deeper: another protest, another collection of money to send to the rebels. By the time she met with her fellow students, Olga herself was the topic of the meeting. They had to find a way to save her.

Olga Rodriguez, age twenty, at the Normal Teachers School in Santa Clara COURTESY OF MORGAN FAMILY COLLECTION

The cops had been working the streets, flashing Olga's picture. They had stopped at the college, trying to shake down the principal. Soon she'd have to flee to another safe house.

Olga didn't know that the SIM had barged into her family's home and had torn the place apart. They searched the rooms, closets, and the yard. Olga's mother stood by the door, trembling. She knew the cops weren't going to rest until they found her daughter. Then they found Gilberto.

Four years older than Olga, Gilberto had lived with the family since he was a boy. He was her cousin, but he was still a family member and it was perfectly acceptable to wail on the male relatives to make a point. Two of the SIM cops found him on a street corner and demanded to know her whereabouts. Gilberto looked at both men and shook his head. He wasn't going to give her up. They demanded to know, but Gilberto dug in. Not a word.

One of the men grabbed him from behind, while the other punched him in the face, chest, and stomach. The blows kept coming, blood gushing from his nose and mouth. The agents carried him to the car and threw him inside.

It was time to take him to the Rodriguez home. By the time Olga's mother rushed to the door, Gilberto had crumpled to the ground, a bloody pulp.

"Gilberto!" she screamed, falling next to him. She pleaded for the cops to stop.

"This is nothing," one said, compared to what was in store for Olga.

———

Olga had to leave. She needed to save herself and, more urgently, save her family. She had thought about it, and now realized she needed to make a drastic move: She had to head to the mountains. The secret police would be heading back to Olga's home and would surely harm other family members. It was a matter of time before they found her, too.

"I need to be with the rebels," she said.

At first, the students helping her were doubtful. Just getting her to the Escambray would be difficult, but the bigger problem was there were no women with the rebels in the mountains.

"It's not possible," her handler told her.

Olga pushed back. She argued that women had joined the rebels in the Sierra Maestra. If her fellow students wouldn't help her, she'd find a way. She wasn't going to stay.

One of the students finally agreed to talk to a faculty member in the underground movement. If they could find an escort to take her, they would allow it. But if they couldn't, Olga had to wait.

That night, Olga closed her eyes, but sleep didn't come easy. The hours dragged as she thought about her predicament. In just two short years, she had gone from being a student from an obscure family to a revolutionary wanted by the president's secret police. Getting to the rebel camp would be one of the toughest journeys of her life.

First, she had to reach the foothills. The soldiers had set up checkpoints and were stopping vehicles suspected of going to the mountains to aid the rebels. Buses went to Manicaragua, but the army stopped and searched those, too. The cops had photos of her, which made the trek that much more risky. Before she did anything, she needed to change her appearance.

She grabbed a pair of scissors and went into the bathroom. With her dark hair and eyes, she had once been one of the most beautiful girls in her school. But none of that mattered anymore. As her long locks fell to her shoulders and the floor, she realized it would be a long time before she could ever come back again—if ever. The life she knew in Santa Clara was over.

Taking a bottle of hair color that a friend had left at the house, she poured it onto her head, rubbing it in. Slowly, she was looking at a new person in the mirror. Her face and hair looked different. Now all she had to do was pull a cap over her eyes.

As she finished, Olga heard a knock at the door. The students had found her escort.

"I will help you," he said. "But you have to listen to everything I say. We don't have much time."

As he stepped into the house, he reached behind his waistband and pulled out a .22-caliber revolver. Olga needed to carry it where no one could find it. Without flinching, she turned around and shoved the gun into her panties. Then tucking in her shirt, she turned around again.

"I am ready," she said.

The plan was simple. They would both board the bus, but they would do so separately and sit apart. If they were caught, Olga's escort would fire on the soldiers so she could flee.

"It is better that you don't even know my name," he said.

They walked to the station, each on opposite sides of the street, and boarded the bus. As they moved down the aisle, they made sure they sat across from each other.

As the bus pulled away, she thought about her family. She never had a chance to say good-bye. She wondered whether she would ever see her mother again. Before sundown, she'd reach Manicaragua. If she was lucky, she would reach the central mountains in a day. She had taken this familiar route while carrying packages for the rebels, past the grassy acres that rolled endlessly from Santa Clara to the foothills of the Escambray.

She thought of her grandmother, Inocencia Pozo, who had fled to these same mountains a half century earlier during the war for independence. Olga would sit for hours listening to her "Mambisa" describe her own experiences as a young girl, smuggling weapons under her dress to the rebels. She was taken prisoner but ended up marrying the man who captured her, Rafael Rodriguez, a Spanish captain who stayed in Cuba after the war. He died on the day Olga was born.

The vehicle jolted as it slowed and stopped. Suddenly the door opened, and several men in uniforms boarded. Olga gasped. She didn't know what to do. She looked over, but her escort wasn't moving. She needed to stay calm. She needed to breathe deeply. The men walked down the aisle, staring at every passenger, one by one.

One of them came to Olga. *Just stare straight ahead. No eye contact.* He looked at Olga as he held up a photo. He glanced back at Olga, and then he slowly turned around and walked away.

Olga looked over at her escort. They had made it. But they also knew there were many more miles to go.

When the bus came to a halt at the next station, Olga's escort stood and turned to her. It was time to get off. They hadn't reached Manicaragua, but it was no longer safe for either one to be on board anymore. They bounded down the steps and began walking down the street, when Olga's escort turned and pointed back to the vehicle. A cadre of cops waving guns had rushed inside.

Olga and her escort needed to reach a farmhouse to get help. Most of the guajiros in the area sympathized with the revolution even if they didn't take an active role in it. Their stories were all the same. They had supported, even gushed over, Batista during his early years. But the longer he stayed in power, the more resentful they became.

When Olga and her escort reached the first farmhouse, the owner didn't hesitate to let them come inside. He told them what they already knew: They weren't safe. The secret police were all over the area, on horses and in trucks.

The farmer agreed to let Olga stay while her escort sent for help. She had no idea how long he would be gone, but at least she was safe for now.

For the rest of the day, she stayed, even taking time to play on the floor with the little girls who lived there. At ten o'clock that evening came a knock on the door. A messenger indicated that Olga needed to leave. Soldiers were drawing closer, searching all the farmhouses. She was in imminent danger.

A short while later, she heard noises outside. Just as the farmer was taking her out of the house, she spotted two men with long, stringy beards, clad in olive fatigues, on horses coming toward the farmhouse.

The farmer walked out to his stable—a rudimentary wood-frame structure with a roof—and led one of his own horses to Olga.

"I had never ridden on a horseback," she recalled. "But I didn't say anything."

With one of the men riding in front of Olga and the other in the rear, they took off in the darkness. The area, known as Callejón del Coco, was crawling with soldiers. The barbudos knew the area well, but it was a long ride to Guanayara.

As they moved along the trail, Olga began shivering. The higher in the mountains they went, the colder the air. Olga was entering another world. Other than short trips to the farms outside Santa Clara, she had never been this far from home. Huge trees seemed to grow out of the rocks, so tall in some places that you couldn't see anything else. The path they were riding on was so deep in the woods that the trees formed a canopy over the trail.

As they rounded a bend, Olga noticed a faint light in the distance. At first, the men thought it belonged to some peasants, but they quickly realized it was two army patrol cars set up for an ambush.

"We threw ourselves on the ground," recalled Olga.

Suddenly their trip had taken a wrong turn. It was time to get off the horses and send them off in another direction. Now they had to walk on foot on a new path, one far longer and more treacherous. It started to drizzle. Olga was freezing. Her body ached, and her shoes had torn. Her feet bled on the rocky terrain.

"*¿Estás cansada?*" one of them asked. Are you tired? Olga said no. She wanted to keep going. She didn't know how much longer she could go, but if she could make it to morning, they stood a chance.

She began to count the trees she passed just to keep her mind from drifting off. With each one, she pretended to be that much closer to her destination. Don't stop, she would tell herself. If she did, she might not get back up.

As the sun broke through the trees, Olga was lagging, but at least she could see better in the morning light. Just a few more hours, and they could make it to the rebels.

As they reached an area known as Escandel, Olga heard a strange noise. The men stopped. Olga watched as one of her escorts repeated the noise, cooing like a bird. Seconds later, several bearded men in olive fatigues broke from the brush.

She had arrived. This was the first camp, an outpost, the men told Olga and her escorts. The main camp lay several kilometers away.

"*Venid*," one of them said—come—motioning for Olga and her handlers to follow them to an open area with a fire. The fresh aroma of thick, dark coffee hung in the air as the men gathered. Her escorts described the close call with the enemy. It appeared the soldiers were moving in Jeeps along the main roads.

Olga recalled having a strange feeling come over her. She was now with the rebels, the men fighting the war. Other than being with her family, she had never felt more at home, as if she had been gravitating toward this moment her entire life.

One of the men noticed that Olga's feet were cracked and bleeding. "Why is this lady not wearing any shoes?" he asked. Another handed her a pair of worn leather boots. "They are not new, but I hope they will fit you," he said.

Olga smiled. A day earlier, secret police and soldiers were hunting her, and at least now, she had survived to see another day.

But she had only a few hours to rest. Her handlers needed to get her to the main camp, Veguitas. There she would meet Menoyo and the others preparing for their first major offensive.

10

Menoyo split the men into smaller units—roughly ten to a team—and ordered them to set up satellite camps, each a couple of miles away. The largest lay in the center under Menoyo's command, and an intricate network of peasant runners linked the units.

The rebels were putting their stamp on the mountains, creating their own revolutionary village. It was the best way to take on Batista's larger, well-armed units. Menoyo was creating strike teams, fast and able to move through the mountains more quickly than the soldiers.

Olga had run into one of the satellite camps with her escorts and was coming close to the main camp. Menoyo had gotten word from the runners that Olga was coming, and he had agreed: She could stay, but she had to bunk in a nearby farmhouse.

The sun was setting over Veguitas as the men gathered, some breaking down their rifles to clean, others stringing up their hammocks. The sentries made for their posts on the outskirts of camp.

Olga had never seen so many men with guns. Most were young and dark-eyed, dressed in olive fatigues.

Menoyo was standing in a circle with several others when he spotted the visitor. He already knew about Olga's brush with the secret police and her escape from the soldiers. As he walked over to her, he could sense she was nervous. But he assured her: She was among friends. This would be her home.

"You're with us now," he said in a calm, reassuring voice.

One by one, the men approached her and extended a hand. Some, like Armando Fleites, had come from Santa Clara, and others had been in the student directorio network. At least she didn't feel like a total stranger.

Roger Redondo was unlike many of the others. Though he came from a hotbed of rebellion, Sancti Spiritus, his parents didn't approve of him joining the cause. The movement was breaking up families. They wanted him home. But he couldn't just watch as his friends fled to the mountains to fight, knowing they could die. "I had to go, too," he said.

Across the camp, a tall figure in a group of men had his back to her. The group broke out in laughter, and one of the rebels motioned to the central figure and said, "Be careful, we have a lady among us now."

The man with wide shoulders and thick arms turned around to face her. He had blond hair and rugged features, and when she looked into his eyes, all she could see was blue.

Morgan extended his hand to her and said something in broken Spanish, but she could barely understand him. She felt her head go light as she stood and stared

Roger Redondo, lead intelligence officer with the Second Front COURTESY OF RAMIRO LORENZO

into the stranger's eyes. She had never seen anyone like him.

Morgan smiled. "I am very pleased to meet you." He let go of her hand and stepped back.

Olga tried to act as though nothing had happened. She nodded and walked across the camp with her escorts, but after several minutes, she found herself looking over her shoulder and searching for the stranger.

—⁓—

Near the Veguitas camp, a young couple with children agreed to give Olga a cot in their home. It was a simple farmhouse with a wood-burning stove, small windows, and a wood floor.

As she lay down to sleep, Olga kept thinking about her own family. Whatever problems they experienced, they could always depend on one another.

The next morning, the young mother saw her guest's sadness. "*¿Qué pasa?*" she asked. What's wrong?

Olga looked around the farmhouse and could see that the woman was like her own mother. The clothes for the children hung on a line strung in the corner. The pot on the stove was brewing coffee. Flowers stood in a simple vase.

Olga told her about her life in Santa Clara, the police hunting her down, the other students arrested and tortured. But as they talked, Olga realized that the people in the mountains were even more vulnerable.

Her own problems paled in comparison to what the campesinos in the Escambray had been enduring. City life offered some protections. In Havana, revolutionaries could seek shelter in foreign embassies, and the more sophisticated among them could turn to the press corps. Here in the mountains, there were no safe havens. The Rural Guard could get away with anything. Some of them pulled locals from their homes and beat them senseless in the middle of the night. Until Menoyo and the other rebels showed up, the peasants had no advocates.

"Thank God they are here," the young mother said.

Olga watched the children playing with dominoes, the tiny wood pieces crashing to the floor and then the shrieks of laughter. No one could guarantee this family that it would survive.

As the sun began to crawl down over the mountains, Olga walked outside. The peaks of the Escambray rose above the trees, creating a cavern of raw nature and elegance that made time stand still. She had never realized how beautiful her country was until now. It made no sense to her that so many bad things were going on in Cuba when places like this, the Sierra del Escambray, were so divine.

As she peered across the open field, she could see someone on a large white horse riding in the distance. As he came closer, she recognized the rider as the stranger she met at the camp, the man she later learned was an Americano. He was the last person she expected to see.

As he dismounted, he was whistling the "Colonel Bogey March," better known as the tune whistled in the movie *The Bridge on the River Kwai*.

"*Hola*," he said. "How are you doing, Olgo?"

Olga held her tongue for a moment. "I am fine, Commander, but my name is not Olgo. It's Olga—feminine."

Morgan smiled and stepped back for a moment. "Forgive me, I am still trying to learn Spanish."

Morgan had finished training the young recruits for the day in target practice and had been thinking about the woman he had met the night before. He didn't know how to break it to Menoyo, but he asked for permission to go out riding. Several of the farmers had made their horses available to the rebels, so when Morgan showed up at the makeshift stable, he picked the only white mare.

As Morgan and Olga stood outside, the woman came out of the farmhouse. She had recognized the Americano, his presence already known in the close-knit villages around the camp.

The woman had been cooking a meal of roast pork with beans and rice. "*Tienes hambre?*" she asked.

Morgan looked puzzlingly at Olga, making it clear that he didn't understand.

Olga motioned to him as if eating.

Morgan smiled. "*Sí*," he said.

Some of the peasants feared the rebels coming too close because of the Rural Guard, but the family hosting Olga had long believed in the revolution. They knew Morgan as one of the leaders. They talked about the fighting and the hardships coming to the mountains. Olga stopped to explain to Morgan in what English she knew what they were saying. The greater the rebel forces grew, the stronger Batista's retaliations against the peasants. The wrath of his soldiers was growing.

Between bites of food, Olga and Morgan kept staring across the table at each other, shifting uneasily in their chairs. Olga had never seen an Americano other than in photographs. The men were usually cowboys with guns, the women decked out in fashionable dresses on the covers of magazines. She was intrigued with Morgan but knew very little about him.

After dinner, over a cup of café con leche, Morgan leaned against the wall in a *taburete*—a small armless chair used by Cuban farmers—and pulled out a cigarette. Every few minutes, he stopped talking and looked at Olga.

Olga had wanted to see him again, but now she didn't know what to say. They were in the midst of a revolution, and no one knew where they would be a month from now, or even a week. She followed him outside into the cool night air, the stars looming large and bright.

The rebels were heading out on a mission the next morning, and it could be a while before he returned. The revolution was taking on a new course. What had started as a cat-and-mouse conflict had now become a war.

Morgan lifted his hat, then turned around and faced her. "It's yours," he said, surprising her as he placed it on her head. "I'm giving it to you."

Again, she didn't know what to say.

Morgan leaned in—as though to kiss her—and smiled. "I will see you. Take care of yourself."

He mounted his horse and waved good-bye. Olga watched him ride over a steep hill and wondered whether she would see him again.

11

MENOYO CREPT TO THE EDGE OF THE TREES AND PEERED AT THE ground below. "*Mira*," he said, pointing to the rows of coffee plants and the sprawling farmhouse just beyond the brush. Government forces had taken over La Mata de Café, a large plantation owned by the Lora brothers, members of one of the wealthiest families in the Escambray.

Morgan and the others stared down the same ledge. In an open area dotted with farmhouses and wooden structures, they saw soldiers—everywhere. Menoyo and his men knew that when they set out they might run into Batista's men; they just didn't know how many. Of all the places in the vast Escambray—two hundred thousand haunted acres—this is where the army had chosen to camp. Either the officers knew the rebels' location, or they had a remarkable sense of intuition. It had to be more than just a coincidence.

Menoyo lifted his binoculars and scoped the trouble below. In the center of the plantation stood a large stone and wood chalet, through which officers were moving. To the sides, outbuildings served as temporary barracks for the soldiers. He wasn't sure, but there was a good chance the unit was hauling mortars and other heavy artillery.

"*Esperamos*," he said. We wait.

The rebels needed time to strategize. Menoyo, Morgan, and the others formed a circle. They had only thirty-five men with them, and it was too late to gather any more. At this point, the other camps were far away on their own patrols. The main rebel unit could wait and regroup with the others days later, but no one knew how long the army would stay put.

Menoyo recognized that this might be their only chance to hit the two hundred or so soldiers, unaware and unprepared, and inflict serious casualties. If the soldiers were plotting to attack Menoyo's central position, the rebel unit needed to ambush them now. The other option was to wait until the cover of night and surround them from every corner.

"See that?" Menoyo pointed to the chalet serving as commanders' quarters. That was their first target. If a few rebels could get close, they could lob grenades inside. If they landed the explosives properly, they could wipe out most of the leadership right away. That could force the rest to retreat and scatter, as had happened days earlier.

The rebels formulated their plan. They would split into several smaller groups, and each would take up position around the four-acre spread. Menoyo and Morgan would approach the front and rear of the chalet and, on the commander's signal, would toss explosives into the command house, thereby signaling the beginning of the assault. In the darkness, the soldiers would have no idea how many rebels surrounded the farm.

"Terrorize them in their sleep," Menoyo said.

The rebels could see that he and Morgan were growing closer, spending hours together every day talking strategy and other business. Morgan was speaking more Spanish, and Menoyo was picking up some English as well.

More and more, Menoyo was depending on Morgan to take the young men under his wing and teach them the rudiments of fighting. When they were scared, he needed Morgan to buck them up and shake out their heebie-jeebies.

Darkness edged in as the men huddled in the brush. This was no hit-and-run field exercise. This was a direct attack on an army camp. They had to hit the soldiers quickly.

It was time.

Menoyo motioned for the others to take their positions. "Let's go," he said.

He and Morgan darted toward the camp. The last thing they wanted was to run into a sentry. If shots were fired, the ambush would fail. Both men peered through the darkness but didn't see anything between them and the chalet.

They bolted toward the main building, Menoyo clutching his M3 submachine gun and Morgan his Sten. By sheer chance, they passed unnoticed through the sentries, halting in the dark, hearts pounding, as they reached the side of the chalet. Next they had to get inside. Quietly, both men inched up to the entrance. They swung open the door, hurled their explosives inside, wheeled around, and ran to the perimeter before they could become targets themselves.

Within seconds, the grenades exploded, sending shards of glass and wood flying into the air. The rebels surrounding the camp opened fire.

Soldiers ran screaming from their makeshift barracks. Others remained inside, reaching for their weapons to return fire. All they could do was hunker down and try to withstand the assault. They had mortars but no idea where to fire them. In the darkness, they couldn't gauge the position or even the size of the rebel forces.

Back and forth, the two sides exchanged shots. Just when the soldiers thought the attack was over, the rebels launched another barrage. Had the army known how few men were attacking, they might have stood their ground. But in the chaos, they wanted only to escape while they still could. Some of the soldiers fell back and found an opening between the rebel positions. One by one, they ran.

Menoyo knew right away the soldiers were retreating just by the fewer shots they were firing. The battle was over. The plan had worked.

The soldiers who survived escaped into the nearby woods. The Second Front had achieved another significant victory. Once again, they had taken on a unit more than four times their size. But they had little time to savor their success. They had to move yet again. The army would return, this time with hundreds more.

12

OLGA LEANED OVER THE YOUNG MAN MOANING ON THE GROUND, HIS fatigues soaked in sweat and blood. He had been shot in the torso, but no one could do anything for him at the moment. It would be a while before anyone could get him to a clinic.

Olga reached for a wet cloth and gently dabbed his forehead, calmly brushing back his hair. He was just a teenager, maybe fifteen or sixteen years old, trembling, his breathing deep and strained.

She looked into his eyes as he stared up at her. "It's OK," she said. "You're going to be OK."

But even Olga knew that she couldn't make that promise. In her short time traveling to some of the area camps, she had seen the bodies of young boys wrapped in blankets and screaming for help.

Quietly, she held onto him, holding him close as he shook under the covers.

"You have to fight," she told him.

As she tried to steady his breathing, rocking him back and forth, she felt someone tap her shoulder. It was Morgan.

It had been days since she watched him ride off on a horse. "How are you?" he asked.

She had thought about him every day, wondering whether she would see him again. She had heard about the battle at Chalet do Lora but didn't know what had happened to him.

"Thank you, Commander," she said. "I am well."

Morgan smiled and pulled a bouquet of wildflowers from his side. "For you," he said.

Olga's eyes lit up. She reached for the flowers and then took one, gently placing it in her hair.

To her surprise, Morgan leaned over and kissed her forehead. She could feel the heat rise around her, and for a moment, just she and Morgan were in the camp beneath Tico Puerto, one of the highest peaks in the Escambray. This wasn't supposed to happen in war, and yet for a brief moment, she forgot about everything else.

Morgan broke the silence. "I have come here to tell you that you have been transferred to another camp. My group and I will leave tonight, and you will go with us."

Rather than ask questions, she nodded. She was excited at the prospect of leaving with him. But she didn't know that she was about to be drawn into one of the most dangerous areas of the Escambray, where the soldiers and rebels were staking out their territory for the final push.

———

Olga gripped the reins tightly as her horse made its way down the steep trail winding around the rocky slope. For most of the night, she leaned back in her saddle, never straying too far from Morgan. Even as the sun broke over the peaks, the rocky path didn't get any easier to travel.

They began their slow climb upward. Every few hundred yards, they had to leave the trail to avoid the steep ravines. This was unlike any other part of the Escambray: mist and vines so thick and tangled around trees that in some places they could barely see the sun. On some of the narrow trails, they had to travel single file.

As the rebels began to ride up a hill, Olga suddenly felt her saddle come loose. Within seconds, she slid off the rear and tumbled down the steep embankment. "Help!" she yelled, as she felt her body bounce along the rugged terrain and down a gorge. By the time she hit the bottom, she almost blacked out. She could feel a sharp pain in her back and arms.

Most of the unit had already made it to the top of the hill when one of the rebels noticed that Olga's horse had made it, but she wasn't on it.

Morgan quickly turned around, his face white. He wound down a cow path until he reached the bottom of the ravine.

"Olgo, are you OK?" he shouted, jumping off his horse.

"I am all right," she said. Embarrassed, she tried to sit up, but Morgan told her to stay down. He reached over and gently squeezed on her right arm and then on her left to make sure nothing was broken.

Olga looked up, smiled faintly, and then inched herself up, trying not to let anyone know how much her body ached.

"I'm all right," she said, still woozy.

Slowly, with Morgan lifting her up, she sat and then looked around at everyone surrounding her. She waited for a minute, then stood up before walking slowly to her horse.

She didn't want anyone to know that pain was shooting up her back. They needed to get out of the area. The soldiers were coming.

——◆——

Morgan rose in his saddle, and then reaching for his Sten, thrust the weapon in the air. They had finally arrived.

One by one, the rebels at the camp came out to meet Morgan as he rode into the center. Covered by ferns and pines, the camp was actually a large farm in the heart of the Escambray in an area known as Nuevo Mundo. Because the topography was so different—an abundance of ravines, caverns, and thickets of trees—the area was ideal for a rebel camp.

Morgan and the others didn't even have time to untie their horses before they learned they were in danger. Farmers had spotted a scouting party of Batista's army in the lower mountains. It was just a matter of time before they set up their base.

The rebels more than likely had enough time to rest for the night. By morning, they would be fresh. Then they could begin their own series of hit-and-run attacks and protect the new camp, which would serve as temporary headquarters.

One of the men had pointed to the farmhouse, where the owner, Doña Rosa, was brewing hot, thick cortaditos for the new arrivals. Tough and outspoken, Rosa was one of the most well-known members of the resistance, a wealthy landowner who loved the rebels almost as much as she loathed Batista. A round, middle-aged woman with an infectious laugh, she equipped her home with a shortwave radio to listen to rebel broadcasts from Santa Clara and to communicate with other operators.

Olga immediately took to the motherly figure, who invited her to stay in one of her rooms. Born in Galicia, Spain, Rosa was like so many others in Nuevo Mundo whose families were fiercely independent and opposed anything that resembled dictatorships. They were better educated than many of their Cuban counterparts, and their pride in craftsmanship was obvious. Large roof tiles, wooden walls, wood floors, and stone foundations comprised Rosa's house, a stately home with a sweeping view of some of the most magnificent mountains in the Escambray.

Rosa was risking her life by associating with the rebels, but she didn't care. If she died, she died on her land. Morgan and Olga gathered around a table as they listened to her talk about the hardships the farmers faced under Batista's Rural Guard. She was tired of it. Too many people had been tortured and run off their land.

A light drizzle fell outside as the rebels tried to keep warm, some gathering around the wood-burning stove and listening to a rebel broadcast crackle over the shortwave. Olga leaned in, trying to listen, when she felt a tap on her shoulder. Morgan motioned for her to walk outside.

"Now?" she asked.

"Yes, right now."

She had already been briefed about all her tasks, including making sure messages were sent for supplies. She wasn't sure what he wanted to tell her, but she followed. He led her to a corner of the camp and sat down. From his pocket, he took out a photograph of his daughter, Annie, and another of his son, Billy. The boy with his gaping smile looked unmistakably like his father.

"This is my family in the US," he said.

She stared at the photos but didn't say a word. Olga didn't know that he had children. She didn't know he was married. Morgan placed his hand on Olga's shoulder. He told her not to worry. He was no longer with his wife. The only people who mattered to him were his children and mother.

He reached over and handed her a piece of paper with writing in English on it. "This is the address of my mother," he said. If anything happened to him, he wanted Olga to let her know. "I know I can trust you," he said.

She nodded and put the paper in her pocket. For a moment, neither of them said a word. Morgan was trusting her with something almost as important as his life. Olga wanted to ask him so many questions. She wanted to say so many things. But it was better to stay quiet. Morgan stood up and hugged Olga, and then they went in opposite directions: Morgan to his hammock and Olga back to Rosa's house.

She tried to sleep that night but couldn't. When the sun finally broke over the mountains, she went to look for Morgan. His hammock was empty. He was already gone.

13

MENOYO STARED ACROSS THE VALLEY, LOOKING FOR SIGNS OF THE soldiers—a glint of light, a shimmer of smoke. The army was coming, that much he knew. But if the rebels could track their movements, they had the advantage.

Batista already had sent some two thousand soldiers to the Escambray, the most he had ever sent to the central mountains. If the ungrateful farmers wanted his firepower, they were going to get it. He also planned to send the B-26s to bomb key positions.

Menoyo knew the worst was yet to come, but he was far better prepared to deal with the confrontations. His unit was growing and finally trained in the basics. He was especially pleased with Morgan. He had become popular among the young barbudos, many of whom had asked to serve in his small unit.

One night, Camacho came over to Morgan, and the two began talking. The other rebels watched as the two huddled over an old Winchester, piecing together the parts to put it back together. They had patched up their differences.

By the morning, the two had devised a homemade assault rifle. Using the frame of a 1907 Winchester and combining it with other parts, they created a base so the gun could fire with interchangeable barrels, depending on what ammo was available. They called it the Cuban Winchester.

Morgan's progress wasn't lost on the other Second Front comandantes, including Carreras, Fleites, and Artola. After meeting in a circle at the end of a long July day, they called Morgan over to them. They had all agreed: It was time for Morgan to lead his own column. He was being promoted to comandante, the highest rank accorded a rebel in Cuba.

Morgan had been running smaller patrols, but Menoyo wanted his guerrilla trainer to lead now. For Morgan, it was bittersweet. He was elated over the confidence that Menoyo and others expressed in him, but no one from his family knew—not his mother, not his father, not his children. Amado and some of the others approached Morgan to congratulate

him, but he downplayed the moment. Every one of the men was important to the unit, he said. If there was any consolation, it was that he had
proved his detractors in the US Army wrong. He was a good soldier.

Menoyo wanted to launch patrols in the new area, but even before they
could gather supplies, a runner rushed to camp with bad news: The Rural
Guard had just looted Escandel. Some of the villagers might have been
beaten.

Menoyo called his comandantes over. This was serious, he said. The
people in the village were dirt poor, but they had still scraped together
food and supplies to send to the Second Front camp a day earlier. Perhaps
the Rural Guard had found out.

"We have to get over there," Menoyo told his men.

Menoyo and Morgan led their teams together—over wire fences and
steep slopes—along the long, winding trail that led to the hamlet.

Menoyo peered through his binoculars. "There," he said.

The runner had reported looting, but this was worse. Some of the huts
were smoldering in burned heaps. Thick, black smoke still hung in the air.
They spotted the body of an old man sprawled by the side of the road and
a villager hunched over him. Another villager ran up to Menoyo, shaking
and crying. The Rural Guard had discovered that the hamlet had been
supporting the rebels.

Hours earlier, the guards—some of them drunk—had burst into the
structures, overturning tables and chairs. They grabbed a seventy-two-
year-old man doddering with mental illness and demanded to know the
whereabouts of the guerrillas. Dumbfounded, the old man had no idea
what they were asking.

A tall sergeant struck the man in the face and ordered him to tell
them. The soldiers forced the old man into a chair, the sergeant waving
a knife in front of him. Still, the old man didn't know what to say. The
sergeant then reached over, pulled on the man's lips, and in one motion
came down with his knife and severed them from his face. Blood spurted
on the man's clothes and the floor as he screamed. But the soldiers weren't
finished.

The sergeant pulled the old man from the shanty—while the villagers pleaded for him to stop—and fastened a rope around his neck. Pulling the rope like a leash, he yanked the man to the back of a truck and tied the rope around the rear bumper. One of the guards jumped behind the wheel and, revving the engine, sped away.

To the wild delight of the guards, the truck dragged the old man over the dirt road, his feet and arms flailing in the dirt.

By now, the whole hamlet had come out, all of them screaming at the guards to stop. A woman ran to where her grandchild was hiding. She fell to the ground as one of Batista's men fired a round of bullets into her. Then the sergeant gave the order for his men to torch the huts. One by one, the guardsmen lit the walls and thatched roofs.

Morgan's face flushed with anger, his fists clenched. He had never seen anything like this. He had known for a long time why the Cuban people had rebelled against Batista. But he hadn't witnessed the depths of the brutality until now.

Morgan had fought in battles. He had killed. But this was different. These were innocents. The Rural Guard had targeted and extracted a gruesome vengeance on farmers caught in the middle of a revolution over which they had no meaningful control. Morgan could barely look at the old man on the ground, his face contorted and mutilated. Only an animal could do something like that to a defenseless person. There was going to be hell to pay.

The remaining villagers told the rebels where the guardsmen were heading. The guerillas came up with a plan: They would shadow the soldiers and wait for the right moment to attack. But instead of traveling on the road behind them, the rebels took a side route.

Through his binoculars, Menoyo could see men in army fatigues moving along the road, making sure they were heading in the right direction. For the next hour, he and the others jogged along a deer trail on the edge of a huge ravine. Most of the men were tired, but wouldn't have stopped for anything.

As the sun was setting, Menoyo came up on a ledge and looked down. The soldiers had stopped and looked to be setting up camp in a row of houses. If they could surround the army camp from above, they could launch a surprise attack.

"We hit them tonight," he told the others.

Menoyo split his thirty men into groups to surround the houses. Morgan took a dozen rebels and waited in the rear to repel any escapes. The trap was set.

As they waited, Menoyo said it appeared there were more soldiers than just the ones who had ransacked the village. There was a chance they were packing more serious firepower: mortars, grenade launchers. If they could stun the soldiers with the first shots—even just to scare them— Batista's men wouldn't have time to set up any artillery. Hopefully, the enemy wouldn't be able to discern the size of the rebel force.

Menoyo gave the order. The rebels opened fire on the houses where the soldiers had camped. As expected, the troops panicked and ran from the buildings. The rebels fired relentlessly into the scrambling guardsmen, watching as their bodies fell to the ground. Within minutes, dozens lay in the mud, dead or badly wounded. Others crawled or ran from the camp and bolted down the road.

Morgan, waiting in the bush, gave the second order to fire. Rebel rifles cracked along the roadway, but it was too dark to tell if they were hitting anyone. Morgan and his men ran toward the soldiers, but they did so at their own peril. They could be running into an ambush.

The rebels stopped. It was time to head back and join Menoyo and his men. In the morning light, they could see better and stood a better chance of finding the soldiers. As they walked back to the camp, they learned from some of the other rebels that the big, hulking sergeant—the worst of the culprits—wasn't among the dead. Morgan had wanted to find him. For now he had to wait.

Shortly after rising the next morning, Morgan and his men spotted Batista's soldiers walking along the road to Camagüey, some of them carrying wounded comrades. Morgan ordered his men to hurry to the pass before the Rural Guardsmen set up an ambush on both sides of the road.

Just as the soldiers appeared, Morgan raised his hand. "*Tres, dos, uno,*" he counted, just loud enough for his men to hear. The rebels opened fire on the stunned soldiers. Some fell to the ground, while others tried to run.

The leaders in front didn't know what to do. Most of the enemy guardsmen had nowhere to go. They threw up their arms. They were surrendering.

Morgan lowered his gun and ordered his men to stop.

The rebels walked forward, slowly, carefully scrutinizing each of their captives. There he was: the sergeant. "We have him," Morgan said. Without hesitating, the rebels pushed the man away from the other captives. And then, without waiting for orders, they sprayed his body with bullets, even after he had fallen to the ground, a bloody pulp of flesh and bones.

14

SITTING BY HIMSELF, MORGAN LOOKED OUT OVER THE MOUNTAINS, THE
peaks rising into the pale summer sky. It was rare that he caught moments
like these, but after returning from the ambush on the Rural Guardsmen
who had terrorized the villagers, he wanted to be alone.

Months had passed since he had left his family on a chilly December morning, months since he had ventured into the mountains to
throw himself into a revolution. His son, Billy, would be walking by
now. Annie, his daughter, would be close to starting kindergarten. He
had never gone this long without talking to his mother. Most of the
time, Morgan had to push everything from his mind just to stay alert.
One day at a time.

At this point, he had no guarantees that he would survive the war.
Too many soldiers were coming to the mountains with too many weapons. He knew he had to do something—something he hadn't done since
he arrived. He reached for paper and a pen and walked over to a corner.
It was a letter he had needed to write for a long time but could never get
the time or muster the will.

For now, nothing else mattered.

Dear Mom,

*This will be the first letter I have written to you since I left in
December. I know you neither approve or understand why I am here—
even though you are the one person in the world—that I believe—
understands me.*

*I have been many places—in my life and done many things which
you did not approve—or understand, nor did I understand myself at
the time.*

*I do not expect you to approve but I believe you will understand—
And if it should happen that I am killed here—you will know it was
not for foolish fancy—or as Dad would say a pipe dream.*

Morgan described what he had experienced: the villagers terrorized by the soldiers and the killings of the old man and the woman who was trying to save her grandchild.

If Loretta understood anything about the revolution, it was crimes against defenseless people. If she had taught Morgan anything good, it was to stand up for them.

"I am here with men and boys—who fight for a freedom for their country that we as Americans take for granted," he wrote. "They neither fight for money or fame—only to return to their homes in peace."

He had been thinking about his wife, Terri, and their life together. He rarely talked about her, but he expected her to press for divorce. He was right: She had filed the necessary paperwork four months earlier. "If I live through this, perhaps I can make things easier for the kids."

He reached for another piece of paper.

These were the hardest letters for him to write. He never stopped carrying pictures of his children. First to his doe-eyed little girl, who would squeal in his arms.

> *When I saw you last you were a little tyke who was into everything all of the time. You used to sit in the window and when you saw my car drive in you would say—daddy, daddy—and I think those were the first words you spoke. And I know when I did not come home any more I know you missed me and looked out the window for your dad—this was a long time ago baby and possibly you don't remember—but I do—And always will.*
>
> *You are going to grow up to be a beautiful girl with a fine disposition. Stick close to your mom. I don't think you can find anyone better.*

Morgan cautioned her that if she grew up and met a man who "dreams of castles in the sky," then let him go. She didn't need that kind of man in her life. "Remember, your dad was one of those people. And it is very hard for those to love such a man."

He folded the paper neatly.

The last letter was for Billy. It would be a long time before his son would be able to read it, but he knew it could be the last time he could ever communicate with him.

"When you read this I expect you will be a big boy who wants to whip the world. Always defend what is right and work to get ahead but do so in a way—that does not interfere with others."

Morgan then alluded to something about which he rarely spoke.

> *Love your God—and your country—and stand up for both. I can say very little to you except this, Bill—and I think it is the best advice I can give you.*
>
> *Always be a man. Defend your rights. Respect the rights of others. Listen to what your mother tells you. You may not like what she tells you but believe it she is right. Study and work hard son and I know that your country and your mother will always be proud of you.*
>
> *Love always, your dad.*

Morgan carefully folded the last letter and slipped each into an envelope. One of the camp runners would take the parcel to Havana. Eventually, it would be smuggled out by guerrilla supporters to Miami. He could only hope it would reach his family.

15

OLGA HAD BEEN AWAKE FOR HOURS, RUSHING BETWEEN THE REBELS WHO had fallen ill with a virus. A B-26 had been flying over and bombing the nearby bohíos, straw huts. It hit farmhouses. It blew out part of the trail. If an army unit marched into the camp right now, the sick rebels were dead.

A familiar, hulking figure entered the camp, other rebels following him. Her heart began racing. She hadn't seen Morgan in days. He had been making the rounds to the other satellite camps, but now he was coming back to Nuevo Mundo. He was looking around, and their eyes met.

Olga trembled. *He is alive,* she thought to herself, not knowing what happened.

Morgan walked over and reached out to hug her. For a moment, Olga forgot about everything. She could feel her legs shaking.

Morgan was carrying something on his shoulder, a bird perched perfectly still. He reached behind his head, let the parrot walk onto his hand, and gently placed it on her shoulder. Then he handed her another gift, a bouquet of wildflowers. "These are the only presents I can give you here in the mountains," he said.

Olga stared at the flowers, surprised, then glanced at the parrot on her shoulder. A bird and flowers were the last things she expected after a day of tending to sick men.

The two walked away from the others while Olga gently held her new parrot. She had never received a gift like this. "I am grateful to you," she said stiffly.

The two walked through the main camp, then continued toward the brush beyond the perimeter. For a moment, Olga was nervous. She had never strayed this far from the safety of the other rebels. She had never been completely alone with Morgan.

By the time they reached the trees, no one was around. Morgan reached over and gently touched Olga's hand, then both clasped hands. Olga didn't know what to say. They were in a war, and she was growing closer to her commander.

"I don't know you," Olga finally blurted out. "I don't know anything about you. We must talk calmly since I don't know anything about your life and you don't know anything about mine."

"The past is already past," he replied, then pulled her close and kissed her—a long kiss that Olga didn't expect.

She felt her legs go weak and pulled away. "Now is not the place, Commander."

Morgan looked at her, surprised. "Why?" he asked.

Olga looked at him squarely. Neither one knew if they would survive the fighting. Morgan had fought in more than a dozen skirmishes and could have been killed in any one of them. Olga herself could be killed, she said.

Morgan shook his head. He told her that he was convinced the Second Front was going to end this war. They would do all they could to drive the soldiers from the mountains and take control. If Castro and the others could do the same in the Sierra Maestra, they were that much closer. When the war was over, he wanted Olga to be at his side, he said.

Olga pushed back.

"Now is not the time—or the place," she said. "We are in a war."

———

No one wanted this meeting, not the rebels, not even the runners who had been carrying messages back and forth. It was no secret that Menoyo and Chomón didn't like each other, but they had stayed clear of each other during most of the revolution—until now.

Chomón had arrived at the camp with ten bodyguards to deliver a message to the Second Front. Menoyo brought his commanders, including Morgan. Both sides gathered across from each other at the Dos Arroyo camp.

The two former friends greeted each other, but soon their voices rose as they had before. The worst of the fighting still lay ahead. Chomón said he came to the mountains with a message: Menoyo needed to step down.

Menoyo had been a warrior, true, but Chomón didn't believe he had the experience to wage war on large army units carrying heavy artillery. Chomón was still leader of the Directorio. Technically, the Second Front fell under his command. His choice was to appoint Rolando Cubela, a veteran who made his bones years earlier killing Batista cops.

Menoyo gritted his teeth and glared at Chomón. Menoyo was the first rebel to arrive in the mountains. He formed the structure of the rebel militia. He recruited the members and trained them. How dare Chomón come into the mountains and insult him in the middle of the war.

"I am comandante!" he shouted, his face red.

Chomón stopped himself for a moment but then reared up. Menoyo had to follow orders. He was still a part of the Directorio.

"No!" Menoyo shouted.

For a moment, the other rebels thought the two were going to come to blows. This wasn't good for the young rebels to witness, and it certainly wasn't good for the revolution. The soldiers were coming. They soon would be heading from Cienfuegos from the south, and Santa Clara from the north. In a matter of weeks, they would reach rebel territory, their goal: to split the mountains. There was no way the rebels were ready for a direct confrontation. They needed to stick together to have any chance of taking the mountains. But now it looked as if the real war was among the Directorio.

Menoyo stood. That was the end of their meeting. If it meant breaking from the ranks of the Directorio, then so be it. That was Menoyo's final decision.

Chomón stood. As far as he was concerned, Menoyo was committing treason, he said. But Menoyo had already made his decision.

As Chomón and his men walked away, the comandantes of the Second Front, including Morgan, gathered around Menoyo. "Gallego," they said. "We are with you."

They had fought together and risked their lives. At times, they barely survived. What was Chomón thinking by coming back into the Escambray like this after months? Fleites, Carreras, Artola, Morgan—they all pledged their allegiance to Menoyo and the Second Front. If the revolution failed, they would all fail together.

16

EVERY MORNING, OLGA STOPPED AT DOÑA ROSA'S FRONT PORCH TO VISIT her baby parrot. Perched on a small stand, it shuddered and cooed as she approached, offering Olga a welcome escape. She joked that the parrot could say her name but not Morgan's.

One morning, after checking on the camp, she found her pet wasn't on its perch. Frantic, Olga ran to every corner of the camp, looking to see if the green bird had flown somewhere else.

"Did you see my parrot?" she asked the rebels.

Soon the entire camp was looking for the bird. The young rebels searched the trees around the camp. They looked inside the hammocks. They searched the trails just beyond the camp grounds. Then they found a tiny, furry ball on the ground. It was Olga's parrot—dead.

With tears in her eyes, Olga walked away. She wasn't supposed to leave the camp, but no one was going to stop her. Staring straight ahead, she passed the bohíos and the rows of coffee plants beyond the camp's boundaries. She disappeared on a trail into the dense brush.

She never should have grown so attached to the little bird. She never should have allowed it to become part of her life. She had taught it to talk. She taught it to perch on her shoulder. She held the little creature close and felt its soft green feathers against her cheek.

Olga had lost her home. She had lost contact with her family. The one little thing that gave her joy in life was gone. Like everything else in this war, it had died. Deeper into the woods she went. Her legs grew heavy. It felt like she hadn't slept in days. She reached the side of a creek, but now she had no idea where she was. Light streamed through the leaves, but nothing looked familiar. She had never veered this far from safety. She might be able to follow the creek bed, but the light beyond the trees was fading. Even if she knew her way back, it would take hours to return to camp.

She was so tired.

She found a clump of thick bushes alongside the running water, lay on her side, and closed her eyes.

Morgan rushed through the camp, yelling for Olga. He had checked Doña Rosa's house, looked in her hammock, and began rousting the others.

"Where's Olga?" he asked, raising his voice. No one knew.

He ran to the edge of camp and stared across the plantation, but saw no sign of her. He yelled for his men. They had to find her. They strapped on their guns and made for the main trail that led from the camp. Except for the plantation, dense forest covered most of the area. She could have taken only a few well-worn paths. But the longer she was away, the more dangerous it became. Batista's men had been sending scouting units into the area, trying to pinpoint the rebel positions. If they ran into Olga, they'd kill her.

Morgan motioned for his men to hurry, but even they knew finding Olga was going to be difficult.

"Olga!" Morgan yelled.

But there was no response.

He never should have let her out of his sight. He knew she was upset over the parrot, but he had no idea how bad she felt—not to the point where she would risk her life. He stared into the trees and kept moving along the path, oblivious to anything else but finding her.

As he neared a thicket near a brook, he spotted something near a clump of bushes in the distance. It was Olga. She was breathing, her eyes closed.

He gently shook her shoulder as he whispered her name. Startled, Olga sat up and looked up at the man standing over her. He didn't care that the other rebels were present. He bent down, took her into his arms, and kissed her. Both put their arms around each other and embraced.

Morgan saw something in her that he had never seen before. He had been with many women in his life, but no one had sacrificed so much. She had given up her life for a deeper cause and risked it all. Morgan would never let this happen again. From now on, it would be different.

For Olga, it was all happening so fast. She had already lost people close to her. People she loved. The last person she wanted to lose now was Morgan.

Both knew at this moment their lives were about to change. Neither one could afford to hold back their feelings, not anymore.

17

Jesús Carreras Zayas paced back and forth, his eyes glazed. Even his men knew to stay away from him. For months, the farmers in the eastern Escambray had been picking up faint radio signals from Sierra Maestra that delivered tidbits about the latest skirmishes. But this was different.

The announcer was talking about the Escambray, and the rebels hadn't expected the message. The broadcast was urging people to sever their alliances with other rebel units and join the 26th of July Movement.

"La verdadera revolución está en la Sierra Maestra," the voice proclaimed. The real revolution is in the Sierra Maestra. Then the announcement that caught everyone by surprise: The movement was coming to the Escambray. Get ready.

Carreras and the others reeled. This was their territory. They had spent the last year fighting for every inch of ground, every deer trail, every road. But it was more than that. The Second Front was making a name for itself. Who was Castro to take over another unit that was holding its own?

The column leader of the Second Front wanted to know more. If the 26th of July Movement was sending men into the Escambray, they had to pass through the North Zone, his operations area between Fomento and Sancti Spiritus. There was no other way.

To Carreras, it was also personal. He had lost men over the past few months while sticking and running on the soldiers. He had just discovered that one of the new recruits who came in July was a Batista spy responsible for the deaths of six rebels in Havana. To carry out justice, Carreras took the spy to the back of the camp and shot him in the head.

Carreras meant business, and if the barbudos from the Sierra Maestra were coming, he needed to alert his men in the field to keep watch. He also had another plan. He would leave a stern warning at the camp: No one—not even the leaders of the Sierra Maestra revolutionaries—was going to pass through the territory and call it their own. The blood of the men of the Second Front had soaked into the soil of the Escambray. Not even Castro himself, the most recognized leader of the rebel forces, was going to diminish their position.

After he finished writing, he stood up, walked over, and tacked a message to the side of a wall for all to see. The words were clear: "No troops could pass through this territory," under any circumstances. If they did, "they would be warned a first time," but if it happened again, they would be "expelled or exterminated."

———

Menoyo had to scramble. The soldiers were coming, some in Jeeps and others on foot. Because of the airstrikes, it was getting tougher for the Second Front to move, but the biggest problem was that the rebels were running low on ammo. If they had to take on a battalion, it would be disastrous—especially a head-on attack. The government wasn't just sending raw recruits. These men came from the 11th Battalion, a unit already bloodied from fighting Castro.

Unlike most of the military cronies who served under Batista, the 11th was led by Ángel Sánchez Mosquera, a tough commander who led search-and-destroy missions in the Sierra Maestra. During his sweep through the mountains, he burned the bohíos of peasants suspected of helping the rebels and executed the rebels he captured.

The Second Front needed a plan. It wouldn't be easy, especially with a shortage of ammunition. Menoyo had to gamble. He would set up his attacks through small, mobile units. If each man could fire three rounds and then fade into the brush, they could make good use of their limited ammo. Then, by sending in another team and repeating the strategy, they could also lead the enemy to believe the attacks would keep coming. The idea was to inflict as many casualties as they could.

It was a risky strategy, but Menoyo didn't have a choice. He was in danger of losing his mountain stronghold.

———

Ernesto "Che" Guevara stood in the open field, a bend of the Jatibonico River rushing behind him. With his long hair and ragged fatigues, no one would have taken him for the leader of the column. He and his men were exhausted, their feet covered with blisters and blood from trudging across difficult terrain. This land was strange and unfamiliar to the rebels, but they had finally made it.

For Guevara—Fidel Castro's trusted lieutenant—the river was the starting point into the Escambray. He and his men had dodged the Rural Guard not once but four times during their trek. They had gone without food for days. With the rising foothills before him, Guevara knew they stood just days away from reaching their destination.

If anyone had doubted he would make it, he had just proved they were dead wrong. If anyone thought he couldn't cross the swamps in Camagüey, he had disproved them. He showed them all, even Castro himself. Now he'd show them again. From the map, it was now a straight, westward jaunt to the camp near Banao. It was time to unite the other factions. It was time to take the Escambray.

A trained doctor from Argentina, Guevara was rising in the revolutionary movement and just as eager as Fidel to make his mark. He had first met Castro in Mexico City, where Fidel and Raúl Castro had fled to avoid being arrested by Batista's secret police in 1955.

Guevara hit it off with the brothers in the Mexican capital. A hotbed of revolutionary intellectualism, the Latin bohemia of the Distrito Federal had become a cauldron of bitter anti-Americanism. The Castros talked about their long struggle in Cuba, while Guevara recounted a life-changing motorcycle trip he took through South America—a trip that opened his eyes to the ugly sides of the continent.

Guevara volunteered to join Castro and other guerrillas when they boarded the *Granma*, a rickety cabin cruiser, for a clandestine journey from Mexico to Cuba to launch their efforts. When the wooden craft ran ashore, the rebels waded through a treacherous swamp before government soldiers ambushed them. Guevara, the Castro brothers, and nine others survived the attack, escaping into the Sierra Maestra. In time, the small group grew into a formidable force, launching attack after attack on government soldiers. Guevara impressed the other rebels during those battles by refusing to back down.

When Castro decided to expand his base into the Escambray, he turned to Guevara, warning the Argentine that he would face opposition from Menoyo's rebels.

By the time Guevara arrived at the Second Front outpost, he was ready for confrontation. At first glance, there wasn't much to it: a few huts and what looked like the remains of a campfire. Guevara inched closer, running into the sentries. The guards knew he was moving into the mountains, but they didn't know where. Guevara didn't waste any time. He walked right past them to a parked Jeep at the edge of camp.

Hoisting himself up on the vehicle, his back against the autumn sky, he faced the men gathering curiously around him. In a clear and steady voice, Guevara told them that he had come to deliver a message from the Sierra Maestra. He needed to make this clear: This was going to be their land. It didn't matter what had happened before now. The 26th of July Movement was about to make some of the biggest moves of the war. Everyone—including the rebels surrounding the Jeep—either had to join or be left out. It was their choice.

From across the camp, Carreras spotted the men crowded around the Jeep. He rushed over and broke through the line. "*Para ahora mismo!*" Carreras shouted. Right now!

Guevara looked down. The rebels on both sides grabbed their guns. As the men later recalled, the Argentine said he represented the forces of the revolution. He had a right to be there and didn't need anyone's permission.

Carreras glared at his counterpart. "You have to talk to me before you talk to these people," he said.

For Guevara to pass through this region, especially in crossing the Hagabama River, he needed permission that could come from one man only: Menoyo.

Guevara jumped down from the Jeep.

Everyone watched the two men to see what was going to happen next. Either man could have killed the other right there, a shooting that would have triggered internecine combat.

Guevara didn't expect such a test of his authority. No one had talked to him this way. But he knew that Castro would disapprove of any bloodshed—at least now. Guevara had to stand down if he wanted to accomplish Castro's mission.

He stepped back and began talking to the others present. If the rebels of the Escambray wanted to join him, they should do so. They could come over to the 26th of July.

He then spun around and walked away. No blood was spilled that day, but the feud between Carreras and Guevara was far from over.

18

It began as a drone over the mountains, a moan that barely echoed down from the clouds. At first, no one noticed. The sound rose into a low rumble, like thunder in the distance, but still no one paid it any heed. Morgan and Olga just wanted to be alone.

As they walked along the path leading to camp, Olga looked up and saw what appeared to be an airplane in the distance cross over the mountain. Then she saw another.

Morgan quickly pulled her close and moved them toward a mound of bedrock. Within seconds, the two planes were rumbling above them. Olga covered her face as a hail of bullets fell from the sky, kicking up dust just a few yards away. Morgan threw her to the ground and rolled on top of her. Neither one moved.

The planes circled, unleashing a steady stream from the air guns. Olga could hear the planes directly over them, the earth trembling from the shots raining down. Shaking, Olga gripped Morgan.

"It's OK," he told her. "It's OK. It over, *finito*."

She had many close calls, but never anything like that. Morgan kissed her and held her for a moment. Olga didn't want to move. She always prided herself on being brave, on facing anything: the police, the soldiers. But this had come so close.

"*Dios mío*," she said.

Slowly, they both stood, Olga's knees trembling. It was time to get back to the camp. God only knew what had happened there.

They rushed back along the trail. Morgan dashed to the first hut, then the second. Some of the huts had been peppered with shots, but so far no one was injured. The other rebels were scrambling through the camp, making sure the nearby farmhouse and equipment were unharmed. The planes would return.

Olga and Morgan turned to each other. Either one could have died. Either one could have been left without the other.

"I love you," Morgan said.

Olga hugged him. She had seen for the first time how quickly they could be shot—and killed. They had survived by a matter of inches.

—◆—

Menoyo paced like a cat.

The planes were picking up. They had hit near Nuevo Mundo, and they had dropped bombs near Manicaragua. Batista wasn't going to let up with the air power. That was the only way he could force a surrender. With every report of damage, Menoyo was getting angrier.

Batista's men had been beaten at Charco Azul. They had been beaten at Chalet de Lora and Finca Diana. It was clear the army's strategy had suddenly changed. Instead of moving deeper into the mountains, the troops had been ordered to halt. Batista was trying to bait the rebels out of the mountains by bombing.

If that's what Batista wanted the rebels to do, then Menoyo would meet that challenge. But it had to be planned carefully.

As long as the rebels remained encamped in the mountains above Batista's men, nothing was going to move forward. Menoyo pointed on the map: Trinidad. The southern coastal city southwest of Sancti Spiritus would be the perfect target. It would send a clear message that the rebels were going to take the fight to the cities. If that's what Batista wanted, that's what he was going to get.

Trinidad had an old stone-and-wood garrison loaded with machine guns, grenades, and other weapons. The US government had cut off Batista's supply, but he had gotten around that obstacle by going directly to Britain, of all places.

The Second Front didn't have a lot of ammunition, but it now had four hundred men. Menoyo and the other commanders would lead them.

—◆—

With his men gathered around, Menoyo spelled out their plan of attack. Two main roads led directly into Trinidad, with a few—but not many— entry points to the rear. The garrison was here, he pointed out.

One bad move, one wrong entry, and the rebels could lose the element of surprise. Then they became targets. There were simply too many soldiers, and they'd be attacking from all over, including the garrison. The rebels needed to come like bats out of hell.

Menoyo had already thought this out. They would gather at a place known to the locals as Mangos Pelones—a farm on the edge of a highway ten miles from the city. They could get trucks from the local plantation owners to haul everyone into the town. Once they got to the entrance, they would split into groups and surround the garrison, while the point men took on the guards.

Menoyo wanted no surprises. If Batista's soldiers were effective anywhere, it was in the cities, where they could control the buildings and the people. Months earlier, the army led a brutal attack on civilians in Cienfuegos as punishment for a revolt at a nearby naval base. Soldiers stormed the streets, arresting and killing people even suspected of helping the insurrectionists. Menoyo looked at his commanders. Get ready, he said. They were embarking on a plan that was close to a suicide mission.

———

Olga stared over the tops of the coffee plants as the wind blew across the plantation. At the highest point of the camp, it looked like a sea of green. There was still no sign of Morgan. He should have been back by now, coming up the trail with his men. He had left on patrol, but he wasn't supposed to be gone this long.

She had tried to keep busy, but she couldn't stop thinking about him. She should have heard from the runners by now. She remembered the paper he had given her on that cool, rainy night with his mother's address. She remembered the promise that she had made. "If anything happens to me, let her know," he had said. She turned sadly and walked back to the farmhouse, where the grower, Nicholas Cárdenas, had opened his plantation to the rebels.

One more hour, she said to herself. *Una hora mas.*

She didn't know everything about what the commanders were doing, but it was no secret that the fighting was about to get more intense. She could see that every day with the rebels arriving at the camp. If Morgan died, she would regret that she had never told him everything that she wanted to say, that she wanted to be at his side—even if they both died.

In the distance, she heard voices just beyond the farmhouse. She rose and walked to the edge. Straining to see over the plants, she saw men coming up from the trail. Looking closer, she spotted him. "He's alive," she said as she rushed across the camp.

He was exhausted but managed a smile when he spotted her.

Never again would she let a moment like this pass. "You won, commander," she said, staring up and smiling.

Morgan looked around for a moment, confused. "I won?"

"I believe I have already given it enough thought," she said. Olga didn't care that everyone was now staring. "I will marry you."

Morgan threw down his gun, leaned over, and kissed her. He knew this wasn't a good time. He knew that he might never leave Cuba alive. But if he died without marrying Olga, somehow his life—and all that he had sacrificed so far—would have been for nothing.

It was time.

19

Ventura Hernandez glanced outside and beckoned for Morgan and Olga to come in. Batista's men had camped just miles away, and the Rural Guard had been prowling the area, dragging the guajiros from their bohíos to find out who had been helping Menoyo.

In the middle of the mess, Hernandez and other farmers were just trying to live their lives. The Second Front rebels had been their saviors. No unit did more for the Escambray, protecting the people from the dreaded soldiers. For months, Hernandez had helped the Second Front, sneaking them bananas and coffee, warning them about trouble in the valley.

He turned to Olga and Morgan standing in the middle of his stone-and-wood farmhouse. "I will be your witness," he said.

Hernandez would prepare the documents for them to be married and seal them: "The free territory of the Escambray." But before the ceremony, he instructed his daughters to take Olga down to the creek that meandered through his small farm. "Be careful," he told them.

His girls grabbed a towel and soap and led Olga down the hill. The sun was setting over the mountain as they reached the end of the trail. The creek bubbled up at the end of the small road. The girls led Olga to a bend where the water was rushing over stones and branches and a nearby waterfall cascaded down from a ledge. One of the girls told Olga that she could bathe here.

As she slipped off her shirt and slowly removed the rest of her clothes, the girls huddled around her, giggling. Olga slipped into the water, first to her knees, then her waist, and finally she immersed herself.

"Oh my God," she said aloud. It had been months since she had had a full bath.

She stared up at the sky, a cool breeze blowing across the valley, the tops of the trees waving as if they were moving just for her. She thought about all that had happened: her escape, the war. If she could stop time— now—just the way it was . . .

"We should go," said one of the girls. They worried that the Rural Guard could be coming.

The Hernandez daughters shielded Olga as she stepped from the water. Shivering in the cool air, Olga followed them to the trail. Each walked next to each other to make sure no one could ambush them from the brush.

At the door, Morgan met Olga, still wrapped in the towel, her hair cascading down. For a moment, he stood and stared. She had never looked so beautiful. Morgan, too, looked different. While Olga was gone, he had gotten a pair of scissors and cut off his beard. She had never seen his full face. Even his eyes seemed different.

Hernandez had decorated the table with a vase of wildflowers and a bowl of bananas, oranges, and mangoes. Olga knew he didn't have much. Hernandez's wife had walked out on the family one day, but the girls stayed with their papa. He worked the land mostly by himself, making sure they had enough to eat and sell at market.

Through the door came Onofre Pérez, a big round man with thick forearms, who served as one witness. Francisco "Panchit" Léon, an aging, gray rebel twice as old as the others, would be the other.

Hernandez quickly stood up. "We must start," he said. But first he asked that one of his daughters take Olga into a bedroom.

When Olga walked in, she saw that they had laid out a blouse along with a floral skirt and a pair of shoes. "You can wear them," said the farmer.

Olga was speechless. She had never been treated so kindly since arriving in the mountains. For this family to do this for her—they didn't even know her. She slipped into the clothes, careful not to crease the fabrics.

Hernandez wasted no time. He handed Morgan and Olga their vows on a piece of paper. As Morgan read his lines, tears welled in Olga's eyes. She couldn't believe it. She lost her family in Santa Clara when she fled to the mountains. She might never see her mother or sisters again. But here—now—she had gained a new family, William Morgan—someone she would hold in her heart for the rest of her life.

"I love you," she told him.

They kissed, and then looking up, everyone clapped.

Pérez had spent weeks with Morgan in the mountains but had never seen his comandante so much at peace. Hernandez offered the group a pitcher of punch made of homemade rum and fruit juice. Everyone took turns toasting the happy couple.

Morgan put his arm around Olga and motioned for her to walk outside. In the darkness, they walked down near the river, the moon casting shadows on the ground below. Twigs snapped under their feet as they found a quiet corner of the farm.

Morgan and Olga in the Escambray mountains, with assault rifles, smiling lovingly into each other's eyes COURTESY OF MORGAN FAMILY COLLECTION

Morgan reached into his pocket and took out a present: a jar of cream—a luxury in the mountains during a war. Olga smiled. Even when she lived in Santa Clara, she hadn't received a gift like this.

"I don't have anything to give you but my love," she said.

"Your love is more than enough for me," he replied. "When your country is free, we will be very happy and love each other more."

Above the mountains, the stars shone brightly, lighting up the black sky. They embraced, kissing, slowly sliding down to the ground and rolling on the grass. They didn't care that it was cold or that the others were nearby.

In the darkness, Menoyo and his men crept past the row of faded pastel storefronts, lights flickering inside. One more block, and they would stand within reach of the garrison.

Trinidad had dozens of neighborhoods. A virtual maze of concrete blocks with barrel tile roofs lining narrow cobblestone streets covered the center of town and offered plenty of hiding places. Even with two hundred soldiers running around the city, the rebels could find plenty of spots where no one would find them. For most of the afternoon, they had been filtering quietly into the city and then ducking into the homes of supporters who had been waiting to host them.

To keep a low profile, Menoyo had split the Second Front into strike teams, the same strategy as in the mountains. Each would converge on the garrison from a different street. He motioned for his men to gather at the block just beyond the target. They had just seconds before their actions drew the guards' attention.

Menoyo had reviewed the attack plan for weeks with his commanders, each group taking a post fewer than fifty yards from each corner of the building. It was no different than positioning themselves for an ambush in the bush, taking the high ground behind thick brush and ridges.

Menoyo and his men crouched down and positioned their rifles. Taking aim at the looming stone structure, Menoyo eyed the windows, the doorway, the guards. Then he threw up his hand: "*Fuego!*" he shouted.

The men squeezed the triggers of their rifles, bullets flying into windows and the yard around the structure. They took turns, careful not to expend all their ammo, trying to make each shot count. Menoyo fully expected a return volley from the soldiers in the garrison. But what he didn't expect—what he didn't rehearse while planning the attack—were gunshots in the distance.

The soldiers weren't just in the garrison. They were in the street, just beyond the plaza, firing at his men. The strike team led by Anastasio Cárdenas Ávila had started to bolt from the buildings to join the main unit, but these soldiers had surprised them. Men in uniforms jumped out from the buildings, firing into the street. Others seemed to come from nowhere.

What the rebels didn't know was that Batista's commanders had just sent 150 reinforcements before they arrived. Add that to the 200 soldiers entrenched in the garrison, and they were up against a group the size of the entire Second Front.

The rebel who was most in trouble was Cárdenas, pinned down with his men on a street called La Reforma. They tried to escape but couldn't. One of his men, Hector Rodriguez, was clutching a .12-gauge shotgun that protected him but split in two when hit with enemy fire. Cárdenas wasn't as lucky. He died, along with five others. The other guerrillas tried to help, but the soldiers fired on Cárdenas and his men, riddling their bodies with bullets.

Across town, Menoyo was beside himself. He grabbed the twenty-pound bomb that he and the others had built from sticks of dynamite. He lit the fuse and heaved it into the side of the barracks. The sticks exploded, tearing a giant hole in the side of the wall and sending chunks of cement flying across the street.

But the soldiers didn't let up. With all the ammo that money could buy, they kept firing into the rebel groups from all directions. The rebels didn't have a choice: They had to retreat.

Menoyo pulled the radio close, calling the other teams. It was time to pull out, he screamed. *Pronto*. Each team knew what to do. Some converged at the north side of town where they had parked the trucks borrowed from the farmers. Some of the men jumped into the vehicles, while others bolted into the brush beyond the outskirts of town. But the army wasn't done. The soldiers gave chase, firing at the rebels on foot.

Morgan kicked into gear. He could see that the others were in trouble, and he ordered his men to set up their own counterattack.

Gripping his Sten, he stood as the soldiers were charging and fired into the unit, unflinching. He didn't give a damn how much ammunition he expended. He needed to hold back the soldiers.

Keep firing, he yelled to his men. Don't stop. After several minutes, the soldiers were forced to run for cover and halt their pursuit. Menoyo and the others had a clear road.

The Second Front lost six men, including Cárdenas, one of its comandantes. Eight other rebels were shot up, but still breathing. They had less ammunition than before and were retreating. But they had done something that no one—not even Castro—had accomplished. They had entered a major city and boldly inflicted casualties on Batista's army. Dozens of soldiers lay bleeding in the streets. Morgan in the rear guard ensured that most of the rebels stayed alive.

20

MENOYO HAD ALREADY DECIDED: HE WASN'T GOING TO TAKE HIS COLUMN. He wasn't going to take his full complement of bodyguards. He wasn't going to call on Morgan or the other comandantes. He would meet with Che Guevara alone.

One word, one crossed look, and it could all end. The two sides already hated each other, and the situation was getting worse. If he didn't reach some sort of an agreement with Guevara, a civil war would form between the two largest rebels groups of the revolution.

Too much was at stake.

With a personal guard of two men, Menoyo walked east down the long hill from the camp toward El Pedrero. He felt the fate of the revolution on his shoulders. He had hoped to have seized enough weapons and ammo at Trinidad to arm all the rebels, but that didn't happen. He had hoped to have pulled the soldiers into the upper mountains, but that didn't happen either.

He had tried to stop the bombings, but now Batista was sending even more planes over the eastern mountains. Then there was Guevara, skulking in the background like a moonlight shadow.

Menoyo got word from the guajiros near Sancti Spiritus that Che had been going from village to village, trashing the Second Front, telling the farmers that he represented the one, true rebel unit. Guevara even found a way to drive a wedge between the Second Front and the Directorio by signing an agreement with the latter group on December 1, declaring that they were now joining military forces.

He was also making waves on other fronts. He had disrupted the national elections in Las Villas Province weeks earlier by mobilizing his column and blocking access to voting booths in key areas.

Now, he wanted the Second Front.

After trudging across the tree-shrouded mountain near Pedrero, Menoyo could see the camp just over the hill. At the top stood the wood farmhouse covered with palm branches that had served as Guevara's

Escambray headquarters. He had launched a rebel newspaper from the house, the *Minuteman*, setting off a propaganda machine with one goal: Pull the region under Fidel's control.

Menoyo nodded to the sentries as he passed, yanked on the straps of his M3 submachine gun, and inched closer to the house.

Both sides were eyeballing each other already. Guevara appeared in the doorway, standing next to his men. The two rebel leaders shook hands, sizing each other up like gunslingers in a Western. Then they ducked into the dark bohío.

They immediately went to opposite sides of the table. It was obvious that neither man liked the other. It didn't help that Guevara began by ripping into Jesús Carreras and the shabby treatment that he had shown Guevara and his men.

"He's one of my comandantes," Menoyo responded with a shrug. "You were coming into our territory. He had a right to challenge you."

Guevara's eyes narrowed. "No," he fired back.

Guevara represented Castro. They had launched this revolution. They had every right to be in the Escambray, and they didn't need Carreras's approval.

Che had called this meeting, he reminded Menoyo. He wanted to cover important ground and had waited for this moment. First, Che spoke of his sojourn across the mountains near Sancti Spiritus all the way to the Las Villas border. He had two words: land reform. The land in the Escambray needed to return to the guajiros. They toiled on the plantations, but they weren't getting anything back—barely subsisting. The plantation owners were drinking the blood of the peasants.

Guevara wanted Menoyo to implement a plan to carve up the land and divide it among the workers. Only then would there be a true revolution. No one would own one thousand acres anymore, as it was now with many estates scattered across the mountains.

"No," Menoyo said, shaking his head and pushing back from the table.

Menoyo had long thought about what was best for Cuba, and in his mind, the landowners were far from the worst people. Some of the biggest landowners in the mountains had supported the revolution. They had supplied food and guns. They had fought for their independence generations earlier against Spain. Menoyo suspected Guevara of Communism—it was that simple—and he despised all forms of Communism.

"I cannot do that—and I will not," said Menoyo.

Neither man was going to back down.

Menoyo had slept in countless dirt-floor bohíos across the Escambray. He had broken bread with its families. He knew their struggles better than this interloper. Menoyo reminded Guevara that when the Second Front was driving out the soldiers at Charco Azul and Rio Negro—paying with their own blood—the 26th of July Movement was off in another mountain chain. Menoyo and his men had fought this war on their own.

Che looked up, frowning. If Menoyo persisted in opposing him, it was going to mean war. The enemy was in Havana, Che insisted, and it was critical that all rebel groups fall under one roof. The revolution had reached a point at which all the rebels needed to go on the offensive—in the Escambray. This is where the revolution will be won, he said. This is the time to strike, he added.

"I know that," Menoyo shot back. That's why the Second Front had staked their claim in the heart of Cuba, not at the far end of the island. "This is our territory."

Before Menoyo could finish, Che lit into the Second Front. Within seconds, both men were ready to go for their guns. No one moved. This was exactly what Menoyo feared would happen. Even he couldn't control himself. Both men stared at each other, each one waiting.

Guevara broke the stalemate. If Menoyo wasn't willing to agree to everything that Che was proposing, it was important that the groups reach a military accord. If they could move on Batista now, they could move him out. But they had to do it now. Camilo Cienfuegos Gorriarán, one of Castro's trusted column leaders, would take the northern part of Las Villas Province. Guevara would sweep across the center to Santa Clara. The Second Front would take the southern end, including the city of Cienfuegos.

"We need everyone," Guevara said.

Menoyo listened. He knew his men could march to Cienfuegos. They could take the army fort at Topes de Collantes. He thought for a moment about what his men had endured. This plan offered them a chance to finish the fight in their own territory.

He nodded. "You have an agreement," Menoyo said.

Guevara presented a document that he had prepared in advance. They wouldn't sign the agreement for land reform, but they would settle on the military pact.

Menoyo read the document and signed it. Guevara countersigned and handed it back to Menoyo. His signature at the bottom read simply: "Che."

Menoyo looked up. "What's this?"

Guevara replied that it was his favored name.

Menoyo angrily crossed out his name and wrote above it "Gallego," his own nickname, which meant Galician.

Even in the agreement, the two men had disagreed. Both sides knew that each man would lead his unit into battle—but it was just a matter of time before they turned their guns on each other.

MORGAN SLIPPED INTO THE OLIVE-GREEN SHIRT AND FASTENED THE buttons, closing each one except for the top. Reaching over the cot, he grabbed his belt with the large silver buckle and pulled it through each loop on his pants. He picked up his .38-caliber Smith and Wesson, spun the chamber, and snapped it into place before tucking it in a holster on his right side.

Olga watched as her husband reached down to tug on his boot laces, making sure they were tight. He dug into his pocket and yanked out a rosary, unfurling the beads and placing them around his neck.

"Be careful," she said.

She had watched him many times as he readied to leave the camp, but this was different. He and his men would be leaving for days—forty miles from camp—in an offensive that would be either disastrous or the boldest move of the revolution. There was no room for mistakes.

Once again, she felt herself growing anxious. She promised herself this wouldn't happen, that she wouldn't fret about him leaving. But she couldn't hold it back anymore.

Morgan placed his arms around her. "Please, don't worry," he told her. "I will be back."

It was another suicide mission: thousands of soldiers waiting in Santa Clara, B-26s circling the skies, barricades set up along major roadways. Sooner or later, their good fortune was going to end. Morgan would be lucky to get to the first town in the next province without a firefight. From there, he still had to descend into five more towns along the north–south highway between Santa Clara and Cienfuegos. She had heard the plans. Each time, her heart beat faster, and she pretended not to listen.

Menoyo's plan was to sneak across the river valley to Topes de Collantes, a sprawling white tuberculosis sanitarium that Batista had built a few years earlier before it became a military stronghold now housing 150 soldiers. Artola and Carreras would join the attack and then take up with 26th of July Movement forces to the north.

In the coordinated sweep, Che would move with his men thirty miles across the center of the province, Camilo Cienfuegos would position his men even farther north, and Jaime Vega and his men would ride in from the east—the units all trying desperately to stay in step. Castro would remain with his men in the Sierra Maestra.

Across the camp, Menoyo ordered his men to pack their gear. They were anxious to begin their march, packing all the ammunition they had. But before they could even gather in the center of camp, a messenger barged into the middle of a commanders' meeting.

Menoyo walked over and grabbed the paper the man was carrying. The leader paused for a moment, puzzled. The note was from Che Guevara: Stay put until further notice. Do not mobilize. Menoyo turned to his commanders. Why would Che put the brakes on?

There was no reason to pull back. In fact, army leaders were feuding among themselves, and rumors were running rampant that one of the generals was secretly meeting with Castro in Oriente Province to remove Batista. It was time to strike. Menoyo ordered a messenger to stop at the next Directorio camp that had aligned itself with Che to find out what had happened. The Second Front still had friends in the unit.

Menoyo didn't like taking orders from Che, but he had to abide by the pact that he had signed. They had gone over the map numerous times, studying the roads and trails where the men would travel as they moved toward their targets. The rebels were on edge, pacing the camp, waiting.

The messenger returned. The look on his face said the answer wasn't good. What the rebels learned infuriated Menoyo: Che had tried to sabotage the Second Front's plans. While the Second Front was waiting, Che had ordered Raúl Nieves, one of the commanders of the Directorio, to attack Manicaragua, a key city.

It was all a ploy. Manicaragua lay in the center of the area reserved for the Second Front.

"¡Hijo de puta!" yelled Menoyo. It was clear the 26th of July was trying to take credit for everything and wanted to leave the Second Front out completely.

"Take your column, go to Manicaragua," Menoyo ordered Artola. "Get there before those bastards."

Che had broken his word. For all of his pontificating about loyalty to the cause, he had crapped on his own pact.

"It's time to fight," Menoyo ordered his men. The Second Front might not live to see the New Year, but at least it would die with honor.

Morgan slung the Sten over his shoulder and stormed onto the trail. Nothing was going to stop him and his men from reaching the first town, Cumanayagua. From the edge of the camp, Olga watched as her husband's green fatigues faded into the trees. In just hours, the column would march into the valley of death.

More than a hundred miles to the east, government troops had ambushed a 26th of July column, killing eighteen rebels and wounding eleven. But no one knew when the army was going to attack the southern positions. During these tense, unsure moments, Morgan stared straight ahead, clenching his weapon like a sacred object. For most of the march, he kept to himself, looking occasionally at the map to make sure he was keeping pace with Menoyo. Every now and then, a messenger on horseback pulled up to the unit, giving bits and pieces of information on the locations of the other comandantes.

In the distance, the tops of the buildings of Cumanayagua rose above the long road. The town lay just a dozen miles from Cienfuegos, the major port city and lifeline for the government.

Morgan instructed his men to break into teams—just as they had done in the mountains—and enter the city at different points.

Their first target would be the garrison for the army's weapons and ammo. In addition to encountering government troops, it was Christmas Eve, so there might be civilians on the streets. The men needed to stay hidden as much as possible, using the storefronts for cover, and they needed to take one street at a time.

Leading his team, Morgan moved along the side of a road that ran directly into the city. Coming from above, the rumble in the air began to get louder. As the rebels looked up, two B-26s broke from the clouds.

Some of the men froze. Morgan didn't flinch. He quickened his pace for the town and then ducked into a row of stucco storefronts. Moments later, the planes swooped over the town and let loose a barrage of bullets across the dusty road. Pedestrians ran for cover, jumping into stores and hiding under trees. Suddenly, the other rebels watched as Morgan appeared on a roof.

With his silhouette against the sky, he screamed while lifting his Sten in the air, firing upward at one of the planes. Even as the plane veered and flew away, Morgan kept aim, firing round after round.

As quickly as they had circled in, the planes disappeared.

The town's pedestrians saw the crazy gunner on the rooftop and applauded. The rebels soon learned that most of the soldiers had left the town for Cienfuegos before they had arrived. The few who remained surrendered. William Morgan had taken Cumanayagua.

—◆—

Menoyo and his men trudged along the trail, flushed and tired from moving under the glaring sun. As they broke through the brush at the base of the mountain, they spotted the looming structure. To the rebels, it looked like a battleship on the peak of a mountain. Few of the guerrillas had ever seen anything like Topes de Collantes.

The science fiction sanitarium was everything it was billed to be. Set in the middle of nowhere, the sprawling building was created as a grand experiment by the government to treat tuberculosis patients half a mile above sea level. Once holding one thousand beds, the ten-story tower now held government soldiers guarding the road to Trinidad. Built on a peak of the Escambray, the concrete edifice was nearly impenetrable. But if the rebels were to win the southern mountains, they had to take it.

Menoyo ordered his men to break into teams. One would take the southern side of the building, another would take the opposite. They were to wait for his orders. Menoyo then told his own team to set up firing positions. He didn't want anyone wasting ammo, but he wanted the soldiers to feel the heat. Normally, he would have waited. But this case was different. They had to open fire first. The only way they were going to force the soldiers to fight would be to let them know they were outside.

Menoyo scanned the huge structure and then lifted his hand. "*Fuego!*" he called, dropping his arm. The rebels fired, aiming at windows and doors. The shots rang out, waking the soldiers inside. Moments later, the troops began shooting back. For several minutes, both sides fired volley after volley. But the rebels had the upper hand. The soldiers had nowhere to go. If they tried to escape, the rebels were waiting.

Then one of the rebels approached Menoyo with an idea. He had once worked in the sanitarium as a nurse and knew of a tiny door on the side of the building that was chained with a padlock. If they could get inside, they might be able to disrupt the army's operation. Menoyo nodded. He called on others, including Ramiro Lorenzo and José Casanova, and filled them in on the details.

As darkness fell, the men scoped out the building. One by one, they jumped across the terrain but stayed several hundred yards away in the shadows. Menoyo studied the door and nodded to the others. "Let's try it," he said.

They crawled on their hands and knees to the side of the building. Then, taking out a pair of metal cutters, they severed the chain and quietly pushed the door open.

Still on their knees, they squeezed through the opening and found the narrow spiral staircase just inside that led to the main offices upstairs. Menoyo and the men slithered up the stairs and reached the main floor, where they crept down the hall. They passed each door until they came to the offices, where a light was shining through the crack under the door.

Menoyo jumped in and surprised an army officer before he could grab his gun. "You are under arrest," said Menoyo as the man turned white. He introduced himself and asked who he had the pleasure of arresting.

The officer looked up at Menoyo, shaken. "I am Commander Perez Corcho," he said.

Their gamble had paid off.

Corcho put up his hands while the men frisked him. Menoyo walked over to the PA system. "This is Comandante Eloy Gutiérrez Menoyo, commander of the Second Front of the Escambray," he said, his voice echoing through the building. "We have already taken over the town square, and we are in the building. Everyone needs to throw their weapons in the hallways. Come out with your hands in the air."

The soldiers tossed their rifles and machine guns down and went to the main floor, where the armed rebels secured them.

Topes de Collantes was theirs.

22

Lázaro Artola crawled atop the ledge. He and his men had trudged along trails choked by thick brush, trying to reach the town before the others. They successfully had avoided a plane buzzing over the mountains. Now, staring down the long road, he could see into the streets of Manicaragua, a dozen miles from the provincial capital of Santa Clara and a gathering point for soldiers.

Much of the city had been laid out in square blocks of old, ornate storefronts and high arching columns. People passed through narrow street corners. The stench of horses and trucks wafted through the air. Artola motioned for his men to get ready.

One by one, they fixed their rifles. Artola had one of the most disciplined columns in the Second Front, but this was dangerous work. He had no time to look for road mines, no time to take cover if the planes arrived.

"Move out!" he yelled.

Like clockwork, his men fanned out toward the town square. Some crawled along the storefronts, others jumped behind trees. Just as they reached the plaza, civilians popped their heads out from the shops, some even venturing out to the sidewalk. "*Los soldados han desaparecido,*" some said, waving their arms. The soldiers are gone.

The locals pointed to the road leading out of the city. The soldiers had packed up and left for Cienfuegos, they said, forty miles west. Artola discovered no one at the garrison. He had expected a fight, but the townspeople were telling the truth. The rebels had taken Manicaragua without any resistance.

Artola signaled for his messengers. His men would go to Cumanayagua and let the Second Front officers there know that the Manicaragua garrison belonged to the Second Front and that the government soldiers were heading to Cienfuegos. They probably were moving along the highway since they hated going into the mountains. Make haste.

Nearby, people came out onto the streets, erupting in cheers. The local farmers hated the government almost as much as the droughts that had killed their coffee plants. As his men shook hands with the people, Artola noticed another group of rebels entering the plaza. But they didn't belong to the Second Front. They were Che's men. At the head of the column was Directorio captain Raúl Nieves.

Nieves stopped for a moment and shook his head. Che would be disappointed. He had wanted the 26th of July to plant their flag in the ground here. The Second Front had beaten them.

In Cuba's military headquarters in Havana, General Francisco Tabernilla Dolz stared grimly at the dispatches coming in from the Escambray: Fomento, Cumanayagua, Remedios, all critical garrison towns. This wasn't supposed to happen.

It was early yet, but something in the mountains was starting to worry the top generals, including Tabernilla. First, there was Manicaragua. Not only had the town been taken without a fight, but the rebels had blocked off the area. Then the main rail line through the heart of the region had been cut at Zaza del Medio. Now Caibarién, forty-five miles northeast, had just surrendered to Che's men, which meant the government had lost one of the key ports.

The army was learning that Che's men would take one town and Menoyo's men another. It was like a chess game. One swept through the central mountains and the other, the south. In any war, setbacks occur. But the army was losing ground on multiple fronts.

North of Cienfuegos, a rebel team led by Publio Ruiz, a young captain trained by Morgan, had overwhelmed the soldiers in a charge, killing several. At Yaguajay, the rebels led by Camilo Cienfuegos of the 26th of July Movement had stunned the army by surrounding the town and pinning the troops in their barracks.

Tabernilla was beside himself. "Two years of a prolonged campaign" were taking a toll, he said. But it wasn't just the fatigue of war. The rebels were starting to show their experience.

For an entire year, they had been mapping and patrolling the mountains, which now allowed them to snake through the back roads and trails they had learned so well. Artola made it to Manicaragua in just a few hours. Morgan reached Cumanayagua before anyone else. Both rebel forces were linked by scores of messengers.

In all the months of fighting in the Escambray, the army never created permanent bases in the mountains. Towns such as Cumanayagua and Manicaragua remained vulnerable because the army had no significant presence.

Perhaps it was arrogance on the part of the military or a lack of any real concern on the part of the generals, but after reading the battle reports, Batista was disgusted. He stripped his commanders in the Escambray of their power and put in Colonel Joaquín Casillas Lumpuy to restore order. Batista then sent an armored train loaded with weapons.

He only hoped it wasn't too late.

23

PEERING THROUGH THE MORNING HAZE, DOMINGO ORTEGA GOMEZ lifted his rifle and took aim as the soldiers moved within striking distance. *Just a few more seconds*, he thought, propping himself up. *Just a few more . . .*

Ortega's team members stood by with their rifles raised just as the army men came into view on the narrow dirt road. It was no surprise the soldiers would show up. This road—the stretch of highway between Manicaragua and Cumanayagua—was their only route to reach the southern coast. The trails through the mountains were too dangerous for the men in uniforms and their vehicles.

Most of them had left the small towns and were now trying to reach Cienfuegos, where they had a chance of joining other units. For Ortega, it was a test. The young Second Front captain just happened to be patrolling the area when he got word the soldiers were coming. The rebels knew that taking control of this stretch of highway would cut off the army's escape.

Ortega motioned for his men to get ready. It was hard to figure out how many soldiers were in the unit. If it was a company, Ortega couldn't possibly stop them with just a few rebels. But if he could at least inflict damage, he might be able to send a message the road was no longer safe.

He squinted for a moment, aimed, and then squeezed the trigger. The other rebels fired on the stunned soldiers. Some jumped to the side of the road, others fell. The rebels stood and continued firing as the soldiers ran. It ended as quickly as it started, with nine soldiers dead in the road. The rest escaped. It wouldn't take long for word to reach the other army units: The Second Front had just cut off the army's lifeline.

———

Just after dawn, Morgan summoned his men together. He rarely called these kinds of meetings, but he had just received an urgent message.

The information was sketchy, but hours earlier, a large plane was seen taking off in the darkness from Camp Columbia in Havana. No one knew who was on the flight, but word was that Batista himself had climbed aboard and ordered the pilot to take off.

The rebels looked at Morgan and then one another. Where was this news coming from? They had heard so many rumors about the state of the war, especially in the past week. They had gotten word from a messenger that Che had taken Santa Clara, a major victory. Was it possible that the dictator who once ruled over the entire military machine of Cuba would just leave?

Batista had been the driving force of Cuba for sixteen years. He was the face of their country. He was *el hombre*. If anything, he would fight to the bitter end.

Morgan didn't disagree with anything they were saying, but that wasn't what mattered. They still had a war to fight while they waited for more news. As far he was concerned, they were going to take their next steps in the offensive.

For a long time, the Second Front had needed to take the fight to one of the most important cities in central Cuba: Cienfuegos. With a thriving port, the city provided a crucial link to the sea. The sun had risen over the eastern mountains as Morgan and his column took to the road, leaving their camp.

Soaked in sweat and dirt, they clutched their rifles as they walked on the same road where dozens of soldiers had passed days earlier. Morgan and the rebels were tense. They had no idea what they were facing. Cienfuegos was a maze of winding narrow roads that eventually led to the wide-open bay and the navy base in the center. It wasn't just a garrison they were targeting. It was a military installation with hundreds of men and a great deal of firepower. The soldiers there had rocket launchers and mortars. They had bazookas, and if they needed, they could call in the P-47 fighter planes.

Morgan had no idea what was going on in the rest of the mountains. But he knew he had to reach Cienfuegos before the city was lost. Once they reached the first set of roads, they could break up and enter the city at different angles, different streets. Gripping his Sten, Morgan picked up the pace. The rebels could see the outline of Cienfuegos just over the pass. Keep moving, he told them as they reached the first main road into the city.

In the distance, the rebels heard what sounded like gunshots. As they closed in, they could see men, women, and children hanging over the balconies, waving flags and shouting "*¡Libertad!*" as the rebels approached.

One rebel stopped and talked to the pedestrians hugging one another in the streets. The news was already crackling over the radios: Batista and his generals had fled the country. Morgan ordered his men to keep moving. There was no time to celebrate. They had one important stop: the road to the bay. If Batista had indeed fled, the Second Front was going to make sure the port and the naval base belonged to the guerrillas. Just beyond the next block, Morgan could see the sparkling blue waters of Jagua Bay, the centerpiece of the city.

By the time they reached the end of the road, the naval base loomed over the causeway. Morgan stopped for a moment and stared at the fortress. Then he turned to his messengers. "Tell them they are surrounded. There is no place for them to go." At first, his demands sounded crazy. The navy base could fire on the rebels at any time. It could batten down the hatches and wait for the army.

Morgan held his Sten tightly as he waited for his answer. No one inside the naval base was moving. Morgan was handed a radio. It was the commander, who assured Morgan that the rebels could lower their weapons. The base was surrendering.

Now Cienfuegos belonged to Morgan and the Second Front.

24

THE NEWS BEGAN FILTERING OVER THE AIRWAVES: BATISTA'S REIN OVER Cuba had ended.

The reaction began with shots fired into the air. Car horns echoed down the long boulevard leading to the plaza. The people of Cienfuegos had never experienced anything like it. Overlooking the plaza, they draped Cuban flags over their balconies and waved to pedestrians below. A crowd gathered in José Marti Park and shouted in jubilation to passing cars.

Morgan motioned for his men to gather around. They were in control. They would be moving into the naval base. But that's not why he was calling them together. In a few minutes, the city was going to erupt, and there was no police force to control the chaos. The rebels who had fought in the mountains for the past year were about to become the local police.

The men were exhausted. They hadn't slept in days. They hadn't washed. Some hadn't even eaten. But in minutes, they were going to be the law of the land.

The young barbudos had never been put in this position, but there was no other way for the transition to begin. Looting would start, and some would try to shoot the Batistianos, those loyal to the old regime. The rebels had to guard every section of the city and, if need be, commandeer cars without hurting anyone. They had to remember that they weren't in the mountains anymore but watching over women and children.

Holding their guns tightly, the men split into teams and disappeared beyond the first row of buildings. Morgan strapped on his Sten and started walking toward the naval base. Within moments, people on the streets overwhelmed him. Some reached over to hug him. Others kissed him.

"¡Americano! ¡Americano!" they shouted as he made his way down to the main bridge.

Some Cuban cities still supported Batista, but Cienfuegos wasn't one of them. Batista had ordered so many crackdowns here. Airplane bombings a year earlier had killed four civilians and injured twenty others. The rebels were a welcome sight.

Morgan never could have dreamed about this happening a year ago. A man running from his past, he had arrived in Cuba with little more than the clothes he was wearing. Now the people were mobbing him on the streets, hailing him as a hero of a revolution that was about to change the course of history.

＊＊

Menoyo had no time to celebrate. He had just received word: Batista was gone, but the military was still in control in the capital.

It was impossible to predict how it would end. The crowds had erupted in Havana. The Directorio had taken over the Ninth Street police precinct, and some of Batista's police were shot dead in the streets. The new dawn for Cuba was already turning violent.

The grab for power was under way even before the bodies were buried. Menoyo learned that Che was rushing to Havana. So was Camilo Cienfuegos. Even Rolando Cubela and the Directorio were hightailing it on the Central Highway to the capital. This wasn't necessarily good. There was bound to be more bloodshed. Batista's soldiers were still in Camp Columbia. They were also at La Cabaña, the military prison fortress. Thousands of government troops were still camped in three other provinces.

"It's time for us to go to Havana," Menoyo told Morgan.

The groups heading to the capital either were going to form a provisional government or were going to kill one another. Castro had a plan. Cubela and the Directorio had their plan. The interim government left by Batista was in chaos. All that the Second Front had fought for, all they had died for, their entire future lay at stake.

Menoyo needed to make a stand.

25

OVER THE HOOD OF THE JEEP, OLGA STARED AT THE LONG LINE OF cars jammed along the boulevard and then slumped back down in her seat. A crush of humanity was preventing her and the other rebels from moving any faster. People were standing in roads, waving down cars. Music blared from stores while revelers danced up and down the street. Some were hugging and crying. Women and children bounded out of their cramped stucco homes, waving Cuban flags and shouting to their neighbors. This is why she had been fighting. This is why she had risked her life.

To the people of Cienfuegos, every part of the city carried a reminder of the oppression they had endured: the municipal building, where the insurrectionists tried to create a bunker during the navy revolt; the Rural Guard barracks, attacked by the revolutionary sympathizers; the police headquarters, taken over by the rebels.

As Olga's Jeep pulled up to the main building at the naval station, she pointed to the entrance. "I am going in," she said.

She pushed open the doors and asked for her husband. A rebel guard told her that Morgan was in the command offices meeting with former Cienfuegos government leaders. Olga didn't care. She strode to the door and pushed it open.

Inside, everyone looked up. Morgan was sitting behind a table with papers strewn in front of him, surrounded by people she had never met. He looked serious, but then he broke into a grin.

"You're here," said Morgan.

"Of course," she said. "They are not going to keep me from you."

The moment broke the tension of a long day. Morgan had had to leave the base earlier in the day to stop civilians from looting and hunting down former Batista government workers. He also had to impose a ban on liquor sales as well as a curfew to keep order in the streets.

"We are not criminals," he told the rebels enforcing the emergency measures.

Along the busy streets, people recognized him. *"Weel-yam Morgan,"* they shouted from balconies and cars. He wasn't a hero just in the Escambray. He was getting calls from reporters in Cuba and America as well. Hundreds of newspapers carried an Associated Press feature story about the Americano who had hunted Batista's soldiers in the mountains. The *Havana Post* ran a piece on the *Yanqui comandante* and his exploits in battle. It wasn't Menoyo who was emerging as a major rebel figure in the Second Front. It was Morgan.

For her part, Olga just wanted to find a quiet place where she could be with her husband and talk about their life together. He had survived, and that was all that mattered to her. As they held each other, a messenger barged into the room: People were trying to break into city hall.

Morgan had to go.

She followed him outside to the parking lot, where he jumped into a Jeep and sped away. She climbed into another Jeep with another crew in pursuit. She watched as he wheeled through the streets, rounding corners and vanishing into the darkness.

Menoyo didn't have time to sleep. He didn't have time to eat. Instead of joining the rebels at the presidential palace, he was breaking up fights in the streets. In every Havana neighborhood, people were roaming, some with guns in hand, smashing store windows. At the Riviera, a crowd of angry civilians broke into the casino, turning loose a herd of pigs in the swanky hotel. Others barged into the Sevilla-Biltmore to break open the slot machines. Menoyo had had enough.

"Grab your guns, and get into the streets," he ordered his men. If the other rebel groups couldn't control the neighborhoods, the Second Front would. He broke his men into teams. One would go into the Miramar neighborhood, an upscale enclave of opulent homes with lushly landscaped lawns and pools. Another would venture into Vedado, an eclectic district of stores, hotels, and apartment buildings.

"There will be no looting," said Menoyo.

Alfredo Peña, a soldier in the Cuban army before joining the Second Front, would patrol the businesses, including banks and car dealerships.

Menoyo and his men would patrol downtown to keep troublemakers from breaking what remained of the law.

While Menoyo and his men guarded downtown Havana, a group of rebels and civilians led by Camilo Cienfuegos reached the sweeping entrance to Camp Columbia, the massive military headquarters. Batista commander Ramon Barquin had already looked at all his options, and they weren't good. Even his men knew it was over. Batista was gone. The regime had panicked.

After several tense minutes, Barquin walked out of the base. There would be no standoff or confrontation. He was turning the base over to the rebels.

At La Cabaña, the ancient military prison, it was the same: Che and his bedraggled men showed up at the gates to deliver an ultimatum. Colonel Manuel Varela Castro met them with an olive branch. The army wasn't going to offer any resistance.

In just hours, two of the foremost institutions of government had fallen into the hands of Castro's key men.

26

RINGS CIRCLED HIS EYES, AND HIS FACE WAS FLUSHED FROM THE SUN and sweat. Morgan was exhausted. Olga tried to get him to rest, but he had made the safety of Cienfuegos a personal mission. Traffic was moving down Paseo del Prado, due in part to the patrols he had established. Most of the troublemakers had been locked up.

After pulling into the naval station for another briefing, he received an urgent call. It was a messenger: Be on your guard; you are about to get a visitor. Fidel Castro.

After leaving Santiago de Cuba for Havana, 470 miles away, Castro decided to divert his route. He was coming to Cienfuegos. Morgan had heard rumblings that Castro was crossing the country in a caravan on his way to the capital, but he hadn't given it much thought. Some of the Second Front rebels grumbled about the 26th of July leader's decision to change course. After all, Cienfuegos was the only major city that fell under the control of the Second Front.

Morgan shrugged. His men needed to get ready. Their problems had been with Che, not Fidel. "We will show him respect," Morgan said.

The revolution had far bigger problems looming. The rebel groups were struggling to see who gets power. In Havana, the Directorio members were refusing to leave the presidential palace.

Castro's group had demanded that they vacate the building so his group could move in. From what the Directorio could tell, Castro's people were all but taking over. They had moved into all of the major garrisons and occupied nearly all of the police precincts. During his caravan ride, Castro barked over the radio that the country needed a new provisional president. Then he proceeded to name fifty-nine-year-old provincial judge Manuel Urrutia Lleó to the post, along with a cabinet.

He had iced out the Directorio. After listening to the radio broadcasts, Rolando Cubela had enough. He dashed off a note to the 26th of July Movement, demanding that the Directorio have a seat in the new government and that the "members and the blood shed by them be fully recognized." Otherwise, he wasn't budging.

News of a showdown rippled across the country.

———

Dressed in olive fatigues and a sidearm in his waistband, Castro jumped into the crowd waiting for him. "*Bienvenido a Cienfuegos!*" people yelled as they ran around him. Wearing his rebel cap and sporting a dark, full beard, he wasted no time moving along the line of people, shaking hands. Ever since Batista left, Castro was emerging as the next leader of Cuba, drawing television cameras in nearly every province where he stopped. Many of his speeches in the small towns were being broadcast into the capital.

Unlike the other towns that Castro had visited, Cienfuegos was a bastion of the Second Front. More people in the Escambray unit came from this city than any other. Scores of rebels bearing the Second Front insignia came out for Castro's entrance, leaving no doubt of the unit's strength in numbers.

As he stepped into the welcoming throng on Jagua Bay, Castro wasn't the only person commanding the attention of the crowd. Even as Morgan stood by, watching, people rushed up to him, pulling on his uniform and hugging him. Everywhere he went, he drew his own crowd.

For a brief, awkward moment, two of the most popular leaders of the Cuban revolution were in the same place, the crowd parting as the two rebel leaders came together. Olga watched carefully as her husband stood toe to toe with Castro. Both men reached out their hands to shake. The one thing they shared at the moment was that neither man had slept in days, both pushing on adrenaline. Castro nodded and then slipped back into the crowd. He had just a few hours to make a stand before moving on to Havana for another grand entrance.

Castro and his entourage made their way to Restaurante Covadonga for a celebratory dinner. As everyone squeezed inside, waiters rushed around the tables, handing out plates steaming with fresh paella. Castro barely picked at his food as he worked the crowd, stopping at tables to talk.

Dozens of Second Front members slipped inside as well, but after several minutes, Olga noticed something. All of the Second Front rebels were on one side of the room, the 26th of July rebels and Castro on the other. There was some small talk, but Castro was steering clear of the barbudos from the Escambray. After several more minutes of watching the body language in the room, Olga went over to Morgan.

"I'm not feeling well," she said. "I'm going to leave."

Morgan looked at her, puzzled.

"No," she snapped. "It's time to go."

She slipped out the door.

27

Cursing aloud, Morgan threw his Sten over his shoulder and jumped into the Jeep outside his office. He had just returned to the naval base when a messenger rushed inside, nearly out of breath. Two of the young Second Front rebels had been drinking. No one knew where they got the liquor, but they were staggering down the street.

"You need to get over there," the messenger said.

Morgan and his men had been enforcing the liquor ban, picking up people breaking the law and even locking them up when necessary. But this was inexcusable.

Wheeling down the boulevard, Morgan was intent on hunting them down. "He was angry, angry, angry," recalled Olga.

The pressure on Morgan had been building, and no one could see that more than she could. He wasn't sleeping but a couple of hours a night. He wasn't eating. He listened to the radio, waited for emergency calls, and then drove off in his Jeep. Every time she looked up, he was rushing out the door. He had managed to keep the vigilantism and other activities to a minimum—unlike the peacekeepers in Havana.

But the call clearly unnerved him. If he had to spend the rest of the day speeding up and down the Paseo del Prado, he would find them. Shortly after leaving the base, he rounded a street corner and spotted the two young men down the block. It was bad enough that they were just kids, but they were wearing the patches of the Segundo Frente.

Morgan's face went red and his eyes narrowed. "*Venir aqui!*" he shouted in mangled Spanish.

He tore into them. They not only had disobeyed his orders, but they were reflecting poorly on a unit that had fought for the liberation of their country. "*What's wrong with you?*" he screamed.

The young barbudos stood there, dumbfounded, mouths agape. They had never seen Morgan so angry. They didn't know what to say. Morgan wanted them off the streets. He never wanted to see them drinking again. Not in his town.

He had been hard on them, and he knew it. But he couldn't let it go. In the mountains, he had become a leader for the first time in his life. He not only saw the difference in himself when commanding his column, but in what he was able to do to keep others alive. With everything unraveling in Cuba after the fighting, he was being asked to do it again. Though the war had ended, he couldn't just drop being a commander. Cienfuegos would have fallen into chaos without him and his men. He had to stay.

The demand of keeping Cienfuegos in order wasn't the only matter weighing on his mind. In the early morning, Olga watched him pull out the pictures of Billy and Annie. He stared at the photos and placed them by his side. She knew how much he missed them. The war had allowed him to compartmentalize his life in a way that kept the problems of his past from creeping in. But it was all coming back.

⁓

Che Guevara was just getting started. He had swept the Directorio out of the way for the time being. But there was still the Second Front. They were everywhere. Castro had installed the new government, but Menoyo's men remained a visible force. Morgan was overseeing Cienfuegos, and Menoyo and his barbudos still appeared on the busiest street corners of Havana, toting weapons and wearing their own uniforms. It was precisely what Castro had predicted.

Weeks earlier, under a flashlight in the darkness of his camp, Castro had fired off a letter to Che, complaining that Che never should have signed any pacts with the Second Front. It was going to haunt them. Those same rebels would vie for power with the 26th of July Movement. "They want instead to share the fruits of our victories to strengthen its tiny revolutionary appliance and arise tomorrow with all kinds of claims," Castro wrote.

For two men so close, the letter came as a rebuke. But Che had plenty of time to redeem himself. The 26th of July had more men in its ranks now than ever before. It controlled every military base, prison, airport, and seaport other than Cienfuegos. They occupied nearly every garrison in Cuba and had appointed their own president and cabinet. They owned Cuba.

Castro, Menoyo, and Morgan COURTESY OF MORGAN
FAMILY COLLECTION

Che sent a message to Menoyo for a meeting. The place: La Cabaña, Che's headquarters. The request was marked urgent.

When Menoyo received the message, he looked at his men and shrugged. The last person he wanted to meet with was Che. He didn't like him. He didn't trust him. Che wasn't the leader of Cuba. "Who the hell does he think he is?" Menoyo complained. If Che wanted to meet with the leadership of the Second Front, Menoyo was going to bring everyone. Menoyo, Carreras, Felix Vasquez, a captain, and dozens of others would show up at the gates with their weapons.

The Second Front hadn't asked for anything from Castro. All they wanted was democracy—elections. After breaking his word and ordering men into the southern zone, Che clearly wanted something, but what? The two groups still hadn't settled their differences.

"Everyone was angry," recalled Jorge Castellon, then a sixteen-year-old Second Front rebel.

When they arrived at La Cabaña, Che was waiting. It wasn't a social visit. No sooner had they gathered in the courtyard than Che lit into them. He trashed Carreras, accusing him of being a thief and a drunkard.

"It got ugly," Menoyo recalled.

Carreras jumped to within a few feet of Che. "Let's go out there now—you and I with our guns," he said. For a moment, it looked like both men were going to kill each other. The bad blood from the mountains hadn't faded.

Che glared. The country was operating under a provisional government, which meant the Second Front needed to disband, he said. The revolution was over. Menoyo pulled his submachine gun off his shoulder. No one was going to tell him to disband his unit. "Why don't you take care of your own?" Menoyo shot back.

Castellon recalled gripping his gun, his fingers curled around the trigger, pointing it at Che. "We almost had a shoot-out."

Che saw the meeting heading for disaster. If the Second Front stayed any longer, a bloodbath would ensue. "This meeting is over," he announced.

Menoyo put down his weapon and turned his back on the Argentine. He motioned for his men to follow him through the gates of the ancient fortress. Other rebel groups may have acquiesced to Che, but Menoyo wasn't about to let the Second Front do the same.

—◦—

Morgan hung up the phone and turned to Olga. "This isn't good," he said.

Too much was happening. It was time to pack up and head to the capital. After just a few minutes on the phone with Menoyo, Morgan knew the Second Front was in trouble.

The new revolutionary government was stamping out all opposition. As long as the Second Front existed, its men were in trouble. If they disbanded, it would take the pressure off the men, but then they would lose any authority or protection, said Menoyo.

Che had gone mad. Every other day, he was ordering sham trials of prisoners. The men hearing the cases were mostly rebels with no judicial experience. Then the prisoners were hauled to the wall—El Paredon—and shot to death.

In Santiago de Cuba, hundreds of miles away, it was much the same: A team of executioners led by Raúl Castro forced more than seventy Batista soldiers and police to stand next to a large pit at the edge of town with priests who were allowed to hear their last confessions. Then, in twos, the soldiers were shot to death, falling into the mass grave.

Olga understood when Morgan told her it was best to move to Havana. Some of Morgan's key men would stay behind, but their work in Cienfuegos was largely over. The fate of the Second Front lay in the capital.

28

MORGAN EASED HIS JEEP UP TO THE SIDE OF THE TOWERING HAVANA hotel, checking for any security breaches. After a long, winding drive from Cienfuegos, Morgan and Olga arrived at the Capri to size up the hotel as a temporary home. Weeks earlier, hotel managers thought it a good idea to open their doors to the rebels after Batista fled, so they invited the guerrillas to stay as long as no one trashed the place.

His Sten slung over his shoulder, Morgan walked into the lobby, taking in the smooth tile floor and the sun shining through the tinted glass. No one doubted the elegance of the nineteen-story edifice with glass chandeliers hanging over white-linen-covered tables and a plush casino.

But Morgan wasn't concerned with luxuries. He wanted to make sure that he, Olga, and his men would be safe. The place had plenty of doors and access points in each direction for his men to come and go. The fact that the high-rise had balconies with thick concrete floors gave them an advantage if they had to defend themselves.

Bankrolled by Tampa crime boss Santo Trafficante Jr., the hotel featured a pool on the roof and stood a few blocks from the Malecón, the main road along the harbor. Some of the rebels fanned out around the grounds, scouting the hotel's proximity to the closest major streets in the Vedado neighborhood: Avenida 23 and La Línea. They weren't expecting imminent attacks on the Second Front. After all, Fidel Castro's government was still solidifying its position. But Che and Raúl were taking control and pinpointing their enemies.

As the rebels headed to their rooms, a familiar figure walked through the entrance. Menoyo had waited anxiously for the men to arrive. He wanted the Second Front all together. He was especially glad to see Morgan. Weeks had passed since the two had seen each other.

After greeting everyone, he pulled Morgan aside. "We need to talk," he said.

Menoyo was clearly tense. The angry exchange with Che had stuck in his craw, and by all accounts, it wasn't over. The Second Front continued to feel pressure to disband, he told Morgan. As long as they all wore their uniforms and carried their weapons, they were going to be targets.

Menoyo was most concerned about Che and Raúl. "I don't trust them," he said. If Che had his way, he was going to ram his agrarian "reforms" down the throats of the Cubans. "He is a Communist," Menoyo said.

Publicly Fidel Castro had denied that he was a Communist, saying that he was going to allow elections. But even with those statements, Menoyo was still wary. Castro wouldn't rest until the one rebel force still standing in his way was gone.

Beyond the front doors of the Capri, the black and red flags of the 26th of July Movement hung from balconies along La Rampa, the main drag. Outside the stores and nightclubs along the busy street, men wearing 26th of July armbands clenched their guns.

Morgan turned a corner and came to a stop. As he and Olga sat in the Jeep, he noticed that people in cars were pointing to them. Morgan thought maybe it was the rebel fatigues. But even when they returned and walked through the Capri entrance, it was the same. Other rebels were coming and going in the lobby without attracting attention, but everyone was looking at Morgan.

Finally, one of the bellboys came up to him. "Ju are Weel-yam Morgan?" Morgan nodded.

He wasn't just another barbudo. For days, the newspapers in Havana had been telling the story of the Americano. The Associated Press had just run a lengthy article about Morgan and his leadership of the Segundo Frente through more than a dozen battles. But Morgan remained oblivious to the publicity.

Olga heard people whispering his name as they passed. As he stood near the elevator, a hotel worker asked for his autograph. After signing his name, he and Olga went to their room on the fourteenth floor.

Inside, Olga looked ashen. "I worry about you," she said.

"We're not doing anything wrong," he said. "We have nothing to worry about."

Morgan signing autographs COURTESY OF
MORGAN FAMILY COLLECTION

But she wasn't concerned about the public. Most Cubans in the 1950s had a fondness for America even if they didn't always express it. Many had grown up watching black-and-white movies starring James Cagney and John Wayne. They read about American baseball teams like the New York Yankees. In many ways, Morgan represented the American archetype: a rugged, handsome gunslinger who fought for the Cuban people.

No, Olga worried about Guevara, the Castros, and the Cuban Communist Party reading the stories. Even some Directorio members had trashed the Second Front.

"These people are beyond anything you know," Olga said. "You don't know my people like I do."

No one despised Americans more than Che and Raúl. In his own way, so did Fidel. America was the bogeyman. They blamed the United States for every social and economic ill inflicted on the Cuban people. Nor was it a new stance. Anti-Americanism had been a side note of Cuban politics for generations. "The Colossus of the North" was the familiar name for the United States. Now Morgan was in their midst. The more they heard about him, the less the leaders of the 26th of July Movement liked him.

Raúl Castro ushered the men into the meeting room. He had been waiting for Menoyo and Fleites to arrive. The new government saw the Second Front everywhere. They had camped at the high school in Vedado.

They had camped at Menoyo's family home. They had camped at the Capri hotel with William Morgan.

"What are you doing?" Castro asked. Menoyo had failed to understand there was only one revolutionary army, and it fell under the direction of the new government, Castro stated. There was no need for a Second Front anymore.

Before Menoyo could respond, Che jumped into the fray. First, he said, the Second Front needed to merge with the Revolutionary Army, but he wasn't sure which rebels were worthy. There were so many comandantes running around that he didn't know if the Second Front even had any foot soldiers.

"That's none of your concern," Menoyo said, trying to stay calm. "Why don't you meddle with your own people and leave mine alone."

Che raised his voice and kept going: The Second Front had preyed on the guajiros, he said. They had forced the farmers to buy raffle tickets and had taken the people's money as a tax. "You corrupted the people," Che said.

Menoyo had watched his unit get pushed out of any role in the new government, but he wasn't going to allow Che to fabricate vile stories about the Second Front. He pushed away from the table and pulled out his submachine gun, pointing it at Che. "You are a liar," he said.

To the surprise of everyone in the room, Che ripped open the top of his shirt and displayed his bare chest. "Go ahead!" he screamed. "Shoot me!"

At that point, "everyone pulled their guns," recalled Fleites.

Castro needed to think fast, otherwise he was going to be presiding over a bloodbath. He jumped up on the table, putting himself between everyone, Fleites remembered.

"This meeting is over!" Castro shouted. "Everyone out!"

Menoyo and Fleites put down their guns, turned around, and, without saying another word, walked out the door.

29

MORGAN AND OLGA HAD COME TO HAVANA WITH A DOZEN MEN, BUT each day more showed up in the lobby of the Capri hotel. Wearing old, dirty fatigues, the men hoped to get jobs in the new government, but no one got any offers. When the forlorn rebels came to the hotel, Morgan and Olga couldn't say no. Morgan asked the hotel manager that they be allowed to run tabs, too.

For Olga, it was the worst time. She had gone to the Sacred Heart of Jesus Clinic with Morgan and Isabelle Rodriguez, one of the early Second Front supporters who lived in Havana. Rodriguez, a doctor, saw that Olga was feeling faint and not eating. She convinced her to see a physician for tests. The results: She was pregnant.

Olga was beside herself. She walked across the examination room and hugged Morgan in front of the doctor and nurses. Morgan lifted her up and smiled like he hadn't in weeks. "I'm going to have a son!" he said.

"No, we are going to have a baby," she corrected.

It came as a surprise to them both. They had talked many times in the mountains about having children and raising a family, but that was supposed to come later.

During the ride back to the Capri, Morgan beamed, but Olga grew quiet. She had been feeling ill for days, but she didn't want to believe that she was pregnant. Not now, not with everything happening. They were under so much pressure.

Morgan could tell she was troubled. "I don't want you to think about it," he said. "No one is going to hurt us."

Olga shook her head. If they could get out of Cuba, if they could move to America, no one could do anything to them. They would be able to raise their child without any fear for their safety, she said.

After they returned, they told the rebels staying with them their news, and everyone hugged one another. In their short time in the mountains, they had become like a family. Many of them knew Morgan before he had met Olga. They had watched the couple's love grow during one of the most trying periods of their lives. Now they had an even greater reason to protect one another.

——◆——

At dawn, Loretta Morgan was already bundling up in her thick coat and boots and quietly walking out the door to trudge to the church. Too much was happening for her to feel settled. She had picked up the paper and read about the government turning to firing squads, and that was enough to send her into a panic.

She had pangs for her son, and no one could tell her to calm down. She didn't give a damn what they had to say. The more others told her to stop thinking the worst, the angrier she became.

Billy.

Everything she saw was a reminder of him: The porch where he built his first toy car. The roof he almost jumped off wearing a toy parachute. The backyard where he whirled imaginary swords. Every day was the same: Visits to the church in the morning to deliver the linens she volunteered to wash, and then as the sun filtered through the den, she unfurled her rosary and whispered her prayers into the early evening.

One night, the phone rang. Loretta was always worried about the night calls. They were never good.

"Mom," said the voice on the other end.

He had finally called. Hearing his voice sent her heart soaring, and for a moment, she was beside herself. She knew he was alive from the news articles that had been appearing in the paper, but to hear his voice. *His voice.*

"My God," she said. "Bill, I've been waiting for you to call."

Morgan listened as his mother spoke. She had so much to tell him. She didn't care that it was long distance. Billy and Annie were fine; they were living with their mother in another part of town. Carroll Ann, his sister, was fine.

But beyond that, she worried about him. She had been reading about the executions in Havana. Even members of Congress were talking about it. With the revolution over, he needed to come back to the United States, back to Ohio, back to his family.

Morgan listened. He didn't want to alarm her. "No one is going to hurt us, Mom," he said. He assured her that the new government was moving forward with new plans and that Cuba would succeed as a nation. Then he changed the subject. He had his own news to share.

"Mom," he said, "this is important." He told her that when he was in the mountains, he had met a woman who was helping her people, someone who believed in him. A few months ago, they had married. "Her name is Olga," he said.

Loretta had heard of the marriage from reading one of the articles, but she didn't believe it. She had put up with her son's antics for a long time, but this was all too much. She didn't know anything about this Olga, her family, her background.

But Morgan wasn't finished. He had to tell her the rest. "She is expecting, Mom."

At first, it sounded to Morgan as if the phone went dead.

This was all happening too fast, far too fast. He still had a son and daughter in Toledo. But she would talk to him later about everything else. She was glad he was still alive. She asked when she would see him again.

Soon, he hoped. "I want you to meet her," he told her. He had to stay in Cuba for a while longer. He did have a request for her—just one. Could she send him some money? Just enough to tide them over. Morgan couldn't tell her, but he didn't need the money just for himself. He needed it to help the men. So many were depending on him.

30

MORGAN WAS NO LONGER A PRIVATE PERSON. CUBANS WERE COMING TO the Capri to catch glimpses of him. American tourists asked about him. During walks down La Rampa, people stopped him, wanting to talk. He tried to shrug off the attention. After all, the well-being of his men meant more to him now.

The revolution had become so popular that one enterprising company was printing trading cards of the rebel heroes, including Morgan. The public remained largely oblivious to the tension between the two rebel groups. All they saw were men in fatigues with guns.

By early February, the situation was getting decidedly worse. More and more of the barbudos were coming to him for support, counsel, and even pocket change.

"They need me," he told Olga.

Sitting in the hotel's lounge, Morgan had plenty of time to think. To the emerging government, he was persona non grata, a *Yanqui comandante* who had interjected himself into their struggle. He couldn't broker any deals with Che or the Castro brothers. Other than waging war, there was no way out. Either way, he wasn't going to give up his rank or his gun. He and Menoyo had already made that decision, as had the other commanders.

Morgan looked up and spotted someone who looked vaguely familiar. At more than six feet tall with thick, black hair and dark, brooding eyes, the man was the tallest person in the room. As Morgan squinted through the smoke and haze, he noticed that workers in the casino also knew the man who was now walking toward Morgan's table. It was Dominick Bartone, an old fixer from Cleveland with a penchant for gambling and guns. It had been years, but Bartone looked the same.

A known member of Cleveland's organized-crime family, Bartone ran in some of the same circles as the men who operated Toledo's gambling clubs. In the tight-knit world of racketeers, there were few degrees of separation.

The two men shook hands.

Bartone had heard about Morgan's exploits as a rebel fighter, and he also knew about the split between the rebel groups. As one of the Cleveland mob's point men, he had a keen understanding of the thorny conflicts playing out in the new government. The future of Cuba's gambling wealth depended on Castro.

For years, gangsters such as "Lucky" Luciano and Meyer Lansky had been greasing Batista with millions raked in from the proceeds. Estimates put the Cuban Caudillo's take at between 10 and 30 percent of the revenues. Castro and Che had condemned the casinos publicly during the revolution, charging that the American mobsters had more influence over Batista than his own generals. Cubans already depended hopelessly on the United States for trade, and the gaming houses had become a critical part of the Cuban economy.

But Bartone wasn't in Cuba to gamble. The mob had vested interests in the casinos. If they could sway the direction of the new government, they might be able to save their investments. It was no accident that Bartone found Morgan. The crime bosses desperately wanted a contact with someone who had ties to the new government. Among the Ohio crime families, Morgan still had an impeccable reputation for loyalty.

Bartone had a proposition. If Morgan, Menoyo, and the others wanted to promote the Second Front as the true proponents of the revolution, he would help them. So would the other casino interests. The Second Front's goals for democracy and elections had been drowned by the 26th of July Movement. In America, most of the debate focused on whether the government was going to turn Communist. Morgan and Menoyo could go to the United States on a speaking tour and talk about their unit and its struggles to galvanize support among the public for democracy. That could help pressure Fidel into recognizing the Second Front and, more importantly, cancel out Che's influence.

But Bartone's offer wasn't just about goodwill. The mob wanted something in return: Keep the casinos open. If the Communists took over, the party ended. They'd fold up the craps tables and seize the properties.

Morgan listened. On the one hand, a mobster was giving the Second Front diplomatic advice. But on the other, promoting the Second Front made sense. It could raise the profile of the unit and even help shield the men.

Morgan needed time to vet the plan with other unit leaders. He didn't care what happened to the casinos, he later told Olga. He cared about his men. If they were going to survive, they had to do something drastic.

— ⁓ —

"Fidel would like to see you," said Celia Sánchez Manduley, Castro's social secretary and mistress.

It was odd that of all the comandantes in the Second Front, Castro was asking for him and not Menoyo. Armando Fleites walked down the long hall. Armed guards wearing 26th of July armbands were waiting outside the door.

Cuba's new leader had heard much about the twenty-eight-year-old doctor who had given up everything to join Menoyo in the Escambray. Following in his father's footsteps, Fleites had pursued a medical degree at the University of Havana. But like so many others of his generation, he was idealistic and angry. He left his fledgling practice and joined Menoyo in the mountains. For Fleites, it was about taking back the country.

He reached room 2324 of the Havana Hilton. Waiting near the door, Castro waved him inside. Smoking a cigar, the leader had been pacing the floor inside the hundred-dollar-a-night suite, which he had turned into his headquarters. Castro asked Fleites to sit. Without further niceties, Castro extolled the fighting in the Escambray and the Second Front's efforts to drive the army from the mountains. He put Fleites at ease by telling him that Menoyo impressed him. Castro even knew Menoyo's family history from the days when Menoyo's father and brothers fought Franco in Spain.

"He spoke for a long time," Fleites recalled.

All along, Castro watched the younger man like a cat. Then he slipped into a rant. "I am disturbed about two things. One is William Morgan, who is an American. We don't know who he is. We don't know if he's part of the CIA. This is one thing I am worried about." Then Fidel addressed the other problem: Jesús Carreras. He didn't like him. Carreras drank too much and had executed peasants in the Escambray. As far as Fidel was concerned, Carreras had no place in the new government.

Fleites was taken aback. Castro's government had been executing more prisoners than Batista ever did during his reign of terror. But Fleites held his tongue. Castro was trying to drive a wedge in the Second Front, and he was trying to use Fleites to do it. For all of Castro's kind words about the Second Front, he didn't like the unit, and he didn't like Menoyo. Fleites collected himself and waited for Castro to allow him to speak.

When his opportunity came, Fleites jumped in. First, he defended Morgan, calling him "a brother" and "a good commander. His duty was impeccable." For Carreras, it was the same. Yes, he could be heavy-handed, but every execution Carreras ever carried out was justified. Spies in the mountains needed to be eliminated, but Carreras "never went into battle under the influence of alcohol."

"You know, Fidel, these are our people," Fleites said. "They have our backing. We will remain solid in our brotherhood."

If they thought Fleites was the weak link, they were wrong, Fleites recalled. Castro rose. The meeting was over. As Fleites was leaving, he realized that it wasn't just Che and Raúl who viewed the Second Front as a threat. So did the most powerful person in Cuba.

The Capri was no longer safe. Too many people knew that it had become the Second Front's headquarters. Reporters were milling around the lobby. Morgan and Olga had to leave.

Morgan found an apartment about ten blocks away in the Vedado. At the corner of G and 13th Streets, the upper-floor unit provided far more security than the hotel. It had just one bedroom and one bathroom for a dozen other rebels, but at least Olga would be safe when Morgan was gone.

He and the other Second Front leaders had decided to take advantage of Bartone's offer. Some of the men had reservations about leaving, but events in Cuba were unfolding so quickly that even Menoyo realized it was the wisest action to take.

Castro was wresting away more control of the country every day. After promising a democratic government, he had suspended elections for the next two years and then named himself prime minister on February 15. The only way to counter his momentum was for the Second Front to carry its own message of elections and open doors to the new government.

Morgan, Menoyo, and two dozen other Second Front men would travel to several cities, starting in Miami, with advance men handling the publicity. Mayor Robert King High of Miami already had extended an invitation to meet with them.

During the trip, the Second Front leaders wouldn't say anything negative about the current government. They would talk only about their unit and the democratic values for which they fought. Castro no doubt had people on the ground, watching and listening.

But still, Olga worried. Despite Morgan's assurances, Castro and the others would see their actions as treasonous. The Castros and Che would suspect any efforts to curry favor with the US government, which they blindly blamed for everything that had gone wrong with Cuba. What if Fidel decided to arrest them?

Morgan again assured Olga that no one was going to cross the line. But Olga wasn't budging.

"I know my people," she told him. "You don't."

— ❦ —

The man in the lobby of the Capri said it was urgent. Call Morgan. He wanted just a few minutes with the Americano. It would be worth Morgan's time. Morgan didn't want to go anywhere, but the call sounded urgent. With his men in tow, he hopped into the Jeep and sped to the Capri. When he walked into the lobby, the hunched figure at the desk was waiting.

As the two men walked toward the lounge, Morgan noticed that the visitor looked more like a US law enforcement agent than a tourist. Frank Nelson had been around Havana for a long time. He was a fixer and an ex-con who fashioned himself as a modern-day spook. One day he said he was working for the CIA, and another, serving as a foreign emissary. Havana was a breeding ground for people reinventing themselves, people driven out of other places. Nelson was no different. Whatever his status, he had done his homework on Morgan and the Second Front.

In the lounge, Nelson told Morgan that his unit was in trouble. Che and Raúl were looking for any evidence they could find to start cracking down on the members. So were other government loyalists. The fact that the Second Front had been barred from top positions in government was telling enough, he said. For someone not in contact with the Second Front, Nelson knew a lot.

But Morgan was still perplexed over why he had called him.

Nelson had just returned from the Dominican Republic and had rushed to Havana to deliver the message. He wanted to offer Morgan a deal—an offer that would never be made again. The man making it was one of the most powerful in the hemisphere.

"He has the money," said Nelson.

Castro, he said, wasn't doing justice to the new Cuba. He was arrogant and he was dangerous, Nelson said. The man behind the offer had a simple request: He wanted Castro dead. He didn't say how to kill him, he just wanted Castro eliminated. The man was offering one million dollars for the revolutionary leader's head. Morgan later told members of the Second Front that he was taken aback. Rarely surprised by anything, Morgan was stunned by the offer. He wanted to know who the man was behind the money.

Rafael Trujillo, the legendary dictator who had ruled the Dominican Republic for more than thirty years, was one of the longest-serving rulers in the Caribbean. No one despised Castro more than the man known as El Jefe, a ruthless tyrant who surpassed Batista in his ability to torture and kill his opposition to keep his power. Castro had singled out Trujillo as a brute who relished the support of the United States while he was looting his country's treasury. More than anything, he needed to be overthrown, Castro said.

Trujillo was well aware of Castro's stinging criticism and supplied Batista with arms and ammo to make sure the barbudo never took power. But he had misjudged the rebels. When Batista finally fled Havana, it was Trujillo who reluctantly let the Cuban president's plane land in the Dominican Republic after the United States turned him down.

Over the years, Rafael Trujillo Molino had left a long and bloody trail in his country. Born in 1891 in the village of San Cristobal, he ran in gangs as a youth, stealing and extorting money and goods and at one time running cockfights. After a military career, he won the presidency during a bloody campaign in which much of his opposition turned up dead. In time, he ordered the shooting of farmers who demanded higher wages, labeling them as Communists. He once sent his men to massacre thousands of Haitians living in the Dominican Republic during a border dispute in 1937. Only Trujillo could make someone like Batista appear benign.

But among the conservative element in the United States, Trujillo could do no wrong. A virulent anti-Communist, he was America's antidote to Communism in the islands.

Still startled, Morgan told Nelson that he would think about it. They would talk again, and Morgan would give him an answer. In the mountains, Morgan knew the identity of his enemy. Now he realized for the first time that he was venturing into a world where the lines had blurred and the dangers were growing.

———

The plan was set. The tour was booked. The venues were ready to receive the Second Front in nine US cities, including Toledo, Morgan's hometown.

Then they got word. The Castro government was shutting down the tour.

Furious over the Second Front's moves to promote the unit in the United States, Raúl Castro moved quickly to halt the unit from leaving. They weren't going to allow the Second Front to have its own voice. As far as Che and Raúl were concerned, only one voice could speak for the Cuban revolution: the 26th of July.

Menoyo had feared a shutdown. Ever since the heated exchange with Raúl, he knew the Second Front was going to be a target. But the government had no right meddling in their business. The Second Front had no plans to criticize Castro or his underlings during the tour. Menoyo now had to tell his men and make sure the promoters, including Bartone, knew about the power play.

Morgan's mother had read about the event to be held at the Sports Arena. Since then, Loretta Morgan had been waiting anxiously to see her son, even telling her neighbors. It has been a year since she had seen him. She had so much to tell him.

But on the afternoon of March 4, she picked up a copy of the *Toledo Blade* that carried the headline: "Cuba Cancels US Tour by Morgan."

The article gave no reason for the Cuban government's actions. Putting the paper down, Loretta was crushed. Her son wasn't coming home.

31

As darkness set over Havana, the Second Front leaders came to Menoyo's home in the Vedado neighborhood. This was unlike other gatherings.

The unit leaders had reached their limits. They had been stung by Raúl Castro and the others when the tour was cancelled. They needed to do something. One plan was to go back to the mountains. They had the support of the farmers. They had the support of the people in Trinidad and Cienfuegos. Many of them owed their freedom to the rebels and would rise up with them, said Menoyo.

One of the men in the room was a surprise: Pedro Díaz Lanz. His grandfather battled the Spanish in the war for independence in the 1890s, and his father had served as a top officer in the Cuban army until 1930. Díaz, a strapping man with a taut build and penetrating eyes, worked for the new government but had grown disillusioned.

As chief of the fledgling air force, Lanz had believed deeply in the cause, risking his life by flying weapons to Castro in the Sierra Maestra during the height of the fighting. But he was clearly at odds with the new leaders. He didn't like watching Che get chummy with the Communists, and he still resented Castro for not allowing elections to move forward. Díaz came to the meeting at the urging of Second Front supporter Rafael Huguet del Valle to meet the men who were openly defying the new government.

"Ñangaras," said Lanz, using the Cuban slang for Communists.

Morgan had other issues. As the men in the room began talking with Lanz, Morgan pulled Menoyo to the side. "I need to talk to you," he said.

It was rare that Morgan would look so serious. He disclosed his meeting with Nelson as well as the offer from Trujillo. "He said he would pay a million dollars for me to kill Castro."

As Morgan went on to describe the meeting, Lanz's ears perked up. He heard every word that Morgan said. Immediately, the airman walked over to the men. "This is serious," he said. "If this is coming from Trujillo, this is serious."

Morgan looked at Lanz and then at Menoyo. At this point, he wondered whether he should have said anything. But Lanz put him at ease. He would support the Second Front on whatever action it took, but it was probably better to be transparent. "My personal opinion is that you should tell Fidel. If they find out otherwise, they will break your back."

Morgan had been thinking about what he should do. He had serious reservations about Che and Raúl, but he had been trying to keep an open mind about Fidel. If there was any hope for the revolution to succeed, it rested with Fidel.

Ultimately the decision was up to Morgan. He wasn't going to murder Castro. That was never an option. But neither was telling Castro. Now he was having second thoughts. Maybe revealing the plot would help the Second Front.

Going to Castro was a risk. No one knew how he would react. But if meeting with Fidel would buy protection for the Second Front, Morgan had no choice.

—◦—

Light cascaded down on the palm trees growing inside the atrium of the sweeping lobby. Castro's men were everywhere: at the elevators, the front desk, the front doors. By the time Morgan walked into the middle of the Hilton lobby with Menoyo and Artola, all eyes had fixed on them. In their fatigues, the three Second Front leaders approached the front desk and asked for Castro. People didn't just come in and ask to see Fidel. But they weren't people—they were the Second Front.

For days, the Segundo Frente had hovered in the government's crosshairs. They had refused to give up their weapons and uniforms. They openly challenged the government by planning a tour of the United States. Ever since Castro had arrived in Havana in January, the Second Front had been the one group that the government couldn't control.

Castro still didn't know what to make of Morgan. He could have gone back to America by now to capitalize on his newfound fame. But here he was . . . still.

Morgan and Menoyo knew this wasn't going to be easy, but Morgan made the first move. In broken Spanish, he said that he and the others were coming of their own accord because Fidel himself was in danger. He laid it all out: A bagman from the mob had visited Morgan—but not about a casino deal. The man had a proposition: For one million dollars, he wanted Castro dead, and Trujillo had ordered the hit.

Castro looked up quizzically from his chair. Morgan filled in the details, but Castro's mind was already spinning. He wanted to know more. Who else was part of this plot?

Morgan shook his head. He didn't know.

Castro rose, excited, waving his cigar in the air. If the offer was bona fide, then it wasn't coming from Trujillo alone. Others insiders were involved. Castro's brilliance was showing itself. No other man could compete. This is why he was on the twenty-third floor of the Havana Hilton above everyone else in the country.

"I want you to play along," he told Morgan. "I want you to act like you are going to take the offer."

Ever the supreme strategist, he wanted not only Trujillo but also all the rest. Don't just stop with one plotter. Reel them all in. To do this, Morgan would play double agent, Castro and his men working closely with him at every step. It was the perfect opportunity for Castro to root out his enemies and solidify power. It gave Morgan an opportunity to exert the kind of influence over Fidel that only Che and Raúl enjoyed at the time.

Morgan had just wedged himself between Fidel Castro and Rafael Trujillo, two of the Caribbean's most dangerous men.

———————

Olga ran to her room and threw herself on the bed. The men had been talking long enough for her to pick up everything. She couldn't believe what she was hearing. "Why are you doing this?" she yelled.

It was one thing for her husband to fight in the revolution against a dictator. But this was suicide. This was Rafael Trujillo, *el Monstruo del Caribe*. No one had been as ruthless and unforgiving to his people. After all the battles Morgan had survived in the mountains, he was going to thrust himself into a plot that could end up devouring him.

All Olga wanted was to settle into her new home and have a baby. She was already surrounded by men sleeping on her floor and kitchen, everyone sharing the same bathroom. Now she had to worry about Morgan going into battle again.

Morgan walked into the bedroom and closed the door. He assured her that everything would be all right. No one would hurt him. "I have to do this, Olga," he said. The steps he was taking were to help everyone. He wasn't looking forward to it. He didn't ask for it. But he had a chance to make things safe for their family and the Second Front. Che and Raúl hated them. If it was up to them, they'd all be walking to the wall.

Olga understood what Morgan was saying, but she didn't like it. What if Trujillo found out? "I don't want to suffer anymore," she said. She just wanted to leave. It would be better to live in the United States, where at least it was safer. "I want to get away from the politics. I want to get away from these people."

Morgan told her that they would leave but not now. Too much was at stake. Too many people were depending on him. The young men who fought with him in the mountains were vulnerable, too. "These are my boys," he said. "I can't just leave them."

$\sim$

Castro wasn't going to let this overture from Morgan pass unheeded. He met with his secret police and staff, instructing them to keep a constant dialogue with Morgan. But Castro didn't want the operation run by the Second Front. Like all major undertakings in the new government, Fidel insisted on total control.

Morgan's rebel entourage was staying with him; surely he wouldn't mind a few more men. Castro pushed for a couple of his own men to bunk at Morgan's.

Pedro Ossorio Franco had been an agent only for a couple of months, but he was tough and trusted. For more than a year, he bellied up in the mountains with the Directorio, fighting in some of the fiercest battles in Pinar del Río Province. After the revolution, he joined hundreds of rebels who took up military positions to ensure the army remained loyal to Castro. The lanky, twenty-one-year-old Mexican was summoned to the headquarters of the Technical Investigations Department, which carried out undercover police work. He was to stay at Morgan's and keep his mouth shut. Just observe. Every few days, phone his commanders.

He also had another duty—delicate, dangerous, and never to be divulged, even to other members of his military unit. He was to spy on Morgan. If he saw any signs of betrayal, he was to report it immediately to the secret police. Under extreme circumstances, he could use his weapon.

Ossorio didn't know what to expect when he arrived at Morgan's apartment. He had heard a lot about the Americano and his exploits in the central mountains. But he didn't know how Morgan would react to his presence.

"You are welcome here," Morgan told him. "Everything here is yours. Everything I have is yours."

Ossorio didn't say anything. But he was surprised by Morgan's overture. He hadn't expected the American to welcome him like a friend. But Morgan clearly put him at ease. Ossorio noticed that all of the other Second Front rebels gathered around Morgan to protect him. Armed with machine guns and sidearms, the message from the rebels was clear: Mess with our comandante, and you will be staring down a dozen gun barrels.

For Morgan's part, he wasn't concerned about Ossorio. He was facing far bigger challenges. Trujillo's people were calling and asking him to meet them in Miami as soon as possible. The plans were changing already. What had begun as an assassination was morphing into something bigger and more nefarious. He had gone into battle dozens of times, but now forces on both sides of the Greater Antilles were closing in.

32

MORGAN STEPPED OFF THE ELEVATOR ON THE ELEVENTH FLOOR OF the DuPont Plaza Hotel and strode down the long hallway. He always thought his first trip back to the United States in more than a year would be with Olga to see his children. But not this time. This was a quick, secret trip to Miami. He was expected to meet with Trujillo's consul, a man with a gravelly voice who had called him to set up the meeting. But when he opened the door, he was greeted by somebody else.

There was no mistaking the broad shoulders and dark, slicked-back hair. It had been weeks since he had seen Dominick Bartone. Morgan thought he was being summoned to Miami to meet the operatives who Trujillo was sending from the Dominican Republic to get the plot under way.

But as he shook hands with Bartone, Morgan had already figured out what was happening. He should have known the mob would have a seat at the table. The casino owners had as much to lose as anyone in Havana. Lansky, Trafficante, and others had poured tens of millions into the ritzy gaming hotels, including the historic Nacional. They weren't going to give up their empires without a fight.

Mob involvement introduced yet another dangerous twist. Now, in addition to plotting secretly against Trujillo, Morgan had to deal with Bartone and the crime families. The best he could do was play the street soldier and keep Bartone at ease.

The mobster hadn't spared any expense. Windows ran ceiling to floor, offering a spectacular view of Biscayne Bay. The room, 1133R, was as swanky as any suite in the hotel.

The men had gathered and were waiting. Augusto Ferrando introduced himself. The Dominican Republic's consul in Miami, Ferrando was Trujillo's bagman. If El Jefe needed a favor from someone in Miami, Ferrando whipped out the paper bag stuffed with cash.

Next to Ferrando stood Manuel Benítez, once one of the most corrupt cops in Cuba. Benítez made a splash during World War II when he joined the FBI investigation of a Nazi spy hiding in Havana. Both he and

J. Edgar Hoover took credit for the arrest of Heinz Lüning, a low-level, eccentric operative. But the real credit belonged to British postal inspectors who turned up the leads that led to the mole's arrest.

Under Batista, Benítez had commanded the national police force and an intelligence network that infiltrated every level of Cuban society. During his tenure, Benítez was brutal, putting his most savage cops on the revolutionaries plotting Batista's overthrow. By all counts, he was responsible for more dead bodies turning up on remote, dirt roads than any single person. While he was kicking ass on the student rebels, he was amassing a small fortune from the casino owners.

Benítez had been itching for days to finalize a plan to take care of Castro for good. No one knew the underhanded methods of getting things done in Havana better than he did. In a snake pit, he was a rattler. He would advise Morgan, and after Castro's death, he would help lead an insurrection.

Morgan learned in just the first few minutes of the meeting that this wasn't about just Castro. Benítez and Batista wanted the whole damn country back. They would send as many as three thousand mercenaries to the island if necessary. They even had one of Batista's former generals ready to lead the charge: José Pedraza Cabrera.

Morgan seized the moment. First, his job was to flush them out, every one of them. So far, it was working. If they wanted to launch an invasion, he was game. In fact, he and Menoyo could rustle up more than a thousand men themselves. If an invasion was to succeed, there would have to be a simultaneous internal revolt.

Castro controlled every branch of the military except the navy and a good part of the air force. Morgan could recruit some of those men, too. "We could win the country tomorrow," he boasted.

That's all that the men in the suite wanted to hear. Bartone jumped in, saying he could supply the guns, the ammo, and the C-47 transport planes. He already had a Globemaster parked in a hangar in Miami.

The plan was in motion. They would meet again. From now on, they would communicate by shortwave radio only—no telephones. They would make sure Morgan got his transmitter, and they would adopt fake names to disguise each man's identity. They also insisted that some of their own men camp with Morgan, just a few. That way, they'd have a front-row seat. Benítez already had people in Havana, so he'd send them.

Bartone agreed that he'd start funneling some of the money to Morgan so that he'd have some start-up cash. In fact, Bartone was already prepared. He reached over and handed Morgan two envelopes. Inside were two cashier's checks, each for five thousand dollars, from the Pan American Bank of Miami, both dated April 27. Morgan needed to set up two bank accounts under aliases and deposit the checks. Bartone would be in touch. Whatever Morgan needed, he had only to ask.

The men cleared out of the suite.

By the time Morgan boarded the plane for Cuba, he realized that the plans had changed dramatically. His life was about to be turned upside down. He wasn't just beholden to Castro and Trujillo. Now he was about to cross a sacred line, one he had never crossed before. He had prided himself on his loyalty to the streets, the mob. When he had nothing, they were there for him. Though he had embarked on a new direction in his life, he didn't want to do anything to betray them.

Now he had no choice.

—◆—

Castro was pacing. There was nothing he could do until Morgan arrived. The secret police were waiting. Castro's bodyguards were on alert.

When Morgan and Olga came to the door, Celia Sánchez greeted them and ushered them upstairs. Castro was walking back and forth in his bedroom, smoking a cigar. Newspapers and magazines lay strewn about the floor and tables. It looked like Fidel—in his signature olive-green fatigues but with his boots untied—hadn't slept in days.

"Tell me what you have," he said, leaning against the headboard.

Morgan recounted everyone: Benítez, Ferrando, Bartone. This wasn't just about an assassination; this was about overthrowing the entire government. They were planning an invasion and simultaneous insurrection.

Castro didn't say a word. He had been talking about the plot with his aides ever since Morgan brought it to his attention, and was intent on learning everything.

Morgan said it might take weeks before it all came together, but they were determined to make it happen. They had the men, they had the money, and they had people planted all over Cuba, ready to help. It was just as Fidel had suspected. It was also just what he needed to flatten his enemies.

Morgan indicated that all further communication with the Trujillo conspirators would take place over shortwave radio. He was going to host some of the plotters as well, including former soldiers from the regime loyal to Batista.

Castro needed to think. This was indeed much bigger and with more moving parts.

The first thing Morgan needed to do was move into a bigger place, Castro said. With more people being drawn into the plot, he needed more space. Fidel would also add a few more of his men to Morgan's entourage. No one had to know they were loyal to the government.

The secret police would monitor all people coming and going to build files on them for later arrests. Menoyo would help maintain the cover. The Second Front would stay and present themselves as willing to help the plotters. With Castro's help, they would snare as many of the plotters as possible and smash the coup. But that was easy for Castro to say. His life wasn't immediately on the line.

Morgan's was.

33

EVEN IN 1959, THE SPRAWLING ESTATE IN THE HEART OF HAVANA'S Miramar neighborhood was worth a million dollars. A mirror covered the entire wall of the dining room, and the long dining table was made of glass. Paintings adorned the walls, and expensive furniture filled every room. In the rear of the house were a courtyard, a pool, and a cabana bar.

The last owner, Alberto Vadia Valdes, a building contractor who reaped a fortune from government work for Batista, moved most of his money offshore before fleeing. The bar still had liquor in it, and Vadia left behind most of his suits, shoes, and personal items neatly stacked in closets.

Nothing in the house seemed real to Olga. She wanted to pack her bags and get on a plane for America. But Morgan reminded her that they needed to stay. It was the only way for him to save his men. When it was over, they would resume their lives together. No more assassination plots, no more revolutions.

"Listen to me. We are going to be fine. Nothing is going to happen to us."

The Batista people were showing up soon with the radio transmitter. Every room needed to be wired—ceiling to floor. Microphones would be tucked in lamps in the office and living room. The telephone would be bugged. Every conversation in every room would be monitored. No word uttered in darkness would go unheard. But that meant they had no room for error. Every man in the house needed to play his part and keep his mouth shut. They were about to crawl into bed with the enemy.

Morgan set up the shortwave in a room within the main house that shared a wall with the garage, which would serve as the control center. Next to the radio were reel-to-reel tape recorders ready to be hooked up.

Morgan flicked on the transmitter. At first, it emitted a low buzz, and then the dial on the Viking Valiant radio flickered on.

Already the house was attracting more of Morgan's men. Just hours after he and Olga moved in, a handful of grimy barbudos in soiled shirts and old shoes showed up at the door, asking for a place to stay. Most of them had been bouncing around for weeks at flophouses with little means of support. Morgan couldn't say no. With more than five thousand square feet at his disposal, he assigned the new arrivals to various bedrooms, couches, and floors.

Then along came Tony Chao, who located Morgan through other men in Havana. Morgan hadn't seen "The Americanito" for more than a year. It was Chao's heartfelt plea that had convinced Morgan to head to the mountains. The once skinny kid had grown and put on twenty-five pounds. He also looked like he hadn't slept in days. Chao had made it to the mountains to fight in the revolution, and when it ended, he began looking for Morgan.

"You are staying here with us." Morgan hugged him and introduced him to Olga.

———

Olga knew most of the rebels who were settling into their home, but when she went to answer the door, she got scared.

Standing in the entrance was a man sent by the Cuban secret police to help monitor the transmitter. Manuel Cisneros Castro—no relation to the Cuban leader—avoided eye contact as he stepped into the foyer, armed with spools of wiring.

A short, squat mulatto from Bayamo in Oriente Province, Cisneros had hooked up with Castro's rebels in the Sierra Maestra and had risen to lieutenant. Of all the government agents who would be staying in the house, Cisneros was probably the most important. He would monitor all the messages coming from Trujillo. Cisneros immediately went to work, helping to finish connecting the tape recorders to the shortwave.

After he arrived, the doorbell rang again. Standing in the doorway were the men sent by Trujillo's people. Men who were once enemy soldiers were now waiting just inches away. Morgan guided them into the house, pointing to a room where they could stash their gear and belongings. They would find their own corners of the house to sleep, but most of the time, they'd be out recruiting new guerrillas for the invasion.

Olga looked at the visitors and then turned to Morgan. "What are you doing, boy?" she snapped. It was one thing to allow Castro's people inside. Now they were letting in men who had tortured and killed her people.

Morgan tried to calm her down. "Look, we have to bring them in, but we'll watch them." Morgan assured her that the Batistianos were only going to be in the house for a few weeks and that Morgan's bodyguards would keep close tabs on them.

In the driveway, Morgan had parked a blue Oldsmobile equipped with a two-way radio so he could keep in touch with Olga and the others. The car also contained a small arsenal of submachine guns and grenades. Morgan was working with Castro, but he was laboring under no illusions. At any point, it could all blow sky-high.

—◦—

The reel-to-reel tape recorders were running when Morgan walked into the radio room and shut the door. He sat down, grabbed the earphones, and pressed play. Usually they picked up nothing but static. But this time, something on the audio surveillance system caught him off guard. He rewound the tape and turned up the volume. Then he did it again. It was no mistake.

A hidden microphone in another room had picked up a conversation between two of Batista's men, who were bragging about what they planned to do after the invasion. They would assassinate Castro—shooting him in the head—and then kill someone else: the Americano. No one gave them more grief and embarrassment in the Escambray than Morgan. No one beside Castro more deserved to die.

Morgan turned off the tape. Turning to his men, he calmly instructed them not to say a word. He didn't want them to scare off the Batistianos. Play along, he said. "They cannot know we picked this up."

The only other person outside the room who needed to know was Menoyo, said Morgan. After all, he was still their leader. But Morgan insisted they meet with Menoyo in person. Nothing would be divulged over the phone.

Morgan and one of his bodyguards, Edmundo Amado, jumped into Morgan's Oldsmobile and drove to the Peking restaurant on 23rd Street near the Colón Cemetery. Owned by Chinese-Cubans, the eatery was neutral ground where no one else would suspect anything. Menoyo met them at a corner table, puzzled.

Morgan leaned over the table. "They are going to kill me," he said.

Morgan explained what he had heard. They wanted to put Pedraza in power and eliminate anyone close to Castro. The man talking about Morgan's murder was Renaldo Blanco Navarro, a leader of the White Rose Society, an organization of former Batista officers operating in cells throughout the island.

Menoyo was disgusted. He knew they were *chivatos*—informers, rats—but he never expected them to turn on the Second Front. From now on, they needed to stay in contact each day, even if only by phone, Menoyo said. At this point, they could trust only each other.

———

Federal agents were already buzzing at the Miami FBI office. Leman Stafford Jr., a veteran investigator with a soft Texas drawl, pulled up his chair, leaned over his desk, and turned on the recorder to create a report to be sent across the country.

Agents in Miami had just uncovered information that could damage already strained relations between the United States and Cuba. This wasn't just another Cuban operative squawking about his connections in Havana. This came from someone who was once one of Cuba's most influential leaders.

After the meeting at the DuPont Hotel, Manuel Benítez turned to the FBI and told them everything. Under a secret plan, Cuba was about to be invaded. The mob was involved. So was Castro's arch enemy, Trujillo. There was one more twist: The entire plan was being led by an American by the name of William Alexander Morgan.

Stafford couldn't dictate fast enough. The secret report was already being prepared for transmission to FBI offices in the embassy in Havana. "The subject [Morgan] appeared motivated by anti-Communist sympathies, a desire for reprisal against Fidel Castro, who had excluded [Morgan], Eloy Gutiérrez Menoyo and other leaders of the SNFE [Second Front] from recognition in the Castro government," Stafford said.

"[Benítez] said [Morgan] would establish this new revolutionary front in the Escambray Mountains within two weeks, with forces numbering between five hundred and one thousand men at the outset."

Ever since fleeing Cuba, Benítez had wanted to score points with the FBI. He could boost his own stature in America and at the same time send a message to Hoover that he was still a dependable snitch from his days in Havana.

Agents in Cleveland had been backgrounding the *Yanqui comandante* since his name began appearing in the *New York Times* and other papers during the final days of the fighting. This would raise his profile. They were now looking at a man thrust into an international conspiracy that could completely change the course of the Cold War. It was a dangerous game. It wasn't that Morgan was hooking up with the mob—he had done that most of his adult life. He was meddling in the affairs of a foreign country. He was breaking the law and risking America's relations with other nations.

Stafford had one order: Bird-dog him. Watch him carefully. Get the files from Cleveland and keep building on them.

A World War II veteran who graduated from Texas A&M with a degree in accounting, Stafford was a numbers man who always looked like he was heading to Sunday church service: white shirt, sport coat, tie. He was good with numbers—embezzlement, money laundering, bank fraud—but this was a different case. Stafford was now steeped in a shadowy world of mob figures and angry Cuban exiles who were hell-bent on killing Castro.

———

He had been wrestling with a deep secret. So many times he had wanted to pull Morgan aside, but he just couldn't. Sometimes he accompanied Olga on her trips outside the house; other times, he drove with Morgan to his meetings.

"William, I need to see you—alone," Ossorio finally said.

During his time with Morgan and Olga, Pedro Ossorio had grown close to both. His real family lived in Mexico, but the couple had treated him like a son. He had watched Morgan rise to the pressure of an impossible task—first with Trujillo, then Castro, then the mafia. Morgan could have cashed in his fame and split for Miami or even Ohio. Instead, he stayed. He refused to leave his family or his men.

"I was sent here on a mission," Ossorio said.

He was supposed to report everything by phone to the secret police. For a while, he followed his orders. But then he couldn't do it anymore.

Olga, who was listening, walked over to Ossorio and hugged him. "I respect you for telling us," she said.

She had grown fond of the young rebel everyone called El Mexicano. For him to come forward and tell them what was eating at him took guts.

Morgan assured his bodyguard that he had nothing to worry about. They would keep the secret between them. But from that moment on, Morgan knew he had to be careful with Fidel. The Cuban leader had been touting the cooperation between the rebel forces to save Cuba, but it was clear he was still suspicious of the Second Front.

34

Trujillo had been calling on the radio all night. Cars were pulling into the driveway. People were coming to the door. Olga didn't care that Morgan was busy. She wanted to know what was going on.

Morgan had spent so many hours on the radio that he lost track of time. He knew she wasn't going to like what he had to tell her. But it had to happen: They were ready to move forward. Day after day, Trujillo had been agonizing over the plan. The longer Castro remained in power, the more difficult it would be to take him out. It was time to pull the trigger.

Morgan would go to Miami to firm up the details and gather more weapons. He would return by boat just in time to lead the charge. But Morgan wasn't going alone. He had left so many times without her. Not this time.

"I am going with you," Olga said.

"You're pregnant," he replied.

She wasn't going to budge. "Then I will have the baby in the United States. That would be even safer for us."

He had seen that look on her face before. He couldn't tell her no. But he insisted that she travel with Alejandrina, their housekeeper, and Olga's fifteen-year-old sister, Irma. He would send them back by plane after a couple of days. That was the deal.

"I am ready to pack my suitcase," she said.

Morgan let the Trujillo people know that he was on his way, but they weren't the only ones prepared to meet him when he arrived. In the Miami FBI office, Stafford had been working late into the night to track down details of the impending plan when he got a tip from an undisclosed source. Morgan was flying into Miami International.

Bingo.

Finally Stafford would be able to lay hands on the man he had been investigating frantically. He had read everything he could about the Americano: from the background information dug up by other agents to newspaper and magazine articles profiling him in the United States and

Cuba. What struck the agent was that Morgan had been everywhere from the time he was a teenager. He had been a runaway. He had been in the circus. He had worked on ranches in Arizona. He was always on the run. When Morgan arrived, Stafford had one goal: Stay on him.

— ⌒ —

Morgan had one more meeting with Trujillo's people. For months, he had held his ground and kept his secret. He would meet with Ferrando to iron out the final details, from the arrival of the weapons to the invasion in southern Cuba. Then he'd rendezvous with the Batista people to make sure the boat in Miami was ready, that it had the weapons on board.

As the plane lifted into the sky, Olga clutched Morgan's arm. She wanted it to end. If Morgan could pull it off, maybe they finally could find the peace that had eluded them for so long. It had been nearly six months of around-the-clock meetings, phone calls, and radio sessions that lasted until dawn. More often than not, he had circles under his eyes from not sleeping. But through it all, he kept his composure, assuring her at every step that it would be over soon, that they'd finally ensure that the Second Front had a place in the new Cuba. Then they'd move on with their lives.

As the plane descended through the skies over Miami, Olga should have been excited about visiting the United States for the first time. Instead, she was anxious. She knew her husband was about to meet with people who wanted him dead.

As the plane touched down on the runway, Morgan was thinking through his next move. As they walked down the concourse, two men in suits and sunglasses dashed across the walkway toward them.

Stafford flashed his FBI badge. With him was FBI agent Thomas Errion.

"Are you William Morgan?" Stafford asked.

"Yes," answered Morgan.

Morgan told Olga and the others to head to the Moulin Rouge Motel on 41st Street and Pine Tree Drive in Miami Beach. He would catch up with them later.

"Don't worry," he said to Olga.

Stafford and Errion escorted Morgan into the immigration offices in the airport. Morgan remained calm. He had learned long ago how to deal with cops. The same rules applied for federal law enforcement agents. In another time, he would have been dodging questions about gambling raids and illegal proceeds from sawdust joints. But this was different. No one could tell him that what he was doing now was wrong. No one could tell him that he was breaking the law.

"What do you want?" Morgan asked.

Stafford had a litany of questions. For starters, what was Morgan doing in Miami? If his life was in Havana, why come here?

Morgan wasn't going to reveal his mission to Stafford, and he didn't care what Stafford did to try to force him. His reasons for coming were strictly personal, he said.

Then Stafford, jotting notes the whole time, wanted to talk about the Cuban revolution. Much had been written about Morgan's role in the rebellion. What did he do during the fighting? What was he doing now?

The agents didn't stop. They wanted to know who he was going to see in Miami. Where else he was going. Morgan responded to their questions, one by one, but he avoided any hints of what was about to unfold. Halfway through the interview, Morgan suspected the agents knew about the plan. But he wasn't going to break. They'd have to find out on their own. He would tell them this much, though: A representative of a foreign government had approached him to overthrow the Castro government for one million dollars, but he had turned down the deal.

Stafford pressed him: Who? Which government?

Morgan looked intently at each agent. He had said enough. His wife was waiting.

Stafford and Errion knew they had to let Morgan go. They had no legal right to hold him. But they would be trailing his every step.

He needed to act quickly. Morgan had little time to solidify the plans, and now he had federal agents following him. There was no way he would be able to finish if the FBI decided to arrest him on some trumped-up charge. Instead of saying at the Moulin Rouge, he would get rooms at the Montmartre Hotel just over the bridge on Collins Avenue.

They ducked into a waiting Cadillac in the parking lot and were whisked away by the driver down 41st Street and then onto Collins. Even in the dead of summer, Miami Beach was teeming with tourists milling in and out of the Art Deco hotels along the popular drive.

Whoever had been trailing them was now lost in the night traffic. Morgan needed time—time to finalize everything. As soon as he checked into their suite, he picked up the phone and called Bartone.

The Cleveland mobster had made a killing on the sale of guns to the project. Trujillo and Batista both ponied up more than a million dollars, most of it going to buy .30-caliber and .50-caliber machine guns and automatic rifles. Bartone was staying at the Eden Roc down the road. He told Morgan to sit tight. He would send over two cars in the morning, one for Morgan and the other for Olga and her sister to go sightseeing. Bartone himself would play tour guide.

Morgan and Olga looked out over the ocean, the stars scattered like diamonds in the night sky. Olga had envisioned that they would visiting her husband's country—but under far different circumstances.

In just days, their baby would be born. More than ever, she wanted to move to America, where she and Morgan had a chance to build a life together. She didn't care if it was in Miami or even Ohio. She was willing to take that leap forward so they would all survive.

"I wanted so much to have peace," she recalled.

———

With pressure mounting, Augusto Ferrando waited for Morgan at a corner table in the Toledo Restaurant on Biscayne Boulevard. Nothing had gone right for the Dominican consul. Trujillo had been pestering him. The Batista people were constantly complaining. Now he had word that the FBI might be following Morgan. They didn't have much time to talk. From now on, every step was critical.

Out of earshot of everyone in the restaurant, Ferrando and Morgan agreed that the invasion would start in Trinidad. It was the perfect place: the center of the country, albeit to the south. By taking the old, storied city, they could keep the fighting away from Castro's power center in Havana and then work at cutting the country in half. No different from what the rebels did when they took Las Villas Province during the revolution.

At the same time, the Second Front would launch an uprising in the nearby Escambray with the goal of drawing Castro's forces into the mountains for a showdown. By plane and boat, Trujillo's people would drop off weapons to the fighters at secret spots. As icing on the cake, Trujillo would send in his foreign legion, at least two thousand men, to help Morgan and Menoyo on the ground.

Giddy at the prospect of victory, Trujillo began picking Castro's successors. The generalissimo tapped Arturo Hernández Tellaheche, once one of Cuba's most powerful senators, for president. Arturo Caíñas Milanés, a millionaire cattleman stripped of his land by the new government, would be vice president. Ramón Mestre Gutiérrez, founder of a major construction company, would be the next premier. All three had pledged their hearts—and of course their money—to the cause.

In a day or two, Ferrando would have a boat with weapons stockpiled in the cabin. It wouldn't be all the weapons needed for the invasion, but enough to get started. Much of the money to pay for the guns would be given to Morgan in a paper bag.

But the biggest part of the plan was in Cuba. Another cache of weapons was coming from the Dominican Republic, and those would be dropped at other locations. Batista's people had promised there would be people scattered in Havana in safe houses ready to take up arms.

Morgan nodded. Trujillo was making good on his end in grand fashion. Morgan was doing his best to show that he, too, was a player, that he would go along as long as the money was being paid out generously.

But he was wearing thin. Every conversation was getting more difficult for him to play the part. The reality was that he was deeply troubled by everything he was seeing in the operation, from the Trujillo operatives who were trying to curry favor with a corrupt and deadly dictator to the Batista people all trying to jockey for power. None of them gave a damn about the Cuban people or whether they ate tomorrow or even lived another day. Most of them just wanted to line their own pockets while seizing power.

Morgan would do his best to hold up his end by making sure everyone was armed and ready in the Escambray, he told Ferrando. But when this was over, there would be a day of reckoning for everyone.

— ⁓ —

The game of chess had begun.

No sooner did Morgan get back to his hotel than he received a message: Call the FBI. Despite all his careful moves, including switching hotels, Stafford wasn't going away. Agents were watching the hotel and the traffic going in and out. If Morgan was going to keep the plot moving forward, he needed to get the feds completely off his track.

Unless he met with Stafford, he would be hounded every day. The best thing he could do was go directly to the FBI offices. If he could convince them that he truly was on vacation and answer their questions, maybe they'd back off. He needed to buy more time.

When Morgan walked into the FBI's downtown Miami offices, Stafford and Errion were waiting for him. Since the first interview at the airport, they had gathered more information about the suspected coup attempt in Cuba. They demanded that Morgan come clean. Otherwise, they were going to slap handcuffs on him. Americans couldn't serve in the armed forces of a foreign army, and Morgan had done just that.

Morgan stared across the table at Stafford. First, he hadn't served in the military of a foreign country. He had fought in a rebel force during a revolution that had nothing to do with the Cuban army. He had helped the people in the mountains and was still trying to help them—far more than anyone in the US government. Second, the Second Front had been disbanded—albeit on paper—after the fighting ceased, so he wasn't serving in the Cuban revolutionary army either. "I've done nothing wrong," he said.

Stafford shook his head. If Morgan wasn't serving in the military, how was he supporting his wife and living in an upscale home in Havana?

Stafford wasn't going to let it go, but Morgan wasn't going to help him. Morgan's answer was Menoyo. Whatever money he was getting came from his comandante. Right now, in his pocket, he was carrying $350. Back in Cuba, he had about $159 in the bank. "That's it," he said.

FEDERAL BUREAU OF INVESTIGATION

Reporting Office	Office of Origin		Investigative Period
MIAMI	MIAMI	3/9/60	5/21/59-3/9/60

TITLE OF CASE	Report made by	Typed By
	LEMAN L. STAFFORD, JR.	eBB

CHANGED:
WILLIAM ALEXANDER MORGAN,
aka "Sinbad", "Gabby"

CHARACTER OF CASE

INTERNAL SECURITY - CUBA
REGISTRATION ACT - CUBA
NEUTRALITY MATTER

The title is changed to add the aliases "Sinbad" and "Gabby",
as reflected in the records of the Toledo, Ohio Police Department.

REFERENCE: Miami teletypes to Bureau dated 8/6;20/59
Reports of SA LEMAN L. STAFFORD dated
10/14;12/26/59 at Miami, captioned DOMINICK
BARTONE, IS - CUBA, RA - CUBA (Bufile
105-80291)(Miami 105-2006)
Cleveland airtel to Bureau dated 2/18/60

REC 90

CLEVELAND

At Toledo, Ohio

Will attempt to verify subject's presence in Toledo
February 16, 1960, reported by CV-365-C.

Approved	Special Agent in Charge	Do not write in spaces below

Copies made:

10 - Bureau (105-70973)(RM)

See Cover Page B.

5 - Miami (105-1560)
(1 - 105-2006)
(1 - 105-1762)

Pages from Morgan's FBI file NATIONAL ARCHIVES AND RECORDS ADMINISTRATION

FD-204 (Rev. 3-3-59)

UNITED STATES DEPARTMENT OF JUSTICE
FEDERAL BUREAU OF INVESTIGATION

KP 3-19-98

Copy to:	1 - U.S. Customs, Miami (RM)
	1 - ONI, DIO, 6th ND,
	Charleston, S.C.(RM)
Report of:	SA LEMAN L. STAFFORD, JR.
Date:	March 9, 1960

1 - U.S. Border Patrol, Tampa, Fla
1 - INS, Miami (RM)
1 - OSI, MacDill AFB, Fla. (RM)
1 - G-2, Ft.McPherson,Ga.(RM)

Office: Miami

Field Office File #: 105-1563

Bureau File #: 105-70973

Title: WILLIAM ALEXANDER MORGAN

Character: INTERNAL SECURITY - CUBA
REGISTRATION ACT - CUBA
NEUTRALITY MATTER

Synopsis:

Subject, born 4/19/28, Cleveland, Ohio, fought as member Cuban Revolutionary Forces against govt. of FULGENCIO BATISTA which fell 1/1/59. In 4/59 source said subject agreed to establish new revolutionary anti-Castro front in Cuba; in 5/59 was in contact with DOMINICK BARTONE and AUGUSTO FERRANDO, Dominican Consul General, Miami. Said subject had been paid large sum of money for cooperation in counter-revolutionary move. Subject interviewed Miami 7/27/59; claimed in about 5/59 was in Miami, was contacted by "representative" of foreign govt. and offered one million dollars to create counter-revolution. Claimed he refused. Checked into Eden Roc Hotel, Miami Beach, Fla. 7/21/59, thereafter disappeared. Source reported on 8/14/59 subject had departed several days before for Cuba in boat loaded with guns and ammunition. Telephonically contacted Miami Office, FBI, 8/20/59 from Havana, Cuba, claimed he pretended to be head of anti-Fidel Castro counter-revolutionary plot, but actually playing double-agent role in favor CASTRO. U.S. Dept. of State, Washington, D.C., reported 12/17/59 that on 9/21/59 Passport Div. approved Certificate of Loss of U.S. Nationality prepared by U.S. Embassy, Havana, Cuba, for Subject. Subject reportedly seen in Toledo, Ohio, 2/16/60.

- P -

CLASSIFIED AND
EXTENDED
REASON
FCIM, B
DATE OF REVIEW FOR
DECLASSIFICATION

Stafford looked over the notes on his desk. If he could nail down Morgan in the Cuban military, then he'd have him. There was too much scuttlebutt about the ongoing plot. Stafford wasn't going to take any shit.

"What's going on with Trujillo?" he asked.

Morgan dug in. He didn't need Trujillo. He didn't need Batista. If he believed that Castro was selling out the Cuban people, then he would chase him into hell personally. He had plenty of problems with people like Che Guevara—a stone-cold Communist—but he had no problems with Fidel. Morgan had heard the talk about Castro being a Communist, but he hadn't seen proof of it. If he did, he'd fight Fidel himself.

Morgan had said enough. As far as he was concerned, he had broken no US laws, and no one was going to put him in jail.

Both men stared across the table, sizing each other up. Stafford could see that Morgan wasn't going to crack. The session was over. He had no option other than to let him go. But their time together wasn't over.

OLGA HAD BEEN DREADING THIS MOMENT. THE DRIVER WAS ABOUT TO take her and her sister to the airport. In just a few hours, she would be back in Havana.

She knew she had to leave the United States, but she didn't want to go. She had found peace in her brief time in Florida. She didn't have to worry about Castro. She didn't have to fret over Che. She didn't wake up every morning with strange people sleeping on her floors, the phone calls, the cars pulling into the driveway at night.

"I will see you in Havana," Morgan said, his arms around her.

He was about to take on as dangerous a battle as he had faced in the revolution, including the ambushes he executed in the final days. Olga felt crushed by forces working against them. The worst part was that she recognized the land mines as much as he did. Once again, she had to wait for him to come back, alive or dead. She had grown tired of that same sinking feeling.

"After this, no more," she said.

A week or more might pass before she would see him again, and she knew that she probably wouldn't hear from him during that time. The waiting was worse in this case because at least there were messengers in the mountains. Here, she had nothing.

Morgan was going to check out of the Montmartre and rent a room at the Eden Roc for a couple of days. The move to the luxurious hotel just down the street would provide a bit more cover. When Olga arrived back at the house, Morgan's men would watch out for her. At that point, all she could do was wait.

━━◆━━

When Stafford arrived at the office, a message was waiting on his desk. Morgan had called to say he would be boarding a Pan Am flight for Havana in just twenty-four hours, on August 5. Don't worry. He'd phone the FBI before he left.

Stafford had no plans to talk to Morgan over the phone. He was going to make sure he was in the terminal building well before the 5:00 p.m. flight.

Stafford had just gotten off the phone with a confidential informant who had been divulging details of what Morgan had been up to in Miami—and it was anything but a vacation. Morgan's entire trip was about a secret plot to overthrow Castro with the help of Trujillo and his people. He had met with Bartone, and he had met with Ferrando. From what Stafford had gathered, thousands were waiting in the Escambray for Morgan to give them the cue to rise up against Castro.

At this point, Stafford had heard enough. He had been duped. For all intents and purposes, Morgan had obstructed justice. Between now and tomorrow, the FBI agent was going to make sure that everyone's story checked out. Then he would confront Morgan at the gate. This time, he had enough to tighten the noose.

━━

One agent went to the Pan Am gate. Another stood sentinel outside the terminal. A third was scoping the people from inside the doors.

Stafford had doubled-checked everyone's story. Cuba was on the brink, and Morgan was ready to thrust it over the edge. There was no way Stafford was going to let him leave Miami.

The terminal was bustling, but even as the passengers were getting ready to board, there was no sign of Morgan. Stafford angled over to the ticket counter to make sure Morgan was coming. But when he asked the agent to see the manifest, Morgan's name wasn't on the list. By the time the passengers were lining up to board the 5:00 p.m. flight, Morgan wasn't in the terminal.

Stafford waited until the flight gate was shut. He had lost Morgan again.

He immediately rounded up the agents and ordered them to head to the Eden Roc. Stafford was steaming. As he sped through the traffic, he realized that Morgan was much smarter than anyone in the FBI had figured. That's something Stafford didn't glean from the field reports or the background investigation. Every agent had underestimated him. If they didn't find him, they all would have a lot of explaining to do.

The car pulled up to the hotel, and Stafford rushed to the front desk. Just as he thought: Morgan was gone. Stafford had to put out an alert and let headquarters know that Morgan had slipped away.

The teletypes were coming in from Washington. The embassy in Havana was preparing for the worst. US Ambassador Philip Bonsal leaned over his desk and read the messages. It wasn't just that a plot was unfolding to assassinate Castro and overthrow his government. An American was leading it. If the plan succeeded even partially, every US citizen in Cuba—thousands—could be in danger.

The fifty-six-year-old career diplomat—a Yale graduate whose father had covered the Spanish-American War for the *New York Herald*—had spent weeks struggling to restore relations with Cuba.

Bonsal picked up the phone. He needed Cuban Foreign Secretary Raúl Roa to get an urgent message to Castro. The FBI had uncovered critical information about a coup under way to topple the government and kill Castro. No one knew when it would happen, but it was supposed to take place in just days. The man leading the plot: William Morgan.

Roa needed to know that the American government had nothing to do with this, Bonsal said. From the ambassador's perspective, it was better for the United States to disclose subversive behavior from one of its own citizens. His biggest fear was that the coup would be blamed on the United States. That, in turn, could jeopardize the lives of American citizens in Havana.

The ambassador also had to draw up an emergency plan, including the possibility of bringing in ships to evacuate Americans. The intelligence community was on high alert. The only way to stop the plan was to find Morgan.

But no one had a clue where he was.

A cool breeze blew off the dark waters and across the fishing boat. Ahead lay the port of Miami, just beyond the last barrier islands. If they could pass Virginia Key without the Coast Guard spotting their craft, they'd be on their way to Cuba.

Morgan had slept only a few hours the night before, chain-smoking and downing cups of coffee. But he had to keep pushing himself. He needed to get out far enough to avoid the Coast Guard.

Just a few feet away was Francisco Betancourt, a former captain in Batista's army brought in to help Morgan make the journey. Their plan was to meet the other vessel, a fifty-four-foot yacht moored a dozen miles away that was loaded with an arsenal for a small army.

Despite running around to avoid the FBI, everything was going as planned. Trujillo's people were waiting for the signal when Morgan arrived in Cuba. So were Menoyo and Castro. The plan was to get the boatload of arms to the southern coast of Cuba near Trinidad and drop them off to Menoyo and the others.

The ocean was kicking up as the boat pulled farther out, the lights of Miami growing dimmer in the distance. As he looked ahead, Morgan could see the flickering movements of another vessel on the horizon. No signs of any Coast Guard cutters, just the dark open ocean in front of them. They had made it.

It would be twenty-four hours before they cut through the Straits of Florida and circled around the belly of Cuba. But time was of the essence. Trujillo was listening to the radio constantly, waiting for the next update from his people in Miami. Castro was pacing, making sure his men remained in touch with Morgan's at the house in Miramar.

Now it was all up to Morgan.

As the smaller boat pulled alongside the yacht, he climbed aboard, motioning for Betancourt to follow. The man stood on the deck, hunched over. With every mile, Betancourt had grown more nauseated until finally he couldn't go on any longer. There was no way he could make the ninety-mile trip to Cuba.

"I'm sick," he told Morgan.

Morgan didn't have time to wait. It was better for Betancourt to head back on the fishing boat. Two of Trujillo's people were waiting on the yacht, ready to push off. Morgan motioned for them to throw the rope back into the fishing boat, and Betancourt climbed down. As the yacht's engines revved, Morgan braced himself for the last leg of his trip. Surrounded by the numbing drone of the engines, Morgan needed to stay alert. He didn't know the crew. He didn't know the waters. Anything could happen between here and landfall.

As he stared into the night, one of the crew approached him. The look on his face said trouble. "We're not going to make it," the man said.

The captain had been watching the fuel gauge. It was showing far less gasoline than they thought they would need. There was no way the boat was going to have enough fuel to snake around the tip of Pinar del Río and the Isle of Pines before landing near Trinidad.

Morgan couldn't believe what he was hearing. How did this happen? Legions of men were waiting for him in Cuba, and there was the matter of the crazed Dominican dictator who wouldn't rest until there was a bullet in Castro's head.

Morgan was about to get stuck on a boat full of weapons with a fuel tank coughing up fumes. Perhaps they hadn't estimated the extra weight of the weapons or planned on the rough waters in the Great Bahama Bank. But ultimately it didn't matter. They needed to find the closest port. The map provided their answer: Havana.

They could make the capital, but the port was crawling with customs agents who would board the yacht, search the cabin, and undoubtedly turn up the arsenal below. Without any knowledge of Morgan's role in the plot, the bust would blow up everything they were trying to do.

He had planned to unveil his true role when they arrived in Trinidad. But like everything else, he had to change plans. As the two crew members stepped onto the deck, he grabbed his handgun and waited for them to reach the rails. Then, raising the barrel, he pointed the gun at them. The men looked up, startled. He was taking them prisoner.

36

Just before dawn, the men gathered in the living room.

They had been roused from their sleep and told to report to the house in Miramar. After months of planning, it was time. To the anti-Castro operatives, the new government was just a day away. No one was going to deprive them of their rightful place.

Arturo Hernández Tellaheche, the former Cuban power broker, came through the doorway and took a seat in the living room. Arturo Caíñas Milanés, the millionaire cattleman who once backed Castro until the farmers began losing their land to the government, also arrived. Ramón Mestre Gutiérrez, the wealthy thirty-one-year-old contractor who stood to be the next premier, joined his older colleagues at the table. The government-in-waiting, as they were known, had been preparing to grab the levers of power. In the corners of the home, Roger Redondo and other rebels of the Second Front stood guard, keeping an eye on everyone.

As they waited for their next cue, Morgan walked into the house. Dirty and unshaven with dark circles under his eyes, he was a welcome sight. He had just delivered the prisoners and the weapons at the dock in Havana and rushed to his home.

At his side stood Menoyo. Now the final stages of the plan could begin. First, they would send out a signal on the radio to alert the anti-Castro fighters huddled in houses across the city. The signal would go directly to Trujillo, who would be waiting to send in the foreign legion.

As the men stood to talk about the plans, Morgan and Menoyo stepped back, reached down, and pulled out their weapons. If anyone moved, they'd be shot.

Hernández turned around, startled. So did Caíñas. Both men looked petrified. What had happened? Redondo and the other rebels drew their weapons and pointed them at the rest of the plotters in the house. Morgan, Menoyo, and the other rebels motioned for the men to move into one room. No one was going to even think about escaping.

Just then came a knock at the door: Fidel and Camilo Cienfuegos were standing on the front steps. Castro couldn't help himself. It was his moment to gloat and stare into the eyes of his adversaries. Hernández and the others now realized they were done. Morgan had turned the tables on them, and they never had a clue.

Like a cat, Castro circled the men in the room. "Any orders, Mr. President?" he said mockingly to Hernández. Stunned, Hernández looked straight ahead. Wheeling around, Castro turned to Mestre. "So, what were you going to be minister of?"

In a duffle bag Morgan had carried on the boat were wads of cash— seventy-eight thousand dollars from Ferrando in Miami. As Castro pranced about the room, Morgan reached down into the bag and began laying it out on a table. Castro went over to him and nodded. The *Yanqui comandante* had come through.

Now it was time to talk about next steps. For Castro, the first order of business was to round up the Batista supporters holed up in the safe houses. They would never know what hit them. Then came the tough part of the plan: rushing to Trinidad before news about the arrests leaked. Trujillo was still waiting in the wings. They needed to draw out the dictator before he could pull back. Otherwise, the plans they had been forging for months would collapse.

～

The Jeep bounced back and forth as the Second Front leaders gripped the side rails. Menoyo looked at Morgan and smiled. The American had juggled half a dozen competing interests—the mob, Castro, Trujillo, the FBI, Batista, and his own men—while carrying out an incredible intelligence operation that would alter history. Morgan wasn't a secret agent. He was a soldier. And that made his work all the more noteworthy.

The Jeep moved along the dirt road until it reached the stretch of beach just a few miles from Trinidad. They had finally arrived. It seemed like they hadn't stopped moving since leaving Morgan's house, boarding a government plane in Havana, flying to Trinidad, then hopping into the Jeep so they could reach their destination.

Now they needed to launch the plot. Castro's men were waiting in a nearby house with the shortwave. As soon as they hit the frequency, they could connect directly with Trujillo. No doubt the feisty dictator was grousing about not hearing from the leaders of the Second Front.

Grabbing the microphone, Menoyo signaled for the operator to flick on the transmitter. The receiver crackled as the operator moved the dial.

"3JK calling KJB," said Menoyo.

For a few seconds, the waves bounced in and out. No one said a word. Menoyo looked up and then spoke into the microphone again: "KJB, come in, please."

If the Second Front was ever going to get this plot under way with any success, they needed to do it now.

"KJB here," the gravelly voice broke through. "I hear you loud and clear." El Jefe himself was on the other end.

Menoyo gripped the mike a little tighter. "Instructions completed. I am now in the mountains fighting the Communists. The American landed at the appointed spot. Now everything is in your hands."

Trujillo was elated. He had waited months for this moment. The rebellion was in full swing. He insisted on knowing everything. He had put the foreign legion—thousands of the most ruthless fighters in the islands—on alert. All the generalissimo needed to know was that the insurgents on the ground were ready. Then he'd order the legion to land.

The Caribbean stood on the verge of war.

———

For most of the day and into the night, Trujillo was beside himself. Every hour or so, he went to his shortwave and asked his staff whether anyone from Cuba had called. Then he grumbled and walked back to his office. If he could have gone to Cuba to move the plan forward more swiftly, he would have, but at this point, it was a waiting game, with Morgan in charge. Word couldn't come soon enough.

Finally, the shortwave lit up and Morgan was on the other end. He assured the dictator that the men on the ground were taking on Castro's forces. At one point, he even ordered his men to fire their machine guns in the air to create battle sounds. Trujillo was overjoyed. This time, he was really going to make his mark. Castro would never mess with him again.

On the next radio call, Morgan reached Trujillo's chief of security, Johnny Abbes, a sadistic investigator who took pleasure in watching men die. Morgan had good news to share: The Second Front was inching toward Trinidad and a major victory. If they took the southern port city, they were that much closer to taking the entire country.

Trujillo was now fully engaged. He was close to sending in the legion—as close as he was going to come. But some of Trujillo's men had their doubts. Despite what Morgan was saying, they were getting reports to the contrary—news they didn't expect. Some of the news correspondents were reporting that Castro's men were arresting people in Havana and elsewhere. No one could confirm it, but no one had been able to reach Hernández or Caíñas, the two leaders in waiting.

That night, Trujillo took the call when the shortwave lit up. "KJB here, over."

"The American speaking."

"What's going on?" Trujillo yelled. "They say everybody's been captured and you're about to be captured, too. What can you tell me? Over."

Once again, Morgan had to think fast. He knew that eventually the reporters on the ground would get the story. Don't believe it, he said. The Cuban government was fabricating the news. "You know those people are experts in propaganda. It's a plan to create confusion and avoid the reinforcements that they imagine are on the way."

Morgan signed off, but he knew Trujillo wasn't going to buy it for long. They had to do something quick. After talking to his men, Castro came up with an idea that once again demonstrated his Machiavellian might. If they cut the electricity to Trinidad—just for one night—they would show the Dominican pilots flying overhead that the town indeed had been captured and shut down. It was a gamble, but they had to do something drastic to turn their fortunes around.

As night fell over southern Cuba, the entire city was plunged into darkness. The streetlights were turned off, and homes went pitch-black.

Without identifying himself, Castro got on the radio and announced that insurgents had captured the town. "You can now send the shipments to the airport," he said.

Trujillo and the others looked at one another. The news was encouraging, but some of his men still had their doubts. Trujillo agreed to send another plane, but this time, he would send one of his most trusted advisers: Father Ricardo Velazco Ordóñez. The aging Spanish cleric had been a part of the plan since its inception.

No one was better at feeling out a situation than the round man in the robe and collar. He had won the confidence of Trujillo long ago for his role in snitching on the other clerics in the Dominican Republic who had sided with the people over the government. If the priest gave his blessing to the situation, then Trujillo would send in his legion.

At about 7:00 p.m., on August 10, a C-47 transport plane circled the airport in Trinidad and moments later touched down. Menoyo and his men were waiting. As the door of the plane swung open, the priest appeared and waved to the men walking toward the runway. The crew on the plane began unloading more weapons for the Second Front, including nine bazookas, fifteen cases of ammo, and thirty-nine cases of .50-caliber shells. The men in fatigues waved back.

To maintain the illusion the city was still under siege, Morgan's men fired artillery shells and machine guns in the background to make it sound like a battle was being fought nearby.

"¡Viva Trujillo!" the men yelled to the priest.

Velazco smiled and waved. He was convinced. Morgan was on the verge of owning the city. All Trujillo needed was a nudge. One more call to his headquarters, and he'd sic his men on Santa Clara.

If Morgan and his men could convince the Dominican leader that the Second Front was about to take the historic city in the heart of Las Villas Province—just as Che Guevara had done—they'd snare him. If anyone could convince the dictator that the rebels were carrying out the same sweep that had ousted Batista, it was the *Yanqui comandante*.

Morgan gave the signal. "3JK calling KJB."

The hissing sound of the shortwave's static filled the air. Moments later came Trujillo's voice. "KJB here."

This time, the words were urgent: They had captured the town of Manicaragua and were about to launch a drive to invade Santa Clara. It wasn't going to be easy: The Cuban Revolutionary Army was fighting back and had wrested control of the Soledad Sugar Mill. If the Second Front could just get more men, they could complete a sweep of the mountains. Morgan drove home the point: "We must take advantage of the state of demoralization to land our foreign legion which will give them the final kick."

Trujillo had Castro by the balls. Now he could put his own stamp on the counterrevolution and declare himself the conqueror. It was time. But before he could give the order to send in the legion, his own men interrupted. They weren't convinced that everything was as Morgan described. One of the pilots who flew near Trinidad indicated he hadn't seen one dead body. Trujillo's men were also getting reports that Castro had smashed the coup and that the Batistianos were done.

Trujillo was getting angry, accusing his men of losing their nerve. He wasn't going to get a chance like this again. He agreed to scout the scene one more time with a plane, but then he was sending in the cavalry.

Trujillo had his operatives tell Morgan that another plane was coming with weapons aboard. That was all that Morgan needed to hear. He and his men circled the airfield, taking their positions. For Castro, the baiting had lasted long enough. If Trujillo wasn't going to send his legion, it was time to strike. It didn't matter how many men were on the plane or how many weapons they were carrying. Castro was going to send a message to Trujillo.

In the distance, Morgan and the others heard the plane's engines roar overhead. A C-47—a big transport—dropped from the sky, scoping out the darkness below. The men strained their necks to watch the craft descend and come in for the landing. Each corner of the grounds was covered. No one could escape. As the plane roared down the runway, the men whipped out their machine guns and aimed them straight ahead.

For a moment, no one moved.

Turning on the runway, the plane came to a halt. Moments later, the doors flung open. As the crew members bounded off the plane, they were met by Menoyo.

Luis del Pozo, son of the former mayor of Havana, recognized his old friend from their early days and hugged Menoyo in the middle of the runway. For his part, Pozo had a message of greeting from El Jefe. The big man was pleased. If the Second Front needed more men, they'd have them. If they needed more guns, they'd fly them in. Even bomber planes were standing by.

As the two old friends talked, the Second Front members began quietly moving in. Suddenly, the men surrounded the crew members, and before anyone said anything, they lowered their machine guns and pointed them at the guests.

Stunned, the crew members put up their hands. But in the shadows, the copilot pulled out his gun and started shooting at the rebels. The airport erupted in gunfire. Both sides took turns running around the plane, shooting at each other. Within seconds, the entire rebel force was charging toward the C-47.

Trujillo's men fell back and threw up their arms. Two of the rebels lay dead. Two crew members also lay dead—one of them Francisco Betancourt, the Batista captain too sick to ride with Morgan on the boat leaving Miami.

It was over.

OLGA TURNED ON THE BOXY, BLACK-AND-WHITE TELEVISION IN TIME to watch Morgan walk across the broadcast studio floor dressed in his comandante greens.

Reporters had descended on the television station, catching a glimpse of the American who led the international conspiracy that stunned Cuba. The news had just broken about the coup attempt, with stories splashed in the *New York Times* and other newspapers across the Americas. It was the biggest story to break in Cuba since the revolution ended.

Under the heat of television lights, Castro started the press conference by lighting into Trujillo as a "gangster" who pushed for what amounted to a counterrevolution and a desperate plan to kill Castro. "All this is part of a great plot," he told the reporters. "This is not only the work of Trujillo. Trujillo is just one phase of the giant conspiracy against the revolution."

Then Castro recounted every tantalizing detail of the plot, from the mob visit to Morgan to the Americano's trips to Florida to buy guns and boats.

"Trujillo appointed William Morgan the leader of the counterrevolutionary [plot]," said Fidel, pointing to the *Yanqui comandante*. Castro described how Morgan's home had become the command center of the scheme, with radio directives beamed from Santo Domingo. Morgan's undercover work kept the dictator and others believing that an insurgency would take place. "He convinced Trujillo that everything was in order," said Castro.

"All the leaders of the movement were to meet in Morgan's house and receive instructions. Major Menoyo and a group of comrades were living there."

At every turn, Morgan made sure the government knew of the changing invasion plans and where the insurgents were planted. Fidel turned to Morgan and to the reporters. "He is a Cuban," he said. "He is married to a Cuban. He is not a North American."

To the reporters, the story had all the makings of a Cold War thriller, with Morgan as the lead character. He had reached a milestone in his life. No one knew that more than Olga, who was watching the press conference unfold from their home in Miramar.

Reaching over to a table, Castro pulled out the stacks of money, the same bundles that Morgan had carted from Miami on the boat. "We seized some seventy-eight thousand dollars," Castro said. Then, he did something that surprised everyone. He turned to Morgan in front of the cameras and handed the bundle to the American. It was a reward, Castro said, for exposing the Trujillo people.

Like a scene in slow motion, Olga stared in disbelief and then shouted at the TV screen: "Don't take it. Don't take it!"

Morgan stood back for a moment, unable to speak. Fidel had just handed him seventy-eight thousand dollars, turning Morgan into a mercenary on national television. Morgan didn't know what to say. He had asked earlier that the money be sent to the Escambray for special programs to help the people. Castro had just kicked him in the gut.

Morgan put the money back down. Rather than let his emotions show, he stood silent. After a while, he couldn't even hear what Castro was saying.

❧

The door slammed, and footsteps sounded in the house. As he came in the room, she smiled and embraced him.

Morgan's stomach was turning. He could control only his word and the strength of his convictions. It had taken him long enough to find those. "I'm not a mercenary," he said.

There wasn't much Olga could say. She had told him many times before that he didn't understand the politics of her country, but she wasn't going to tell him now. She barely had time to talk to him before he left for the press conference because of all the reporters showing up at their door. When he walked into the press conference, she realized that his stature overshadowed Che's and Raúl's. Neither man had gained this level of fame. That spelled trouble. Nearly all the newspapers in Havana had lionized Morgan in the last day. Castro wasn't used to being upstaged.

"This is why I am scared for you," she said. "I am scared for us."

Olga knew it wasn't a good time to broach the subject of moving, but she wanted to raise it now rather than later. "We need to live in your country," she said. Even though she was about to deliver their child, she wanted to begin preparations to move. It was time for them to settle down to a safer life. "I don't want to worry about you anymore."

Once again, Morgan stopped her. He knew where this was heading, but now wasn't the time. They still had to make sure the Second Front was protected. They still had to ensure the government would hold elections. Plus, after everything that happened with the FBI, he had to make sure it was safe for him to return home. They would wait until the baby was born and then look into moving. Morgan needed more time.

━ ❧ ━

Everyone around Trujillo had failed. Castro not only remained in power, but it would be more difficult than ever to oust him now. In his thirty years of running the Dominican Republic with an iron fist, Trujillo had never been so exposed. He was furious. The generalissimo accused everyone around him of making him look like a fool. He had to clean house. Johnny Abbes was done. He would never serve as security chief again.

Trujillo wanted a complete report on what had happened. But more than that, he wanted to strike back. He wanted blood. He put out word that he would pay anyone one hundred thousand dollars for killing the *Yanqui comandante*. It didn't matter where the hit took place. He wanted Morgan dead.

Three years earlier, Trujillo was suspected of ordering the abduction of a Columbia University lecturer who was writing his doctoral thesis about El Jefe. Jesús Galíndez Suárez was snatched off the streets of Morningside Heights in Manhattan and supposedly smuggled in a private plane to the Dominican Republic. Then he was stripped, handcuffed, and bound with a rope around his feet before being lowered into a vat of boiling water. His body was never recovered. If Trujillo could do the same to Morgan, he would.

━ ❧ ━

Guards stood watch in the corners of the hospital. Even the government sent men to roam the halls outside Olga's room. She had arrived at six o'clock in the morning, doubled up in pain. Morgan inched up to her bed and kissed her.

She had been through so much in the past three months that he could never make it up to her. Their lives had been turned upside down. The newspapers were publishing stories about revenge plots against Morgan for his role in the conspiracy. Olga was assigned her own bodyguards. Armed men were even poised at the street corners near their home.

Morgan got up from the bed as the nurses came to get Olga. He bent over and kissed her. "Remember, darling," he said, placing his hand on her stomach. "This must be a boy."

Smiling faintly, she shook her head. It didn't matter whether it was a boy or a girl, she said. This was *their* child—together.

As the nurses wheeled Olga to the delivery room, Morgan walked to a chair outside the room and plopped down. He had so much to think about. He knew that Trujillo would stop at nothing to see him dead. So would the Batistianos. What troubled him was that he wouldn't be there to protect Olga and their baby, that somehow he would get pulled away and they would become a target.

As he sat quietly, a nurse came up to him. "Comandante Morgan?" she said. "You can come in now."

As Morgan entered the room, a nurse was standing to greet him, clutching a crying baby. "You have a girl," she said.

With Olga just awakening, Morgan walked over and gently lifted the infant into his arms.

For a moment, he stared into her blue eyes and then smiled, looking at Olga. For the first time in a long time, he was at peace.

———

Stafford was rushed. In just a few hours, he had to finish a report for the highest levels of the US government. The orders to file the report hadn't come from his supervisors in Miami. They had come from FBI Director J. Edgar Hoover. The Morgan case had gone from a priority investigation to something far more urgent.

To Stafford, it came as no surprise. He and the other agents had let Morgan get away, plain and simple. Now they were paying the price. Not only had Morgan outfoxed them, but he had pulled off an undercover operation that saved the Castro government. Worse, it had become international news. *Time* magazine ran a feature story on the conspiracy, calling Morgan "the crafty, US-born double agent." The *New York Times*, the *Miami Herald*, the *Washington Post*, and scores of other newspapers carried the story. That kind of exposure invited the scrutiny of Congress and the other big shots. No doubt, they were all asking questions.

No one was more furious than Francis Walter, the powerful Pennsylvania congressman who chaired the House Subcommittee on Immigration. An ardent anti-Communist, Walter, like Hoover, built his political fortune by playing strongly on Cold War rhetoric. He allowed the US government to deport or ban anyone identified as subversive, regardless of evidence. His critics viewed him as reactionary and racist, but he remained popular among his constituents.

The Morgan case made Walter's blood boil. Trujillo may have been a thug, but he despised Communists. If anyone needed support in rooting out Reds in the Caribbean, it was Trujillo. Few others had more impact on immigration matters than Walter, who could pick up the phone to boot someone from the country.

Now Morgan was on his radar.

❦

Olga nudged closer to Morgan on the living room couch as they watched the tropical fish dart across the large glass tank. Since the baby was born, they finally had been able to clear their house of all the radio equipment and settle into their home. They had phoned Morgan's mother to let her know that they had named their baby after her.

Just as Morgan was reaching up to the tank to adjust the filter, they heard what sounded like squealing tires and car doors slamming. Seconds later came a burst of gunfire, with bullets shattering the front windows and walls.

Morgan quickly jumped over to Olga and pulled her down on the floor.

The baptism of Loretta Morgan Rodriguez in Havana Cathedral, with Olga's longtime friend Blanca Ruiz Flores and Eloy Gutiérrez Menoyo
COURTESY OF MORGAN FAMILY COLLECTION

"The baby!" Olga shrieked. "The baby!"

Morgan bolted up the stairs, ran down the hall, and pushed open the door to the baby's room. She was fast asleep.

Moments later, Alejandrina, the housekeeper, joined him. "Get down, Alejandrina, get down!" he yelled. The housekeeper hit the floor while Morgan squatted down with the infant in his arms.

Morgan's entourage was already running across the lawn with guns raised. The two assailants had just enough time to jump into a car, start the engine, step on the gas, and race out of the neighborhood. The escorts ran to their own cars and sped after them.

Olga ran up the stairs and into the nursery. "She's fine," Morgan said, handing the baby to her. Then he ran down the stairs and out the door.

Despite bodyguards at both ends of the block to watch for trouble, the car had managed to slip through security and stopped in front of Morgan's house. Something wasn't right.

Shaking, Olga came down the stairs with Loretta in her arms. There was no way she was going to stay at the house anymore.

38

Morgan spent the rest of the night circling the house, poking his Sten into the bushes to make sure no one was hiding. Their machine guns hoisted in the air, the guards checked every car driving into the neighborhood. No one could come to the front door unless cleared by bodyguards. No one.

Morgan had never hounded his men about doing their jobs, but a stunning security breach had occurred. They had never seen him this angry. What unnerved him was that the attackers had driven directly to the front of the home without being stopped. He could take care of himself and even Olga, who had survived the fighting in the mountains. But the bullets had pierced the wall just under the room where his infant daughter was sleeping.

Olga was packing. So were his men. Morgan had made a decision. He would move into a smaller, more secure location, probably a penthouse unit in the Vedado neighborhood. He could take only about a dozen of his closest men, but they would be carrying .30-caliber machine guns and grenades. Morgan was preparing for another attempt on his life. This time, he would be ready.

He had been working behind the scenes, calling the State Department and other House members, lining up support. The congressman was tired of hearing about the Yankee comandante. He didn't care if the Cubans were calling him a hero. The man had helped Castro. That's all that mattered. Now he was going to pay.

In just days, Representative Walter had convinced government lawyers to make a highly unusual move, one that would leave Morgan as vulnerable as anyone in his position could be. They were stripping him of his birthright.

No longer could he call himself an American citizen. Utilizing a rarely used clause in US law, State Department officials issued a "certificate of loss of US nationality." The reason: Morgan had served in the armed forces of a foreign country. He no longer had the rights given to American citizens. He could be denied entry into the country. By the afternoon of September 4, it was official.

Reporters scurried down the long corridor and into Congressman Walter's office. The paperwork was signed and sent to the State Department. The decision had been teletyped to Havana. Only the public announcement remained. In front of the reporters in his office, Walter lashed out at Morgan, saying his efforts to help Castro "were greatly harmful to the interests of the United States." He clarified that the "State Department agrees with my opinion."

The news trickled over the wire, alerting reporters in Havana. A writer for the Associated Press read the teletype bulletin and called the house in Miramar.

Morgan had spent much of the day packing and making other preparations. He had found a suitable high-rise on Calle 16 just across from the Malecón, but he hadn't heard the breaking news. At first, he was suspicious. No one had said anything to him or even warned him this was coming. The reporter told him the justification for his loss of citizenship. Morgan shot back that he had never served in the Cuban army. The charges had been trumped up.

"I had the good fortune of being born in the United States," he said, "and I am not going to lose my US citizenship."

He hung up the phone. Morgan didn't always understand the machinations of politics, but he concluded that it was the work of Trujillo and whoever was supporting him in the States. He wasn't going to allow anyone to take away his citizenship. He would fight it. His future and that of his family depended on it.

─◆─

Olga watched as her husband met with reporters in their home. He said he wasn't going to blame anyone, but he was getting angry. This wasn't about justice, he said. It was about getting even. He had done nothing wrong.

"What I did, America taught me," he said.

They could have revoked his citizenship nine months ago, right after the revolution succeeded in January. But they were pulling it now, just two weeks after the failed Trujillo conspiracy. He had learned that Representative Walter, Senator George Smathers of Florida, and Senator James Eastland of Mississippi had led the effort.

"Members of Congress bribed by Trujillo gold, who have caused the temporary loss of my citizenship, are no better citizens than I," Morgan said. "Our country knows them well. Public opinion will be on my side."

He was going into battle mode again, except this time the enemy lay a thousand miles away in Washington. If he had to expose people like Walter and Smathers, he would. Morgan reminded the reporters that Trujillo did whatever it took and spent whatever it took to achieve his goals. The dictator had doled out $750,000 to the Mutual Broadcasting System to air favorable stories about his regime. "We have seen how his money poisoned the United States, buying the press in the recent scandal," Morgan said.

The reporters took down every word and filed their stories. Clete Roberts, anchor of KTLA-TV in Los Angeles, showed up at the house with an entire crew, insisting on talking to Morgan. Roberts asked about Morgan's role in the revolution and why he had helped Castro.

Morgan replied that it wasn't about fame. He wanted to help liberate the people from a despot. "People who fought here in Cuba, fought for an ideal, fought for a reason. I think it's about time the little guy got a break. He never had one before," Morgan said.

Roberts wanted Morgan's response to the accusations that he was merely a "soldier of fortune."

Morgan shot back that coming to Cuba was never about money. "I don't believe you should cash in on your ideals. I didn't believe I was an idealist when I went up into the mountains, but I feel I'm an idealist now. At least I have an awful strong faith in an awful lot of people and what they want to do."

But Morgan didn't know what lay in store.

39

EACH MOVE WAS HARDER THAN THE LAST. THIS WAS HER FOURTH HOME since the revolution ended. Olga had hoped to find sanctuary in America, but now that was looking less and less possible.

She was watching the lights moving in the harbor when she heard something coming from the bedroom. At first, it sounded like someone shouting, but she couldn't be sure. Morgan was standing in front of the television set, clenching his fists. On the black-and-white screen, Castro was raising his arms and urging the crowd to join him in denouncing Americans in Cuba.

"*Yanqui, vete a casa,*" he chanted. Yankee, go home.

The studio audience repeated the line, "*Yanqui, vete a casa!*"

She and Morgan had heard it before, but it was resonating with the audience more strongly, whipping them into a frenzy.

"That son of a bitch!" Morgan yelled.

Olga turned off the television, but Morgan was already rushing to put on his clothes. "I'm going down there," he announced. Olga tried to calm him, but he wasn't listening. "I am going down there," he insisted. "Change your clothes. We are going to that program."

Olga went down the hall to alert their escorts, but by the time they gathered their guns, Morgan had already jumped into the elevator.

"You can't do this," she called after him. "This is Castro."

But Morgan was already on his way. Olga and several others ran down the stairs to catch up with him. She didn't know what he was going to do, but it wasn't going to be good. By the time she and the men reached the ground level, the blue Oldsmobile was gone. If they were going to reach the Telemundo studio in time, they had to leave immediately.

Her driver stepped on the gas as Olga frantically looked for her husband's car as they sped along the route to the station. She knew his temperament better than anyone. He was still angry about Castro's antics at the press conference. Then the drive-by shooting, which could have killed the baby. Perhaps he was reacting, after the fact, to the loss of his citizenship.

As Morgan pushed open the door of the station, the employees recognized him and waved him in. He then proceeded and opened the studio doors. As he entered, the audience applauded. "¡*Comandante Morgan!*" they cheered, rising to their feet.

He had become a hero to the Cuban people. Newspapers editorialized in his favor, and civic groups pushed for the government to extend citizenship to him to make amends for the loss of his status as an American. He was bigger now than he had ever been.

Morgan obviously wasn't scheduled to appear on Castro's national address, but he had burst on set with cameras rolling. Castro was still delivering his speech. Ever the showman, the leader acted as if nothing was wrong. But Olga, who arrived moments later with the escorts, could see his head held straight up and his arms folded.

The two men walked away from the microphone and talked away from the audience, with Castro chewing on his cigar. Olga watched as the Cuban leader's eyes narrowed. The escorts nervously held their weapons. Morgan, who had been talking intensely in Castro's ear, backed up, spun around, and walked off the set, the audience cheering. No one heard what they said, but Olga could see that Castro was enraged.

As they walked outside, Olga pulled close to Morgan. "He is going to come after us," she said, shaking her head. "He isn't going to forget this."

———

Even Morgan had a breaking point. Just before dawn, he slipped out of the apartment and climbed into his Oldsmobile with a couple of his men. If he could make it out of the city just for a day, he might be able to rest. He might be able to stop the spiraling.

He had spent barely any time with Olga and even less with little Loretta. The long talks he had with Olga in the mountains about what they would do after the war—it was all becoming a blur. It never seemed to end. Just when they thought they could move on, something else came along. He rarely spoke about his children in Ohio, but Olga could tell that he longed to visit them. He wanted all of his family to be together. He would do whatever it took to protect them and the Second Front, but it all was falling on him. The turmoil of Havana was consuming his life.

The sun was rising as the Oldsmobile sped toward the first row of foothills. The smell of rich earth filled the air as the open expanse of coffee plantations spread out before their eyes. In the distance, the guajiros tended the rows of tall, green coffee plants. This was the Cuba for which he had fought. These were the people who had stirred him, these were the people who mattered.

The car followed a dirt road and came to a clearing. Thick vines covered several shacks that surrounded a larger decayed wooden building. From just beyond the trees came the sound of rushing water.

"El Río Ariguanabo," one of the men said, the Ariguanabo River, a waterway south of Havana.

Morgan walked toward the clump of trees and forlorn buildings. Pushing aside the branches, he peeked inside one of the huts. In the darkness, he saw a row of brick cauldrons filled with green, dank water. At the next hut, he pulled his knife from his leg holster and sliced through gnarled, twisted vines to get inside. Puzzled, the men watched him. He eyed the shacks and paced off the distance between them and the river. It appeared that ditches had been dug to allow water into the structures. The place looked like a fishery, but no one could say for sure.

Morgan got back into the car, the guards following. On the drive back to Havana, he asked about the river, the site, and the local wildlife. Something had clicked with him, but no one could figure out what it was.

—◆—

He couldn't sleep. Morgan had been walking the halls, stepping out on the balcony and coming back in. He hadn't been able to stop thinking about the stop he made with his men. It wasn't some desolate corner of Cuba. To Morgan, it represented something far different.

In that moment, he saw a place where they could become self-sufficient. If he and his men could get enough building materials and dig a network of ditches, they could build a hatchery. No one would bother them. No one would threaten their way of life. It would get them out of Havana, but more importantly, it would allow them to make money to survive. They would never need the government again.

The idea of creating a farm for fish and frogs—food that could be packaged and sold to restaurants—was real, Morgan told his men. The river was teeming with sunfish and bass that could be delivered to restaurants in Cuba and Miami.

The Second Front didn't have a lot of choices. They had nowhere else to go. They either had to leave the country altogether or stay and try to do something in it. All he wanted from the government was to let the Second Front fend for itself on its own land. Morgan would do the rest. It was time for the rebels to take control of their destinies. It was time to assemble their resources and make a stand.

40

Drenched in sweat, Morgan jammed the shovel into the dark, thick muck and turned it over. In just a few motions, he had dug the outline of a trench that would run all the way to the river. Another one a few feet away would run in the same direction.

Morgan had already figured out the layout of the conservation site. Now he needed the men to do the digging. He had taken out books on hatcheries and fish breeding and had even found a conservation map of the land southwest of Havana where the Ariguanabo River meanders into dark lagoons.

He was determined to learn everything he could about fish breeding and another species turning up everywhere: frogs. In the late 1950s, frog legs had become a delicacy at restaurants in the United States, and Morgan saw the potential.

Olga and his men were witnessing a different side of Morgan. They had always known him as a rebel fighter. To see him poring over books and drafting paper was almost out of character, but at the same time, they could see him carrying out his tasks with the same passion that he showed in the mountains.

He had lined up an American investor to buy the concrete bricks and cement to start building the holding tanks for the water. Frank Emmick promised to stay out of the way and let Morgan do the work. Morgan was grateful that Emmick was willing to turn over several thousand dollars, but he remained leery of the Ohio contractor's ties to the US government, including the CIA. It seemed like every investor who had come to Havana after the revolution had bragged about their government connections. After what Morgan had just gone through with the FBI, he wanted nothing to do with the feds.

For him, the hatchery was all that mattered. He had never designed anything in his life, and the level of technology and science required to create a successful conservation site was beyond anything he had learned in school. The design had to be scientifically sound with just the right lighting, temperatures, and chemicals.

Morgan had pressured the government to turn over the land and even prompted the agriculture ministry to loan a few trucks to the project. Nothing like this had been done in Cuba. He was putting everything on the line.

41

WITH THE SUNLIGHT STREAMING THROUGH THEIR BEDROOM WINDOWS, Olga gently nudged Morgan. It was early, but something was wrong. She needed to go to the clinic.

She had been feeling nauseated for days, but she didn't want to bother him. He had been waking up at dawn each day, driving to the hatchery, and working eighteen-hour stretches before dragging himself back home in the dark.

Morgan hadn't noticed how sick Olga had been, but he took one look at her now and knew she was ill. By the time they reached the Sacred Heart clinic, the nurses were waiting. Morgan was worried. Olga rarely complained about her health and never asked to see a doctor. She spent most of her waking hours taking care of everyone else, including members of their entourage.

Both of them had been under intense pressure, but Olga was always better at dealing with it than he was. Morgan walked down the hall, trying to collect his thoughts. Members of his entourage came into the clinic, but he didn't have time to talk. A nurse came out of the examination room, motioning for him to come inside.

Olga looked up from her bed. She wanted to tell him herself before anyone else. "You are going to be a father again," she said, smiling faintly.

Morgan's eyes widened. He couldn't believe what he had just heard. With everything swirling around them, this was the first good news in a long time. He wrapped his arms around Olga and kissed her. "I know this is going to be a boy."

Olga smiled. To her, it didn't matter whether it was a boy or a girl. What mattered was that their children could live in the peace and freedom for which their father had fought. What mattered was that he would never have to fight again.

Soft music from the radio drifted through the penthouse as Olga rested on the sofa, cradling Loretta in her arms. Every day was getting more difficult, but she didn't want to say anything. She had been watching Morgan throw himself into the project, and the last thing she wanted to do was complain. For the first time in their marriage, he was trying to make a life for them.

After laying her daughter down in the crib, Olga heard the wail of sirens outside her window. At first, it didn't mean anything. Fire trucks passed along the Malecón all the time. But the sirens didn't stop. One emergency vehicle after another raced along the promenade in the afternoon sun.

Olga and Loretta Morgan in the penthouse apartment in Havana COURTESY OF MORGAN FAMILY COLLECTION

Stepping outside on the balcony, she strained to watch a steady stream of trucks and ambulances speed along the road. This was more than just a car accident. She walked inside and waited for the noise outside to calm down, but sirens were still blaring in the distance. Now she worried. Hours earlier, Morgan had left the penthouse, with a few stops to make in Havana before driving to the hatchery.

There was no way to reach him at the site and no way of driving there, so she began making phone calls. She tried members of the Second Front, including Menoyo, but she couldn't reach anyone. She called one of the government offices where Morgan was expected to stop, but the lines were busy.

She paced. Alejandrina tried to get Olga to calm down, but she couldn't. Olga was determined to find out what was happening. Before she could make another call, the music stopped on the radio and a man's voice broke over the air. It was urgent. Two massive explosions in the harbor appeared to have come from a docked vessel. It was still too early to report the damages, but scores of people were injured.

The announcer broke off without giving any more details. That explained the sirens, but now Olga was panicking. She wanted to rush down to the harbor, but it was too far to walk. She tried to reach the government office again, but the line was still busy.

All she could do was turn on the television. A report came over the air with more news: There were mangled bodies everywhere, on the docks, floating in the water, lying in the streets. Chaos churned as emergency workers tended to the injured. Some of the people had died.

The two explosions—half an hour apart—came aboard a French vessel, *La Coubre*, which had docked six hours earlier in the harbor. The government was investigating, but there were few details. Olga hung on every word coming over the television and radio. The same reports described the bloodied bodies and a thick, black mushroom cloud lingering over the harbor. By now, teams of photographers and reporters had descended on the waterfront.

At the time, the government didn't even know if it was an attack. There was no way Olga was going to rest until she found out if her husband was safe. As soon as the phone rang, she jumped.

Running across the room, she picked up the receiver. It was Morgan. He didn't have much time to talk. He had rushed to the harbor as soon as he heard about the explosions, stopping to help injured dockworkers. "It's very bad," he told her.

No one knew who or what had caused the explosions. It was like being back in the mountains: Morgan was gone and Olga was left alone to wait.

⌁

Castro was beside himself. He walked up and down the harbor dock, pointing to the vessel and then to the smoke billowing over the water. There was no way this was an accident, he said. Even as rescue workers were carrying bodies to the ambulances, he demanded answers.

It was no secret the ship had brought a cache of weapons for the Cuban military: seventy-six tons of Belgian munitions. The first blast rocked the harbor at 3:10 p.m., the impact hurtling crew members onto the dock and into the water.

Castro, along with rescue workers, rushed to help when another explosion went off from the ship, injuring even more people. Fidel's bodyguards jumped on top of him to protect him from the falling debris. Crew members were burned beyond recognition, and the stench of burning flesh and diesel fuel hung in the air.

Castro told reporters that it was a direct attack on Cuba by its enemies. It was clear this was carried out by people who hated the revolution. He not only wanted to find out who was responsible, but it was just as important that the country demonstrate its unity. They would show the world that they weren't going to stand idly by while the culprits escaped. They would hold a memorial service for the dead. It would be as public and visibly moving as anything they had ever held. Then they would do everything possible to bring the killers to justice.

———

Not far from the entrance to the harbor, the comandantes gathered on the Malecón. Castro was ready. He asked that Che and his handpicked president, Osvaldo Dorticós, join him at the head of the funeral procession. Putting on a show of strength for the international reporters was critical.

Thousands of mourners were expected to line the roadway for the symbolic march as well as television crews. To demonstrate unity, Castro made a surprising request. He asked the two major comandantes of the Second Front to join the others: Morgan and Menoyo.

Both sides were seen as vastly different—one on the outside and the other, running the government. But this is where Castro excelled. It would show the nation and others that Cuba was standing together against the outside forces that did not want it to survive.

The truth is the "Maximum Leader" was shaken by the blasts. Not since the revolution had anyone struck so close to the inner sanctum of the government.

Castro would make this point by including both men at the front of the column. Morgan and Menoyo were both leery of Castro—now more than ever—but they had witnessed the carnage and suffering at the docks. This was the same Cuba for which they had fought. They agreed to join the others at the Malecón.

But Castro had plans beyond the funeral march and services. He was positioning himself to unload on the United States in a way he never had done before. Taking a page from the Spanish-American War six decades earlier, he was about to announce the fiery explosions as the work of the American government. "It could not have been an accident," he said before the procession. "It had to be intentional."

He pointed out that America refused to sell arms to the new government and that it didn't want the Cubans to obtain weapons elsewhere. "What right has any government to try to prevent Cuba from getting weapons, weapons which all governments get for the defense of their sovereignty and dignity?" he intoned.

La Coubre became a turning point not just for Cuba's relations with the United States but also for Menoyo and Morgan as they walked in line with Castro in the procession.

In most cases, the United States would have ignored Castro's anger, but the diplomatic corps in Havana fired back. William Wieland tossed the press release across his desk to Enrique Patterson, the Cuban chargé d'affaires. Wieland wanted to make sure his counterpart read every word on the page. It was one thing to have political differences—especially after America's years of supporting Batista—but it was another to accuse America of bombing *La Coubre*.

"It's unfounded and irresponsible," he told Patterson.

Relations had been tense between the new government and the US embassy, but now they were deteriorating rapidly. The United States had issued its own press release that blasted Castro for trying to use the *Coubre* tragedy to stir up anti-American sentiments. Castro's remarks were "calculated to transform the understandable sorrow of the Cuban people into resentment against the United States," said Wieland.

But Castro wasn't going to budge. At every step, the United States was trying to undermine his leadership. The Americans wouldn't sell him arms. They wouldn't support his reforms. Now they were preparing to cut all sugar purchases, seriously hurting the economy. Some 80 percent of the country's exports depended on sugar. Without it, they'd go broke.

These differences were even weaving their way into the 1960 presidential campaign. Democratic candidate John Kennedy accused the Eisenhower administration of ignoring the crises unfolding in Cuba and the impact of losing the country as an ally at the height of the Cold War. But what Kennedy didn't know was that on March 17 Eisenhower had approved a covert plan to overthrow the new government by creating a secret paramilitary force to invade the island. No one knew when it would happen, but training would begin soon.

Patterson pushed the press release back across the desk. He would pass on the United States' sentiments to the Cuban government. But the truth was that his government didn't give a damn what the United States said anymore. Cuba was done with America. Both sides were approaching the brink.

42

It was time for the Second Front comandantes to meet. They had done all they could to protect their men and survive within the new government. They had put aside their differences to support the leadership during the Trujillo conspiracy. They remained quiet during the agrarian "reforms." They had stood with Castro after the *Coubre* tragedy. But now the government had gone too far.

Cuba was forging official ties with the Soviet Union. Castro had finally pulled the plug on democracy.

Morgan shouldn't have been surprised, but he was. He had watched Castro insist that he wanted nothing to do with Communism, that Cuba was fighting to become an independent state. Now he wasn't just meeting with the Soviets, he was sending the Second Front's old rival, Faure Chomón Mediavilla, as ambassador to Moscow.

Olga watched as Morgan stood near the television. He had spent days with his men toiling at the hatchery, trying to stay above the politics. He had tried to keep the young rebels in his command under control even when they wanted to take a more active role in antigovernment activities. He had already heard the news, but seeing it on the screen made him even angrier.

Menoyo tried to contain his feelings, but the move clearly distressed him, as it did Fleites and Carreras. No military unit opposed Communism more than the Second Front. They had stated this position publicly. They had even expressed their sentiments to Castro. Most of them knew Fidel was still seething over *La Coubre*, but they thought he would wait until the investigation concluded. He had no proof that America pulled the trigger.

With night falling on the harbor, Morgan motioned for the men to follow him to his living room. This was a conversation that only the comandantes could have. The Second Front needed to take precautions. It couldn't wait for the government to make its next move. It was time to hide weapons in the mountains. It didn't mean war. It didn't mean they were going to launch an attack. But they had to start arming themselves in a larger way.

None of the men disagreed. Carreras had been edging to leave the fold and join the younger rebels who were starting to gather for meetings with the growing opposition movement. Fleites had maintained a dialogue with Castro, agreeing to meet with the Cuban leader periodically—but no more. Morgan already had placed a stash of machine guns and grenades at the hatchery, but he would haul in even more weapons.

In one night, everything had changed.

For much of her pregnancy, Olga felt sick, but as she sat in the passenger seat and watched Morgan drive, she grew alarmed. For most of the morning, his hands were shaking, and his face was red. She had tried to get him to pull over and let an escort in the backseat drive, but he refused.

They had stopped to visit her parents in Santa Clara and were driving eastward along the main highway when he started to feel faint. Olga had warned him that he had been pushing himself beyond his limits without enough rest, but he wasn't listening. Every morning, he had been getting up at sunrise, packing his car, and heading to the hatchery. He drove home an hour or two after nightfall, or on some nights even slept in the main building. Now that he was collecting guns, Olga was even more concerned.

"You are going to kill yourself," she told him.

As the sun began to glare off the windshield, Olga looked up to see they were passing through the town of Florida in Camagüey Province. Shopkeepers had just started to put their wares on the sidewalks in front of their businesses.

There were few places in Cuba where Morgan was not recognized. No sooner did they sit down at a restaurant than a man ran up to their table. There was trouble. The police in Camagüey had picked up Elio Lopez. The messenger didn't know why he was in jail, but he suspected that it might have to do with anti-Castro activities. Lopez, one of the Second Front men, was young, impetuous, and angry about how the new government had slighted the rebel group.

When Morgan stood up, Olga could tell he was weak, but he would never leave one of his men in jail. Grabbing his Sten, he motioned for his escorts to follow him to the car. It was like being in the mountains again: Morgan and his men were about to head the soldiers off at the pass.

When they arrived at the jail a half hour later, Lopez's father was waiting outside.

"Don't worry," Morgan said to him. "We are getting him out."

Morgan headed for the superintendent's office, followed by his men. The guards recognized him immediately.

"Comandante," they said, stepping out of his way.

"I want you to release Elio Lopez now," he said.

The guards, ashen, didn't want a fight with the Americano. One of the supervisors explained that the police were holding Lopez and that they couldn't let him go. Morgan ignored him. He demanded to see Lopez.

The guard obliged, sending men to retrieve the prisoner. Moments later, Lopez came out.

"You're coming with me," Morgan said.

Without any resistance, the guards let Lopez go. Morgan was a comandante and had the power to order his release. But that didn't mean the G2, Castro's secret police, wouldn't hunt him down once they knew he was gone. Morgan needed to get him out of there. He headed to downtown Camagüey to secure rooms in a hotel.

With a beet-red face and glazed eyes, Morgan was still struggling. If he didn't see a doctor, he could die. Olga had never seen him this ill before. Morgan insisted he was OK, but as soon as he stepped into his hotel room, he crashed to the floor. Olga dropped to her knees to help him—but this time he wasn't getting up.

❧

The doctors couldn't figure it out.

The ambulance had rushed him to the hospital. The doctors had hooked an IV into his arm and strapped an oxygen mask to his face. Morgan's blood pressure was so high that he shouldn't have been able to function. His vital signs were off the charts, and he was suffering from severe exhaustion.

For the most part, Olga and Morgan had dealt with the pressure of the last year, but they finally reached their limits. Maybe it was the decision to move the guns. Maybe it was the government scrutiny of the

Second Front. Maybe it was that Morgan had become de facto leader of the unit. All of it was taking its toll. He had been smoking more and pacing the floors. He had been waking up with circles under his eyes and shortness of breath. He was just thirty-one years old, but he looked a decade older.

The doctor was blunt: If Morgan didn't rest and reduce his stress, he'd die. The fever, chills, and chest pains were all signs that he was driving himself into the ground.

Morgan just nodded. He'd try to get some sleep, but he wasn't going to stay long. He had to leave by morning.

Olga walked to the side of the bed and placed her hand on his forehead. He always had been the stronger one. He always tended to her when she was ill. Now, curled up under the covers, he looked helpless. She wished they could stay here; she didn't even want to return to Havana. Morgan promised her that he would rest—but he couldn't stop himself. Olga had no idea how it all was going to end. And that worried her the most.

The next morning, Morgan hobbled out of his hospital bed. He couldn't stay. It didn't matter that he was still shaking, or that his temperature was still above normal. He was leaving. After promising the doctors he would find a place to rest, Morgan and Olga walked out.

Instead of returning to Havana, they went to Santa Clara. They had been in the hotel room only for a short time when Second Front rebels pounded on the door. The men knew that Morgan had just been released from the hospital, but this was critical: Jesús Carreras had been thrown in jail.

Castro's leaders despised Carreras, but he was still a comandante. Orders to arrest someone of his rank could come only from the top. Morgan tried to contain himself. He remembered what the doctor had told him: Rest . . . but not now. Among the Second Front leadership, Carreras was the least popular among the new government leaders, especially Che.

Morgan couldn't just leave Carreras in jail. First, he had to make sure Olga stood out of harm's way. He needed to drive her back to Havana so she could rest. Then he would return with more of his men.

Within minutes, he contacted Menoyo on the radio. Morgan needed to reach Castro. He didn't care if it took all day; he wanted to talk to Fidel personally. It wasn't just to help Carreras but to let the government know the Second Front was united. The truth is, Morgan and Carreras hadn't always seen eye to eye. Carreras was quick to get angry and brood, and these days it was happening more and more. Carreras, on the other hand, thought Morgan had gone too far to placate the new government and hadn't demanded enough of Castro.

Whatever their differences, Morgan was determined to get Carreras out. Rather than wait, he decided to check out and drive Olga back to Havana himself.

He was growing angrier. The more he thought about it, the more he believed the government was starting to move on the rebels. A couple of days ago, it was Elio Lopez. Now Jesús Carreras, a comandante.

"We could be next," he told Olga.

Menoyo called back. Castro was willing to talk.

When Morgan pulled the car up to their apartment building in Havana, his men were waiting. Morgan saw Olga safely inside and then phoned Castro. At first, Castro said he didn't know all the details but that he would look into it and call Morgan back.

Despite Castro's assurances, Morgan was going to formulate a backup plan. He had learned more about what happened to Carreras. Police investigating a shooting arrested both him and his driver. Though details remained sketchy, the cops released the driver but were holding Carreras in a brig in Santa Clara. It was hard for Morgan to believe that Castro didn't know, but ultimately it didn't matter. Morgan wasn't going to wait around.

He ordered the men to get ready to make the trip to Santa Clara. They were going to be taking two cars, but they would also be toting their guns.

———

Castro never called. Morgan had slept by the phone, waiting. He had hoped to get word that Carreras would be freed or at least more information on his arrest.

After talking to his men, he finally made the decision. They were leaving for Santa Clara. It was time to load the cars with machine guns and

semiautomatic rifles. The plan was simple: If the jailers wouldn't let Carreras go, Morgan and his men would conduct their own commando raid.

"We had all the guns in the trunks of the cars," Ossorio recalled. "We
were really going to attack."

First, they'd take the superintendent as a hostage. Then they'd storm
the wing of the jail where Carreras was held. They weren't going to leave
without him.

For the entire drive from Havana to Santa Clara, Morgan railed
about Castro and his broken promises. Morgan and Carreras had fought
together from the beginning, when the unit had fewer than two dozen
rebels. They had fought at each other's side, and each had risen to lead his
own column. No matter their differences, the bonds they had forged in
war amid blood and sweat made them brothers. Carreras had fought and
risked his life, just like Castro. He deserved the same respect.

As they spotted the regiment jail, the men gripped their weapons. The
cars halted, Morgan bolted from the driver's seat, and his men frantically
followed. When he pushed open the door to the superintendent's office,
the guards jumped. Morgan demanded to see Comandante Carreras.

The chief jailer responded that he understood Morgan's order, but the
G2 had put a special hold on the prisoner. Morgan wasn't budging. He
told the jailer the order wasn't coming just from himself. He had spoken
to Castro personally.

The jailer looked quizzically at Morgan and his men. The jailer hadn't
heard anything from Castro, but he didn't have time to call anyone. Morgan was a comandante and he had spoken. The chief jailer ordered his
guards to fetch Carreras.

Moments later, Carreras walked in.

"You are coming with me," Morgan said.

Without waiting, the Second Front men gathered around Carreras
and exited together.

As they drove away, Morgan turned to Carreras and said, "I had no
pass to get you out of there. Nada." Both men laughed, but everything had
changed. That the police could jail a comandante from the Second Front
told them all they needed to know.

43

OLGA OPENED HER EYES JUST WIDE ENOUGH TO MAKE OUT THE NURSE carrying the tiny bundle in her arms. The last thing she remembered was being wheeled into the delivery room with Morgan and the escorts waiting in the hall outside. It all had happened so quickly. One minute, she was shopping in a grocery store, and the next, her escorts were rushing her to the hospital.

She reached up and took the baby into her arms.

"Congratulations," the nurse said, "you have another daughter."

Pulling back the covers, Olga smiled as she gazed at the tiny infant in her arms. She and Morgan had already agreed that if she had a girl they would name her Olga. For a moment, she forgot about everything: the arrests, the guns, Morgan's health.

The last nine months had been the most difficult of her life. But looking down on the little baby on her chest, she was overwhelmed. It had been a long time since she had felt this much peace. She barely noticed that Morgan was standing over her, smiling. He leaned down and kissed her and then grabbed her hand.

"A baby girl," he said.

The last thing Olga remembered him saying was that they were going to have a son. But Olga knew her husband couldn't resist any baby—boy or girl. Morgan gently kissed his infant daughter and held Olga's hand. He kidded that they would have more children and he would "finally get my boy."

But Olga stopped him. "Come closer," she said. "I want to tell you something."

He leaned over.

"We don't have any more time," she said. "Remember that we are in the middle of serious problems. Very soon we will have to take another road."

She was right, but Morgan didn't want her to dwell on their problems, not now. "You get some rest," he said. He wanted her to be at ease for one moment at least. Soon enough it was all going to change.

Before sundown, Roger Redondo had all the information he needed. The old cargo ship sat docked in the hidden port. The men aboard had unloaded the containers already. No one was supposed to know the origin of the ship, not the dockworkers nor the townspeople. But Redondo knew everything.

After thanking his sources, he sped toward Havana. He always prided himself on turning up actionable intelligence for the Second Front, whether locating an enemy company in the mountains or tracking down desperately needed rifles. This was different.

Most of the information was sketchy, but Redondo learned that the ship that had just slipped into the port near Trinidad belonged to the Soviets. No one knew where the vessel had last departed, but men speaking Russian had been seen getting off the boat. Russians rarely if ever ventured into this part of the country. Soviet cargo went to Havana.

More details surfaced when one of the men from the boat made a trip to the sprawling sanitarium, Topes de Collantes, fifteen miles away. Angelito Martinez, a Spanish Communist who fought in the Spanish Civil War and later taught military tactics to the Russian army in World War II, had gone to the director's office demanding that the hospital's cook prepare food for the men on his cargo ship.

At first, the kitchen manager refused. "The sick eat first, and then we'll see what we can do for you," he said.

Martinez, whose real name was Francisco Ciutat de Miguel, was fifty-one years old, and he wasn't used to being rebuffed. He ordered that his men be fed and fed immediately.

Redondo needed to get word to Morgan. Soviet diplomats in Havana were no surprise. But Soviet military advisers showing up in a remote area of southern Cuba—a direct threat to the Second Front—certainly was.

Redondo told Morgan everything, including the Soviet agent's demands at the sanitarium. As expected, Morgan bristled. Russian military advisers could have set foot in the country only at the open invitation of Fidel Castro. Worse, the presence of Communist military leaders in Cuba could mean only one thing: They were training Cuban soldiers.

"That son of a bitch," Morgan said.

Morgan, Olga, Loretta, and Olguita COURTESY OF MORGAN FAMILY COLLECTION

He had tried to put everything aside for the benefit of his men and his family. He had promised Olga that they would live in peace. But he couldn't do it anymore—not in light of what he had just learned. This wasn't just Castro's country. It belonged to the people of Cuba. It belonged to the farmers and the workers. They all had fought a revolution for democracy, and now it was falling apart.

The Second Front had to go to war again.

For most of the night, the baby had been crying. Olga walked back and forth between the nursery and the bedroom. Ever since arriving home from the hospital, she hadn't been able to sleep. Morgan had been at the hatchery until late and then came home and met with his men on the balcony.

After an hour, Olga pulled her husband into their room. "No secrets, commander," she said.

Morgan knew he couldn't keep anything from Olga. She knew him better than anyone. But still, this wasn't easy. He told her about the Soviet infiltration in the mountains and what it meant for all of them. They couldn't stand by and watch Cuba being swept into the Communist vortex. He had tried to live in Cuba in peace. No one knew more than Olga all the work and care he had put into the hatchery to make a stable living.

But everything they had fought for was at stake. There was no way they could compromise with what they had just discovered. They couldn't stay in their home. They were no longer just raising fish and frogs at the hatchery. They were storing guns there and moving them to the mountains.

"We have to move against them," he said.

Olga recalled throwing her arms around him. No one wanted to live in peace as much as she did. She was the mother of two children. But she not only understood everything Morgan was saying to her, she completely agreed. They had met in the revolution. They had married in the revolution. If need be, they would die in the revolution.

"I am with you," Olga said.

❧

Once he got the phone call, Rafael Huguet dashed down to the hatchery. The young pilot who spoke fluent English hadn't seen the Americano in weeks, but could sense the urgency in Morgan's voice. The last of the trucks had just left when Huguet showed up, leaving him and Morgan and a few others alone.

Cuban by birth, Huguet had spent much of his life in the United States, attending Georgia Tech and learning his life's passion to fly airplanes. He had opposed the Batista regime ever since his father was beaten by government police during a routine traffic stop in Havana. On the last day of the revolution, Huguet had copiloted a plane laden with arms into Trinidad with bullets flying into the windows of the craft as it landed.

Out of earshot of the workers, Morgan ushered him past the croaking frogs and into a small room off the side of the main building. Before Huguet could say anything, Morgan walked across the room and opened a closet door. "I want you to see something," he said.

Inside were stacks of machines guns, automatic rifles, grenades, and boxes of ammunition. Huguet stepped back for a moment, surprised. "William, what are you doing?" he said. "Are you crazy?"

Morgan shut the door. The weapons were there for a reason: He was heading to the mountains. It wasn't just an idle threat anymore. It had started with hiding weapons near Banao for protection. Trucks had left the hatchery almost weekly. But it had escalated. Castro had crossed a line that the Second Front could not accept. He was inviting Soviet military advisers to the Escambray.

It wouldn't be easy, but Morgan was prepared to train hundreds of men in the mountains, including the farmers who had become so angry with the government. "We have to do something about this guy," he said.

The guerrillas had started to get help from the CIA, which had just dropped a cache of weapons from a plane into the foothills. Morgan didn't want to deal with the agency, but if it was willing to supply weapons, so be it.

The *Yanqui comandante* was taking an enormous risk by moving weapons. "You are open to too many people," Huguet said.

Morgan nodded, but he wasn't going to be dissuaded. It was too late to worry about what Castro was going to do. His reason for calling Huguet was simple: He needed someone in Miami to help procure weapons from anti-Castro activists and if need be to fly them in under the cover of darkness to remote airstrips.

"Would you back me up?" Morgan asked. "Would you get arms for me?"

For Huguet, the timing was right. Once a passionate believer in the revolution, he had grown disillusioned with Castro and others like Che. He had come to admire Morgan over the past two years, not just for what he accomplished during the revolution but what he managed to do after.

Huguet nodded. "I will," he said.

He would be in Miami in two more weeks and would call Morgan when he arrived. Then they could get started. He would have to make the critical contacts to begin raising arms. But the bigger challenge was whether he could deliver the weapons in time.

44

THE CAR IDLED OUTSIDE THE NATIONAL INSTITUTE FOR AGRARIAN Reform (NIAR). Morgan stepped out and grabbed the package on the seat. He had no desire to set foot in a government building, but he had to meet with Pedro Miret Prieto, the agriculture minister, who was getting married in a few days.

Morgan had distanced himself from most government leaders, but he tolerated Miret. Castro had appointed him a year earlier, and the minister had quietly approved of Morgan's work at the hatchery, even allowing him to use government trucks.

Morgan handed Miret the package: a frog-skin wallet for him and a purse for his bride. Miret took the gifts and smiled, motioning for his visitor to sit, but Morgan didn't have time. His men were waiting for him.

As Morgan turned to leave, several guards walked in the door and surrounded him. "Comandante Morgan," said one, "we have to place you under arrest."

Just then, a guard reached for Morgan's sidearm, and the others grabbed his arms. Turning to the head guard, Morgan sternly demanded to know why he was being arrested. But the guard couldn't answer. "We are taking you, Comandante, to the Technical Investigations offices," he responded.

Morgan stayed calm. He allowed the guards to place him in handcuffs.

As he was being led down the hallways, the workers cleared out of the way and stared in disbelief as the *Yanqui comandante* was led out the door.

━━━

Olga ran out of the nursery and headed for the telephone. One of her bodyguards said a call had come from the National Institute for Agrarian Reform. It was Miret's secretary: Morgan was attending an important meeting, but he wanted Olga to meet him at the office.

Olga paused. If Morgan was going to be late, he would call himself. "Why did he not call?" Olga asked.

The secretary repeated that Morgan was in a very important meeting and couldn't be disturbed. But he wanted her to meet him there. Olga's heart raced. She knew something was wrong. She hung up the phone and told Alejandrina to watch the babies. She and the escorts would be driving to the NIAR offices. Olga was hoping she was wrong, that perhaps Morgan was too busy to phone. But as she and the men rounded the corner, she saw the flashing lights and police officers standing around the building. But these weren't just cop cars. These were Technical Investigations Department vehicles.

As they pulled up to the curb, one of Olga's friends ran to the passenger side of the car, where Olga was sitting. "William is not here," she said, out of breath. "They took him to the Technical Investigations Department."

Then the police spotted Olga. Before they could reach the car, she ordered the driver back to the apartment. She didn't care if he ran red lights the entire way. He had to step on it.

Olga wondered whether someone from Morgan's entourage had betrayed him. The only one who wasn't around was Manuel Cisneros Castro, one of Morgan's bodyguards, who had left abruptly the night before to visit his gravely ill mother in Oriente Province. Cisneros had been with them since the Trujillo conspiracy, but to this day, no one trusted him—especially Olga.

Police cars had surrounded the penthouse. Olga ran to the door. She didn't care what happened to her, but her children were inside. On the top floor, standing on the balcony, Ossorio looked down and saw that the building was surrounded. He grabbed a handful of grenades and a Thompson submachine gun and perched near the door, waiting.

"I was waiting to shoot them," he recalled.

Olga walked past the police at the door and headed up the elevator. Policemen were waiting in the hallways between the elevator and the apartment. "What do you want?" she demanded.

"We're going to conduct a search of your apartment," one of them answered.

As they walked in together, she saw Ossorio. "No, Pedro, no," she said. "I am with them. Don't shoot."

Ossorio could see that the police were walking too close to Olga for him to do anything.

"Throw down your gun," one of the officers ordered. Ossorio stood with his gun pointing at the police. He refused to budge.

"Pedro, do as they say," Olga said.

Ossorio tossed down his gun. The police surrounded and cuffed him. After they took him outside, Olga saw that some of the men were rifling through the cupboards and turning over the furniture. Upstairs, her infant daughter was wailing. "Stop now!" she screamed. "This is Commander Morgan's home. You will get a search warrant. I want to see what legal right you have to search his house."

The police captain came down the stairs and stopped his men. "Stand by outside," he instructed them. "We will bring an order back." The police didn't need a legal order for most homes, but this one belonged to a comandante.

As soon as the door shut behind them, Olga ran upstairs. She closed her bedroom door and went to the closet where Morgan had stashed hand grenades and machine guns. One by one, she grabbed them and dropped them down the garbage chute. Then she ran to the dresser and found the maps of the Escambray mountains. She tossed those down the chute, too.

In the nursery, Alejandrina, shaking, had crouched in a corner with Olguita.

"It's OK, Alejandrina, it's OK," Olga said. "Nothing will happen to you."

The police knocked on the front door. Olga opened it, and the captain flashed the order. As soon as he did, the entire squad crashed the penthouse, scurrying into the rooms, turning them upside down, pulling out drawers, knocking over lamps.

"We have to place you under arrest," the captain said to Olga.

———

Even before the presidential debates ended, Loretta Morgan's phone was ringing. The local news reported that the Castro government had arrested William Morgan, but there were few details. One radio newscast said that he had been taken into custody for helping insurgents in the mountains. Another said he was caught hiding guns.

The news broke just hours before the last of the televised Kennedy-Nixon debates, this one, from New York, including strong words about Cuba and the need to stop the spread of Communism in a nation so close to the United States.

Normally, Loretta would have been glued to the TV, watching the young Catholic senator in the final stages of the campaign. But she was a basket case. Every time the phone rang, another friend or church member was calling to ask if she had heard anything new.

Alexander Morgan slumped in a chair, staring at the flickering screen of the television. The broadcasts revealed nothing new, other than what the Cuban government had released in a press release earlier that day.

No matter what her son had told her, Loretta had worried that something like this might happen. The last time they spoke, Morgan talked about the hatchery and how he and Olga were trying to settle down and raise a family. But she knew what a challenge that would be for him. She had no idea what a Cuban jail was like, but it couldn't be good. Her worst fears were coming true.

She went to bed that night with a rosary clutched in her hand, but she couldn't sleep. She kept praying the same frantic, silent prayers over and over.

The next day, the newspaper that landed in their driveway announced: "Cuban Army Disclosed Arrest of Major Morgan, ex-Toledoan." The *Toledo Blade* article mentioned that Jesús Carreras also had been arrested but, again, with few details. There was no information about a trial, nothing about specific charges, nothing about whether Loretta Morgan would ever see her son again.

45

SHE COULDN'T USE THE PHONE. SHE COULDN'T LEAVE THE APARTMENT. She had little food in the cupboards and no money.

Olga had been under house arrest for a few days, but she hadn't been allowed to retain a lawyer. For most of the day, she glared at the guards sitting across from her in the living room as she held Olguita in her arms. She couldn't see her mother or father. She hadn't seen her husband, nor would anyone tell her anything about the case against them. At night, she lay down and cried herself to sleep. Then the babies woke up, hungry and crying.

More than anything, it was the uncertainly of their future that most troubled her. She hadn't been able to learn anything about Morgan's whereabouts. At first, the guards said he was being held at Quinta Avenida, the G2 jail. Then it was La Cabaña. She looked for a way to send a message to neighbors on the balconies below, but the guards were watching her every move.

Finally, without warning, she walked directly in front of the men, reached for a telephone, and ripped it off the wall, pieces of plaster flying onto the floor. One of the guards came over to her, but she warned him to stay away. "I'm tired of this! I'm tired of all of you!" she screamed.

Either she was going to find a way to escape with her children, or the government would haul her to jail. If she stayed in her current situation, she wouldn't make it.

The Second Front men gathered inside the small office in the Vedado neighborhood, encircling the desk. Menoyo sat at the center. No one had taken Morgan's arrest harder than Menoyo. He had stayed up nights, trying to figure out a way to get him out of La Cabaña. Menoyo had never known anyone like the Americano. Of all the men in his unit, no one was more loyal or more willing to die for the others than Morgan. If Menoyo was in the same situation, Morgan would go to war for him.

Menoyo had two choices. He could rally the guajiros in the mountains who respected and supported Morgan and attack the prison. The men probably could overpower the first row of guards to get inside La Cabaña, but the government soldiers would no doubt blitz the fortress before the rebels could get out. It would be a suicide mission.

The second option was to work from the inside, which would be difficult, but not impossible. Not all the guards inside the prison were loyal to Castro. If the Second Front could reach key supporters in the anti-Castro movement, people with direct ties to the guards, they might find a way to help Morgan escape. Those supporters—members of the newly formed 30th of November Movement—were ready to help the Second Front. If Menoyo was going to get his friend out of jail, now was the time.

In the meantime, Menoyo had to make sure the Second Front continued to get weapons to the Escambray. They knew they were going to wage another military offensive—there was no other way to wrest control of the country. But they needed more firepower. They needed recruits. They needed Morgan.

—◦—

Down the long brick corridor, Olga walked with the guards past the dank prison barracks. She had always been leery of La Cabaña: the brutal beatings of prisoners, the executions under Che Guevara, the rotting flesh along the wall. But when the guards came to her home with their orders, she didn't have a choice. They were taking her to the prison for her arraignment.

Looming high on a hill on the eastern side of the harbor, La Cabaña was one of the most visible landmarks of Havana, a fortress built two hundred years earlier to keep out British invaders. Once a symbol of noble defiance, it was now a military prison known for the bullet-pocked walls outside where the inmates were executed.

As Olga was led into the tribunal chambers with the high ceilings and gallery, the guards and observers stood up. It was supposed to be a routine hearing where the judges read the charges and the prisoner made a plea. But as they read the counts against her—treason, bearing arms, conspiracy—Olga interrupted, each time blurting out "No."

They would stop, wait, and then proceed, and each time, Olga would interrupt, "No, that did not happen."

Irritated, the judges ordered her to sign the charges, but she refused. "You are going to do whatever you are going to do," she said. "I'm not taking part." One of the men became angry, telling Olga that she was only making it harder on herself. But she was defiant. "Whatever you have planned is already planned, and we can only wait for the results of all of this," she said.

The guards then turned her around and walked her out of the hearing room. As they headed toward their car, Olga stopped dead in her tracks. "I want to see my husband," she said. At first, the guards kept trying to move her along, but she refused to budge. She demanded to see the head of the prison.

The guards were going to have a scene on their hands. One of the men suggested that they take her to the superintendent's office so Olga could hear the refusal for herself. As they neared the office, Olga looked over to the side where the visitors were gathering to meet with the inmates.

"Olga," one of the visitors called out.

Olga recognized the visitor as a relative of Jesús Carreras and dashed toward the gate, the guards running after her. Before they could grab her, she found out that Morgan and others were being held in the chapel area adjacent to the main entrance. Her heart sank. That was the area for those in trouble and in some cases those who were waiting to be shot.

Without warning, Olga pushed away from the guards. Now there was utter chaos. Guards began running to the entrance, but before they could catch her, Olga had slipped into the superintendent's office. The surprised jailer looked up to see a woman standing in front of his desk.

"Where is my husband—William Morgan?" Olga demanded.

The guards rushed into the room, but the superintendent ordered them to back off. Everything was under control. After listening to Olga, he agreed to let her see Morgan briefly, but she had to follow the rules.

As they walked outside, she peered through one of the gates and spotted her husband. She barely recognized him. His cheeks were sallow, and his eyes were sunken in. She had never seen him so thin.

"Oh my God," she said. "What did they do to you?"

She ran over and embraced him. Tears welled in her eyes as she clutched onto his prison fatigues. Morgan held onto her. "I'm all right, Olga," he said. "Don't worry." He kissed her and whispered in her ear. "I love you," he said.

It was like a dream. Olga didn't want to let go. For a moment, they stared at each other, not saying a word. Morgan had just endured days of interrogation with the secret police, but they had gotten nowhere. When they asked him why he was moving weapons to the hills, he responded every time: "To protect myself."

Later, after sending him back to his cell, one of the jailers served him contaminated food. For three days, he reeled in pain but managed to hold on. The prison itself had also made him sick. The combination of the rainwater seeping through the thick, porous concrete and the ocean wind turned the place cold at night.

Morgan could tell Olga was upset, but the time was running out on her visit. "Listen to me," he whispered in her ear. "I can't say a lot now, but we are working on something—an escape. I will get word to you when we get close, and we will be together again. I promise you." He kissed her. "I will always be thinking about you. You are all I ever think about and will ever think about."

<hr>

The prisoners huddled in a circle on the stone floor, gathering close so that no one could invade their space. One of the men took out a chess board and plastic pieces and carefully began setting it up in the center. The fortress had become so crowded, there were few places the men could go. Each *galería* was crammed with two hundred prisoners—twice the intended capacity—most of them sleeping on the cold, damp floor.

Morgan leaned in close enough for Pedro Ossorio and Edmundo Amado to hear him above the din of the other inmates. News was starting to trickle in from the outside: Their supporters were making contact with guards on the inside, including a supervisor. Someone with authority could make sure the right exit was cleared and the right guards were on duty.

Whatever plan was in place, they needed to bide their time and keep quiet. "These people in here are all traitors," he said. Morgan was getting his information from visitors bringing messages to the other inmates, who passed them to him. It was risky, but it was the only way the two sides could stay in contact. If they needed to get word to Morgan on a day's notice, they could do so.

———

He dropped to the dirt in a corner of the prison yard, throwing himself down for a set of push-ups. As the men gathered around to watch, he slowly pushed himself down and back up. After one set, he did another. Then another.

Morgan had started the day by jogging around the enclosure, picking up speed until he was running. After taking a break in the *galería*, he went back to the prison yard and started the afternoon by doing jumping jacks, barking orders at himself. After one set, he did another. Then another. He had been recovering from his bout with bleeding intestines. No one expected him to jump into a training regimen.

At first, everyone just stared, including the guards. Then he sprinted, oblivious to everyone around him.

"*Comandante Morgan es muy loco,*" one guard said.

It wasn't just the physical exercise. Morgan had started to pray, sometimes whispering just a few quick words in the morning. But in the afternoon, he spent more time at his bunk. For Morgan, it was all he could do to control his own fate. He didn't have any control on the outside. The men working to help him and his men lay beyond his reach. He didn't even know them. But if he could push himself beyond his endurance level, he would be prepared for anything they could throw at him.

———

Families were gathering along 16th Street, setting up chairs and stringing decorations around the streetlights. Along La Rampa, musicians were setting up on the sidewalks.

Olga watched from her balcony as the New Year's Eve celebration was about to unfold on the streets of Vedado. Her visit to La Cabaña had been a disaster. She would no longer be returning to the facility to see her husband. Any more outbursts and she could be sent to the women's prison.

She wrapped the blanket around her shoulders as a cold breeze blew off the Malecón. Two years ago, she was on her way to Cienfuegos to meet Morgan in what was one of the happiest moments of her life. All the promises they had made to each other were about to unfold.

Last year at this time, she took a long drive with Morgan along the ocean, staring up at the stars as they determined to make their life in Cuba. Unless she did something drastic, they would never see another New Year's Eve together. It was that clear. She needed to save her husband.

She thought about her own plan, conceived several days earlier. She wasn't sure it would work, but now she didn't have a choice. She had to make her move. Tonight was as good a night as any to pull it off. The guards would be relaxed, maybe even in a festive mood. They wouldn't see it coming.

She went into Loretta's room and pulled the blanket up. If she was ever going to have a chance, it was now. Olga walked downstairs to see which shift of guards was in place. She was immediately heartened by the men she saw in the living room. These were the guards she despised the most. If they were held responsible for her escape, then so be it. They deserved to be severely disciplined. Olga came into the room and told them that since it was New Year's Eve, she was going to make hot chocolate. Would they like a cup?

It was cold outside and the men looked like they could use some. They all nodded.

Olga went into the kitchen—but instead of grabbing the chocolate, she grabbed a bottle of Equanil, a powerful sedative and muscle relaxer. She then bounded up the stairs and into her room, and then slipped into the bathroom. Removing the pills, she began crushing them with a spoon. After gathering up the powder, she went back downstairs and tossed it into a pot with chunks of chocolate and milk. Stirring the ingredients so that everything dissolved, she poured the hot liquid into three cups. Then, as a precaution, she sprinkled in sugar to mask any bitter taste.

After handing the cups to the guards and setting down a tray of biscuits next to the sofa, she walked upstairs to be with her daughters and wait for the drugs to kick in. Her heart was racing as she closed the door to her room. The guards were either going to discover her ruse or fall asleep. In one move, she had risked everything. If she was caught, she'd be thrown in prison and her daughters taken from her.

She looked at the clock. It was 5:00 a.m. Everything was quiet downstairs as she opened her door. She crept down the stairs and peeked around the corner. One guard was sprawled on the sofa near the main entrance; the others slumped in armchairs. All were fast asleep.

She turned around and bounded up the stairs. First, she went into Loretta's room and woke her up. "Let's go see Daddy, my little one," she whispered. Then she went over to the crib and picked up Olguita. With the baby in her arms, Olga walked with Loretta out the kitchen door. In the darkness, Olga shuffled two blocks down the street with her daughters until she saw a passing car. Running to the side of the road, she flagged down the driver.

"Please, can you help us?"

The man hesitated but then saw the baby in Olga's arms. Flinging open the door, he let them in. As they sped through the streets of Vedado, Olga knew she didn't have much time. In just hours, Castro's entire police force would be looking for her.

46

Clutching the baby in her arms, Olga tiptoed down the hallway, careful not to disturb the other people in the house.

Escipion Encinosa had been giving shelter to members of the underground movement, but he didn't expect the wife of the *Yanqui comandante* to show up at his door. Olga had ended up at the house after fleeing her apartment and begging for help from members of the underground.

The forty-six-year-old father was taking a risk by letting Olga and her daughters stay in his home, but he knew the government would show no mercy if they caught her. Rumors of Olga's escape were starting to leak out, but the government had managed to keep it quiet. How could it explain a twenty-four-year-old woman with two babies fleeing past three dozing guards?

Police were still scouring the neighborhood around her apartment house, and the G2 was rounding up people in the area who might have seen her. She could stay with the Encinosa family, but she would have to leave by morning. There were too many *chivatos* in the neighborhood.

Encinosa walked into his son's room and told him not to say a word. "This is something that I have to trust you with," he said. "I don't want you to tell anyone, not your aunts, not your grandmother."

Eleven-year-old Enrique shook his head, still struck by the image of the young woman clutching her two little girls in the hall outside his room.

For most of the night, Olga peered into the darkness, just hoping her daughters would sleep. She had no money or clothes and nowhere to go in the morning. As the hours passed, she thought about how she and the girls would survive.

If she could get to Santa Clara, she might be able to leave them with her mother, but she worried the police would retaliate against her family. Sooner or later, Olga knew she would run out of time.

That morning, Encinosa reached out to the underground network and learned the Venezuelan embassy would take Olga. But delivering her was like tiptoeing through a minefield.

So many people were seeking asylum at the Latin American embassies that the Cuban government was countering with checkpoints near the entrances. Before leaving his house, Encinosa turned to Olga and warned her, "We have to be careful."

As they moved down the street, they walked on opposite sides until they reached the next block to wait for a driver. The police would certainly be on the lookout for a woman with two children.

When the driver arrived, he looked nervous. Everyone was under watch these days, even the cabbies. As he drove, Olga pulled her daughters close, trying to duck down in her seat. Everything was changing. Apart from the police checkpoints, Cuban army trucks were rolling up and down the main roads. Before the taxi reached the building, the driver stopped and pointed to where she needed to go.

Olga stepped out of the car, holding her daughters. As she approached the front gate, she saw the sign. But it wasn't the Venezuelan embassy; it was the Brazilian. For a moment, she froze. She had no idea if the diplomats inside would even talk to her.

Her other option was to run down the street to look for the Venezuelan compound, but the police would no doubt find her. Just then, a guard in the booth asked what she wanted. She ran over to him. "I am the seamstress for the ambassador's wife, and she is waiting for me."

The guard looked at her suspiciously and ordered her to wait. As he called the main house, Olga quietly told Loretta to scamper into the garden beyond the open gate. That would give Olga an excuse to chase after her and slip into the compound.

Little Loretta did as told. Before the guard could give chase, Olga ran up to a man tending the flowers. "I am in trouble," she said, "and I arrived at the wrong embassy. Please help me."

The man could see that she was desperate. After waving off the guard, he told her to follow him into the house. With two babies in tow and police cars patrolling in front of the gates, her only refuge lay inside.

The first sign that Menoyo was in trouble came from a government agent at dawn. The guns had made it to the Escambray, but the secret police had set up surveillance. The movements had been tracked.

The weapons—M1s, British Stens, and hand grenades—had been stashed in a safe house in an area dominated by the Second Front. With Morgan in prison, someone else in the unit had given the orders. The secret police shifted their attention to the founder of the Second Front. They were following him during his trips to the unit's small, cramped office in Vedado. They drove by his apartment just blocks away.

Menoyo had never been targeted, not like this. In the early morning hours, a government agent sympathetic to the Second Front came to the home of one of Menoyo's most trusted advisers, Armando Fleites. He made it clear that it wasn't a social visit. Menoyo was no longer safe. Castro had taken a radical shift, mostly because of the steady stream of reports that the island was about to be invaded.

The government had built its case against Morgan and Carreras. Now it was going to take down the last remaining comandante.

It all made sense. Just days before the agent's visit, Menoyo and Fleites had gotten invitations to come to the presidential palace on January 26. At first, they couldn't understand why they were being invited to a government gathering. Now they understood.

The next day, Menoyo, Fleites, and others met. "They are going to come after us," Menoyo told his men. They had two choices. They could head to the mountains, or they could go to America and build their own invasion force. In Miami, they could get money and arms from the exile community, recruit new members, and return to Cuba to fight Castro.

They had to leave.

They had twenty-four hours to find boats, fuel, and enough arms to protect themselves. The last jefe of the Second Front was about to depart.

~

With the secret police prowling the streets outside the embassies, it was too risky for Olga's supporters to come to the Brazilian compound. Granted asylum, Olga was one of Cuba's most wanted fugitives. But the man who came to the gate insisted on seeing her.

At first, the embassy guards were suspicious of the stranger. They checked his identification and insisted he answer their questions. After Olga was summoned to see the man for herself, she told the guards she didn't know him. But as she stood with her protectors, the man held up a cigarette lighter. It was the same one that Morgan's mother had sent him.

"This is William's," she said, taking it from the visitor. Olga turned to the guards. It was all right. She would talk to him.

He didn't have much time, but he had something important to tell her from William—the message coming from a visitor at the prison. Morgan was about to break out of La Cabaña. After months of biding his time, he was ready. The messenger didn't know the details, but Morgan wanted her to know that he would be heading clear across the country to Camagüey. More than anything, he wanted to see her.

Olga couldn't believe the words. This is what she had been waiting for. It wasn't going to be easy, but she needed to be there.

Clutching the lighter in her hand, she thanked the messenger and scurried back into the house. The guards warned her that this could all be a setup. How did the man manage to get the lighter if Morgan was locked up? It was too dangerous for Olga to leave.

Olga thought about it, but she was desperate. She knew Morgan had been working on an escape plan for a long time. If anyone could do it, he could. She would get word to her mother that the children would be at the embassy and that she would retrieve them later.

The race had begun. If he was going to be in Camagüey, she wanted to arrive first. After conferring on the phone with one of her contacts, she was told to travel to Cienfuegos, where a car would be waiting for her. It would take a driver at least four hours to reach the city. Olga had to wait until the driver arrived.

During her stay at the embassy, Olga had grown close to the ambassador, who had reached out to protect her and her daughters. He warned her that she could be captured and separated from her children. She could be executed. "I am asking you not to go," he said.

Olga shook her head. If the ambassador couldn't help her, she would find a way. She needed to be with her husband.

He knew he wasn't going to convince her to stay, but he couldn't just let her walk out the gates. He ordered his staff to ready the car. He was risking his own diplomatic status, but he would make sure she got out of Havana.

47

THE GUARDS LOCKED THE GATES FOR THE NIGHT. THE ENTIRE PRISON was on edge. Jailers were prowling the halls outside, making sure the inmates were jammed inside the *galerías*. Bunks were pushed against the walls, leaving most of the men to compete for space on the floors. The sheer number of prisoners was making the fortress vulnerable. There were only so many guards. If enough men rushed the exits, most would more than likely get out.

In the darkness, Morgan heard the inmates breathing in their sleep and the sounds of the guards passing by the *galería*. Then came a crackling sound echoing down the long cavernous hall. At first, it startled some of the prisoners. It was way too late in the night for the dreaded voice. But they all knew what it meant. It was the roll call for prisoners being called to trial. No one wanted to hear their name, but they all listened intently.

They knew the drill: The guards would show up to grab the condemned and take them to the special cells below. There, they would wait until the next day to appear before the court.

The footsteps of the jailers were getting closer as Hiram Gonzalez brushed the sleep from his eyes and looked over at the nearby bunk. Nearly every man was sitting up to watch as the guards came into the room.

Morgan was already waiting as they marched down the aisle. The lights came on as the other inmates sat dazed, watching. This couldn't be, they said to each other. No one expected his name to be called. But it was.

William Alexander Morgan. The *Yanqui comandante* was being called to trial.

——◆——

Loretta Morgan couldn't finish the conversation on the phone. Crying, she had been trying to reach Thomas "Lud" Ashley, the congressman from Toledo, but he had been steeped in House sessions on the Hill.

She had been trying to contact the Kennedy White House, sending a telegram on March 9. She reached out to Cardinal Richard Cushing, one of the most prominent American Catholic clerics. She even tried Cuban President Osvaldo Dorticós Torrado. Since the United States no longer had diplomatic relations with Cuba, the White House had reached out to the Swiss embassy.

This was the nightmare she had been pushing back, hoping it would never come. She had warned Bill. She had begged him to get out of Cuba, bring Olga, and come to the United States. She didn't care what kind of trouble he was in with the FBI. Anything was better than being there.

For the past several days, she had been haunted by the image of La Cabaña. As a young woman, she and her husband had vacationed in Havana, and she remembered seeing the stone fortress looming over the harbor. "That awful prison," she later recalled. "I never thought I would ever have a son there."

She had reached out to members of the church altar society, asking for prayers. If she could travel to Cuba herself and plead with Castro for Bill's life, she would have done that, too.

Ashley had already contacted the State Department about getting Morgan a lawyer. Unfortunately, Morgan wasn't a US citizen anymore, so there was nothing the department could do. "An informal approach to the Cuban government no longer existed," wrote Ashley in a letter.

There was only once place for Loretta to venture: the large, looming cathedral at the end of her block. There, she slipped into a pew, clasped her hands, and prayed.

—◆—

Morgan yanked on his bootstraps to make sure they were tight and then tucked in his shirt. At the far end of the prison, the judges were waiting. After hours of leaning over a table and jotting down notes, he was ready.

In a letter he wrote to his mother earlier in the day, he said all men have "a right to freedom" and that he had a responsibility to finish what he started.

With the footsteps of the guards echoing down the hall, Morgan stood up by the door. In just two more minutes, he'd be facing his accusers.

As he rounded the corner of the chapel and headed to the hearing room, the prisoners came to the front of their cells and the guards stood from their stations to catch a glimpse of the Americano. As he walked by, he did something no one could quite understand. It started with a low hum and soon grew into a melody that caught the attention of everyone around him. Morgan began singing, "The Army Song."

No one knew why he was reciting the lyrics of a tune he had learned when he was eighteen years old and in boot camp, but now he was singing it before captors who held the power to decide whether he could live or die. He bellowed while heading toward the door:

> Till our final ride,
> it will always be our pride
> to keep those caissons a rolling along

The room was packed with scores of spectators, including United Press International reporter Henry Raymont, one of the most prominent correspondents in Cuba. Off to the side, Olga's mother and sister held back tears as the guards escorted Morgan across the room.

Most of the hearings were cut-and-dried, with only family members in the audience, but this was already building as a spectacle. American broadcaster Lee Hall was in the audience. Luis Carro, the government defense lawyer, plopped down in a seat next to Morgan and the others, while district attorney Fernando Ibarra Luis Florez was already strutting in front of the five judges.

Ibarra had earned a reputation as an icy-cold prosecutor who regularly sent men to the wall. As far as he was concerned, they could line up Morgan and the others now or later. It didn't matter. They were traitors who deserved death.

Carro's job was to keep the men alive, but it was getting harder. With only minutes to meet with each man, he couldn't possibly mount adequate defenses. Known as the attorney for the damned, he had been swamped for weeks with men begging him for help, sometimes shaking and crying in their cells. As he looked at Morgan across the table, he felt he already knew him. The *Yanqui comandante*'s face had been splashed in newspapers for the past two years as one of the heroes of the revolution.

But Carro was up against a juggernaut. Morgan and Carreras, both comandantes, were accused of not just moving arms, but leading a group plotting to overthrow the government. The others—like Ossorio, Amado, and even Olga (being tried in absentia)—were all participants in the plan.

Carro asked the military tribunal for a few minutes before starting the trial. Talking to Morgan and Carreras, Carro made it clear the government had a strong case against the men for hauling weapons to the Escambray. Secret police had already found the caches. They had a better chance of punching holes in the government's case that they were plotting to overthrow Castro.

On the other side, Ibarra was confident he had enough evidence to bury them. The prosecutor stood before the five judges and read the charges, his voice rising in anger. Morgan and Carreras used their positions of trust to betray Cuba and deserved nothing less than death. The weapons they moved to the Escambray—the .50-caliber machine guns, M1s, hand grenades, and antitank rockets—ended up in the hands of guerrillas who were actively fighting Cuban soldiers.

To prove his case, Ibarra called Mario Marin to the witness stand. A hush fell over the courtroom as Marin, one of Morgan's drivers, stepped forward. Just before Olga was arrested, Marin fled to the mountains, where he was picked up by Castro's men. Under questioning, he said he not only loaded guns onto the trucks bound for the Escambray but that he drove them, too.

Ibarra pulled out a detailed map seized from Morgan's home with markings of strategic spots in the Escambray. There was no reason for Morgan to keep this map unless he was targeting these areas for future gun shipments.

Ibarra also called on the testimony of two other members of Morgan's entourage, Rueben Dominguez and Manolo Castro Cisneros. Both backed Marin's claims.

Listening quietly, Carro turned to Morgan. The Americano was already walking to the witness stand. A hush fell over the courtroom.

Carro opened up by asking Morgan about the guns. It was critical to deal with those charges first. Turning to the judges, Morgan said that whatever guns he moved to the mountains were only for his protection and that of the Second Front. They were a militia that fought bravely in the central mountains, and they had every right to stockpile weapons. The map the prosecutor was waving around was left over from when Morgan helped save the fledgling Castro government from the Trujillo invasion. They didn't need directions to get to the guns that they themselves stored.

As far as Marin and the other witnesses, Morgan said they were "personal enemies" whom the government sent to spy on him. Their sole purpose in testifying against Morgan was to curry favor with the government.

Morgan had just a couple of minutes to make his case. To Morgan, this wasn't about running guns or unseating Castro. As far as he was concerned, the charges were a sham. This fight was about protecting the principles of the revolution—a revolution they all believed in. Morgan made it clear that none of the defendants in the courtroom had betrayed the cause. The revolution was bigger than all of them.

He looked at Ossorio, Amado, Carreras, and the others and turned to the court. No one did anything to hurt the people of Cuba. They were all still fighting a revolution in which they believed. "I stand here innocent, and I guarantee this court that if I am found guilty I will walk to the execution wall with no escort, with moral strength and clear conscience. I have defended this revolution because I believed in it."

The Yankee comandante had said everything he needed to say.

The judges—Jorge Robreño Marieges, Mario A. Tagle Babe, Roberto Pafradela Napoles, Pelayo Fernandez-Rubio, and Ramon Martinez Fernandez—turned to each other and began to whisper. It was time to decide the fate of the defendants. They had done this scores of times before and would do so scores of times again. Rarely, if ever, was there dissension.

After just a couple of minutes, the chief judge, Robreño, looked up to say they had reached a decision; it was unanimous. With the courtroom quiet, the judge slowly read the charges for each man. Everyone sat still, staring straight ahead.

"Guilty on all charges," he said.

In the gallery, some of the spectators gasped. Olga's mother and sister grabbed onto each another and began to cry. The judges rose from their seats, turned around, and walked back to their chambers.

The guards escorted the defendants from the hearing room. Down the hall, they were led into the solitary cells at the rear of the chapel, where they would await sentencing.

Morgan walked to the rear of his cell, but before the guards could slam his door shut, he asked for paper and a pencil. It might be the last time he would have a chance to write Olga. He wasn't sure how she would get the letter, but he would make sure it was passed to his lawyer. As he leaned over a small table in the cell, he thought about the woman he had met in the Escambray what seemed like an eternity ago. Night was falling on the camp when she walked in, and everyone was tired. But he could never forget the moment.

"Since the first time I saw you in the mountains until the last time I saw you in prison, you have been my love, my happiness, my companion in life and in my thoughts during my moment of death," he wrote. As he thought about their short life together, Morgan couldn't help but mention the regrets of all the external events that came between them: the crowded homes, the emergencies that consumed him. "Such little time we had to spend together, you, the girls and myself, it always seems that we could never be alone, the moments that we were able to, we had to steal them."

What bothered him now was that the Castro government was accusing him of hurting the revolution, but it was Castro who had abandoned the revolution. "Olga, I have never been a traitor or have done any damage to Cuba. I tell you this because you know this is the truth," he wrote. "I ask you to please never allow that my name, the girls and yours get utilized for political reasons. For those who would use them for hatred, wrongs, or to attack Cuba or its people or to represent things which I could never represent."

Morgan went on to caution Olga that he had thought long and hard about his accusers and pleaded with her to rise above her personal feelings. "I do not want blood spilled over my cause. Revenge is not the answer. It's better that I die because I have defended lives. I only ask that someday the truth will be known and that my daughters will be proud of their father."

After he finished the letter, the guards came to the door. The judges were waiting at the dais. The spectators had filed back into the courtroom.

With guards on both sides, Morgan walked down the hallway and entered the room.

After waiting for the defendants to take their place, Morgan and Carreras were told to stand before the court. The chief judge looked up and without showing any emotion, he declared: death by firing squad.

Morgan stared at the judge without flinching. Carreras stood erect. From the rear, one of the prisoners stood up. "I, too, want to die," said Ossorio. "If you're going to shoot William Morgan, then shoot me." Next to him, Edmundo Amado stood and said the same.

The spectators in the gallery stirred and murmured before the chief judge warned Ossorio and Amado to sit down. They were in no position to ask for anything. The sentences had been decided.

48

A GENTLE WIND BLEW ACROSS THE WATER AS THE GUARDS TOOK THEIR place in the dry moat of La Cabaña, just as they did every night before falling in line at the execution wall. In the distance, the faint sputtering of the transport car could be heard at it entered the large gate at the far end of the fortress. Morgan stood next to the priest, John Joseph McKniff, another tranquil night over the vast, dark waters.

The aging priest dreaded these moments. He had watched so many young men lined up against the wall after praying with them that it sickened him. But something stirred in him after meeting Morgan. In the quiet of the prison cell, Morgan had whispered his last confession to Father McKniff and then turned to him calmly and said he was not afraid to die. He was supposed to be executed the next day in accordance with the law, but Morgan and Carreras had asked that their sentences be carried out that night.

"I have made my peace with God," he wrote from his cell. "I can accept whatever happens with my mind clear and my spirit strong."

Now standing next to each other, the men heard a sound coming from the prison that began in a low drone and then started to rise. The wind muffled the noise as it echoed from the center of the compound, but as they listened closer, they could hear the word "Viva" and then another: "Morgan." Then again: "Viva . . . Morgan."

To the guards, this wasn't good. The prisoners were chanting in unison, a telltale sign that something was going to blow. Ever since Morgan was called to trial, the inmates had been uneasy, shouting at the guards and gathering in groups on the concrete patio in the yard. Now they were yelling from the rafters, "Viva Morgan."

There had been rumors of an attack from the outside, prompting some of the guards to keep constant watch on the roof, lugging .50-caliber Czech and Russian anti-aircraft guns. The guards just needed to get Morgan into the car that would take him to the wall. The rush was on.

The transport car rounded the corner of the dry moat, rattling louder. The guards had long ago cut off the muffler of the vehicle so that it would create a loud, popping noise to scare the prisoners.

As Morgan and McKniff stood waiting, the priest glanced over at Morgan. These were the moments when the men began to whimper or shake uncontrollably. Some even refused to get into the car, planting their legs on the ground until a guard mercilessly slammed the backs of their legs with the butt of a rifle. Some even wet their pants. But Morgan waited calmly until the guard swung the rear door open, and he climbed into the backseat without saying a word.

As the car took off, the priest noticed that Morgan's lips were moving. As McKniff inched closer, he could hear Morgan pray. It was as if Morgan couldn't hear the roar of the engine. The vehicle rumbled around the stone wall encircling the fortress until it came to a stop in the center of the dry, grassy moat, the same place where everyone was taken.

Every time the car stopped at this spot, McKniff's heart never failed to skip a beat. Instead of getting easier, the executions were harder. The priest had been in Havana since 1939, but the last two years had been wrenching. The guards opened the rear door.

Morgan stood up, turned to the men, and stepped away from the car. On the other side of the wall, the city was still alive, the faint glow of lights from a carnival breaking through the bleak darkness. As Morgan stood in the shadows, a guard flicked a switch, and suddenly the entire moat was bathed in the glow of floodlights. The guards looked at Morgan, but he was unfazed. As he wrote in the last letter to his mother: "It is not when a man dies, but how."

Morgan raised his cuffed hands to the head guard. "I don't want to wear these," he said. Without hesitating, the guard nodded. Morgan was condemned to die, but he was still a comandante.

With free hands, Morgan turned to the middle-aged priest and embraced him. In just a short time, the two men had bonded. Then turning around, Morgan approached the sergeant of the firing squad. Stopping directly in front of him, Morgan held out his arms and surprised everyone by hugging him. "Tell the boys I forgive them," he said.

For a moment no one said anything.

They had been shooting men every night, but they had never witnessed anything like this. Turning his back to the firing squad, Morgan walked slowly to the wall covered with gouges and bullet holes. McKniff followed him, whispering a prayer and then making the sign of the cross. As the priest stepped away, Morgan stopped him. "Father, wait," he said, removing the rosary from around his neck. "Take this."

McKniff tucked the beads in his pocket.

After waiting for Morgan to take his place, the sergeant shouted for the men to get ready. Standing in a straight line, the marksmen raised their Belgian rifles. Under the lights, Morgan looked larger than life as he stared across the moat at the men with the guns.

"*Fuego!*" the sergeant shouted.

Shots jolted the air, the force of the bullets slamming Morgan against the wall.

Instead of shooting his heart or even his head, they had shot out his legs. McKniff looked up and saw that Morgan was not lying down, but sitting up. The priest could hear him gasping for breath. *The hyenas had aimed for his knees.* McKniff braced himself for the next volley. He could see the pain was shooting through Morgan's entire body.

Breathing deeply, Morgan stared at the guard walking toward him. Stopping just a few feet away, the man aimed his submachine gun at Morgan's chest heaving up and down in the light, and squeezed the trigger. The noise echoed across the prison yard as the smoke rose like mist under the floodlights.

The guards lowered their rifles.

—◆—

Olga woke, her heart racing. In her sleep, she had seen William approach and kiss her. She looked around the room but didn't see anyone. It must have been a dream, she said to herself.

She had arrived at the safe house in Santa Clara and wanted to rest until the escorts came to drive her to Camagüey. The secret police were crawling all over Santa Clara, so it was too dangerous for her to leave the house. The only thing keeping her going was the thought of being with her husband.

William. She had rehearsed what she would say when she saw him in the morning sun. With no radio in the house, Olga had no idea what was happening in Havana. It had been four days since she bolted from the embassy in the trunk of the ambassador's car. She had stopped at a safe house in Cienfuegos and then left for Santa Clara. She wasn't going to call her contacts until she reached Camagüey. She would know soon enough, she told herself.

Just after dark, the owner of the house went to the window and spotted the glow of headlights coming down the street. It was time.

It would take five hours to get to Camagüey, but if there were checkpoints on the main highways, it could take longer. Olga gathered her clothes and thanked the owner. She had stayed in so many safe houses by now that she had lost count. But she was grateful. Every person who hosted her was taking a deep, personal risk. Walking to the door, she looked both ways and then ran to the car with a man and two women crouched inside.

Three years earlier, Olga had disguised herself and jumped on a bus in Santa Clara to escape Batista's secret police. Now she was heading out again, except this time she was going to rescue her husband.

The driver sped down the road . . . and into a phalanx of flashing red police lights. He tried to turn down another street, but more police cars blocked the road. Olga and her helpers were surrounded.

"No," Olga said as she looked out the window.

The car came to a halt, and the police ran toward them with guns drawn. Olga wanted to run, but she couldn't get out. There were too many police.

At the window, one of the officers screamed for them to surrender. Olga calmly exited the car and stepped to the curb. The policeman asked if she was Olga Morgan, but she shook her head. They would find out soon enough.

People gathered in the street, watching. The police were grilling the other two women and the man in the car, but they, too, weren't saying a word. In frustration, the officers swung open the door of a police car and ordered them inside. They were going to the G2 station.

Olga stared straight ahead as the driver pulled away. There was nothing they could do to force her to talk. The police had tried to work the crowd of onlookers, but no one said a word. At first, Olga didn't think anything of it. She was still jittery from the arrest. But as the car bounced along the back road, she realized that the people in the streets could have snitched on her. So could the people with her in the car. But no one did.

From the time she left the Brazilian embassy to her last stop in Santa Clara, people opened their doors to her. In every home, they offered food and clothes to fugitives fleeing the government. She was witnessing the beginning of a rebellion about to catch fire in the same place where she sought refuge three years earlier: the mountains. The rebels whom she had expected to see in Santa Clara—men from the Second Front and their newest recruits—were already in the Escambray.

What Morgan had started with the delivery of guns and supplies was morphing into a new armed struggle. It explained why G2 agents were stationed at every corner in Santa Clara. It explained why so many people were being hauled in for questioning. The occupants of every safe house reminded her of the impact that Morgan had made in the fight for their freedom.

Olga's own freedom was over, she knew that. But she took solace in the fact that maybe Morgan had escaped. Maybe he was still alive. Maybe someday they all would live in peace.

Epilogue

On a cold, windswept morning in January 2002, a reporter pulled in front of the worn, shingled townhome at the end of the long, narrow block.

Peering at the windows covered with ice, Michael Sallah (one of the authors of this book) eased into the parking space in front of the house. As the *Toledo Blade*'s national affairs writer, Sallah had covered stories filled with much of Toledo's history: the mob, the politicians, the captains of industry. But this one had faded over the decades into barely a footnote, if that.

As he ventured to the front steps, a tiny, hunched-over figure ambled to the door, peeking through the crack. Before the dark, diminutive woman had a chance to say anything, Sallah introduced himself and then, without hesitating, asked the question: "Are you Olga Morgan?"

Olga Morgan. It had been years since anyone called her that name. She was Olga Goodwin. She was remarried—a grandmother—and had been living in obscurity in the working-class neighborhood in West Toledo. Few people, including her current husband, knew the secrets of her past.

She looked at the reporter and nodded. Yes, she said. She was Olga.

Sallah asked if he could come inside to talk, just for a few minutes. He had spent hours poring over frayed newspaper clippings about her, even marveling at her photos as a stunningly beautiful revolutionary in the 1950s. He wanted to know more. But Olga was hesitant. It had been years since she opened up about her other life. Years since she left Cuba on a ratty yellow boat during the Mariel boatlift. Years since she arrived in Toledo on a lonely winter day with just a single suitcase.

As she began to shut the door, Sallah insisted on giving her his card, hoping she would not throw it away.

It would be days before she finally agreed to be interviewed, to actually sit and ruminate over her buried secrets. She opened the door to let the reporter into her house, knowing that she could never shut that door again. With a tape recorder on the table, Olga opened up and slowly and deliberately began talking about events that had been stored in her heart.

She had tried to move on with her new life and her new husband and her new home. But the more she talked to the reporter, the more comfortable she became, and within days, she began revealing details about Morgan and a revolution that she tried to forget.

As she rifled through the old photographs and letters in a box on her living room table, she pulled out a grainy black-and-white photo of her and Morgan standing on a mountain peak, clutching weapons and smiling lovingly into each other's eyes.

"This," she said, "sticks in my heart forever."

Every day she was in prison—nearly eleven years—she thought about their life together, their children.

It was during her first day at Guanabacoa prison that she learned from a jail supervisor that Morgan had been executed days earlier, prompting her to lunge at the man's throat in a frenzy until the guards pulled her off.

For weeks, she was held in solitary confinement: a pitch-black room with a hole in the floor to relieve herself and a slit in the door where the guards pushed through plates of old, crusty bread and rice. When she lay down to sleep, the rats and insects would scurry over her body.

For a time, she didn't care what happened.

But after being hauled from one prison to the next and witnessing the brutal conditions, she couldn't stay quiet. She led hunger strikes and eventually emerged as the leader of a group of inmates known as Las Plantadas—the planted ones. At one point, she was beaten with a rubber baton, the pounding permanently damaging her right eye.

In 1971, the United Nations Commission on Human Rights began looking into the conditions of Cuban prisons, particularly the treatment of political prisoners. To rid itself of the attention, the Cuban government agreed to free some prisoners. Olga's name was called. At first, she was stunned. She had already been labeled as a troubled inmate and a lifer. But one day in August 1971, she was summoned to the visitors' room and was met by family members, including her daughters. She was free.

In the ensuing years, she tried to move on with her life. She would walk the streets of Havana, but was constantly reminded of her husband. The pain, sometimes, was worse than what she felt in prison.

One day, she showed up at the Colón Cemetery. She wanted to see his grave. At first, the caretaker hesitated. Someone could be watching. But Olga persisted. "Just for a minute," she implored.

The man relented, leading her down a walkway, past the ornate headstones of Cuban generals and presidents. In a remote corner of the cemetery, he opened a mausoleum door. "I could lose my life over this," he said.

There, Olga saw his resting place for the first time. All at once, the reality of his death hit her like never before. She knew she needed to get out.

She remembered what Morgan had told her: If she and their daughters could ever get out of Cuba, they should go to the United States. His mother would take care of them.

In time, she and her parents and children would get that chance: visas to leave Cuba in 1978. One by one, they boarded the plane bound for Miami. But when it was Olga's turn to board, she was stopped by the guards. There would be no escape for the widow of the *Yanqui comandante*.

From the tarmac, she watched as the plane with her family took off, never to come back again. One more cruel kick in the gut.

She went to live in a convent in Havana, but couldn't stand the thought of being separated again from her daughters. Two years later, she was rousted by one of the nuns. There was a crush of people at the Peruvian embassy, all asking for asylum. "You must go," the nun told her.

Olga grabbed her clothes, hugged the woman, and bolted toward the embassy. The gate was locked, but she managed to climb the fence, with people frantically pulling her over the top to get inside.

After staying for weeks inside the embassy grounds, she was led to a rickety boat at the edge of Mariel Harbor. Her destination: Miami. But after the boat left the shore, the Cuban navy began firing shots into the bow as a cruel joke. Soon, the craft was taking on water. For hours, Olga huddled and prayed with the other passengers until finally she looked up to see a US Coast Guard helicopter drop from the skies to guide the boat to shore in Key West.

Days later, she managed to join her parents and daughters in Miami. But Olga was uneasy. She didn't want to settle in a place where so many of her countrymen had found refuge. Once again, she was haunted by the words of Morgan: *If you ever need anything, my mother will be there for you.* With help from Morgan's old friend, Frank Emmick, Olga boarded a plane bound for Toledo.

As she sat on the plane, Olga didn't know what to expect. She had heard so much about Loretta from her son, but had never met her.

Stepping up the stairs of the apartment house where Loretta Morgan was living, Olga looked up to see the matronly, silver-haired woman gazing warmly from the open door. Olga leaped up the stairs and hugged her.

For the next several days, the two women were inseparable, sharing stories about the man they both loved. Loretta was now a widow, too. Just three years after she lost her son, Alexander Morgan died. Loretta eventually sold the big house and moved into the tiny apartment just blocks away.

Tragedy struck again in 1963, when Billy Jr. died of a head injury at the age of six under questionable circumstances while living with his mother and stepfather on a US military base in Turkey. Morgan's daughter, Ann Marie, was married and living in Indiana.

It wasn't long before Olga made a decision. She sent for her parents and daughters to live with her in Toledo, a place of cold winters and old brick factories. Olga found a job as a social worker, helping migrants find food and shelter. In time, the family blended into their new world.

By the late 1980s, Loretta's health began to deteriorate and she was moved to a group home. As she lay dying in 1988, she made a request to Olga: Bring William's remains back to this country and make sure his citizenship is restored. She had never been able to reconcile with the thought of her son's body entombed in a Havana cemetery.

Olga smiled and nodded her head. No matter how difficult, she couldn't say no. Not to William's mother.

In the years that followed, Olga married Jim Goodwin, a blue-collar worker from Mississippi with kind eyes and a gentle smile. They settled in their small townhome in West Toledo, where Olga began to help raise her grandchildren.

But it pained her that she had not been able to do anything to carry out her promise to Loretta. One year faded into the next, and William's body was still in a tomb in Havana. It was during her interview with the *Toledo Blade* that she brought up the pledge she made years earlier.

Olga didn't know what to expect when the *Blade* published its three-part series on the *Yanqui comandante* in March 2002, recounting Morgan's remarkable journey to Cuba and eventual death by firing squad. Mitch Weiss (the other author of this book), then the *Toledo Blade*'s state editor, had reviewed the stories before they ran and remarked that the articles

Prompted by a *Toledo Blade* series, US Representative Marcy Kaptur of Ohio met with Fidel Castro in 2002 to ask that the Cuban government return Morgan's remains.
COURTESY OF MORGAN FAMILY COLLECTION

could prompt the US government to act on Olga's request.

The following month, two members of Congress, Marcy Kaptur of Ohio and Charles Rangel of New York, traveled to Havana to meet with Fidel Castro and begged the question: Would Castro return Morgan's remains to the United States? After meeting for hours with the lawmakers, Castro said he would consider it.

Meanwhile, a local attorney who read the stories, Opie Rollison, took the liberty to press the US State Department to reinstate Morgan's citizenship, arguing that the government had no right to strip the *Yanqui comandante* of his birthright. After two years, the State Department took a rare step in 2007 by reversing its earlier decision and admitting it acted in error nearly fifty years earlier. Morgan was indeed a US citizen.

Olga Goodwin in 2012 COURTESY OF MORGAN FAMILY COLLECTION

But the issue over Morgan's remains is still unresolved. In 2013, US Senator Sherrod Brown of Ohio joined the fight to help bring the body home, meeting with the Cuban Interests Section in Washington, DC. But so far, the plea has not been met.

Olga, now seventy-eight, vows she won't stop until Morgan is laid to rest in the city where his family is buried. "This was his country," she said. "This is where he belongs."

She admits that some days, the task seems impossible. The political tensions between the two countries flare up. Cuba itself struggles with the notion that it would be honoring a ghost from its own difficult past.

When she needs to keep going, Olga turns to a scrapbook in her basement and an old faded letter that Morgan wrote her from La Cabaña in his final hours.

Since the first time I saw you in the mountains until the last time I saw you in prison, you have been my love, my happiness, my companion in life and in my thoughts during my moment of death.

Acknowledgments

The person to whom we owe the most for this book is Olga Goodwin, widow of William Morgan, who carried this powerful story in her heart for more than half a century. She not only spent endless hours with us during the research phase of the project, but she trusted us with her private memoir—hundreds of pages—that she wrote shortly after arriving in this country during the Mariel boatlift in 1980. The rare details that she recalled of her life with Morgan proved invaluable and provide a much richer perspective of one of the most compelling characters of the Cold War.

We are grateful also to writer and historian Aran Shetterly, whose book on Morgan, *The Americano*, helped uncover Morgan's role in history and bring his accomplishments to the public's attention.

We credit the men who served with Morgan in the Second Front, most notably Roger Redondo and Dr. Armando Fleites, for the long interviews they granted us during the research and writing of this book. Without them, we wouldn't have been able to fully appreciate Morgan's military achievements during the revolution.

We are grateful to others who shared their memories, including the late Eloy Gutiérrez Menoyo, Ramiro Lorenzo, Domingo Ortega, Jorge Castellon, Hiram Gonzalez, and Michael Alvarez.

We recognize author and former journalist Lee Roderick, whose tape-recorded interviews in the 1980s with key people who knew Morgan—including Second Front rebels now deceased—were indispensable in chronicling key events in his life.

We also recognize several historians with vastly different political backgrounds who helped us gain a greater understanding of Morgan by virtue of those differences. They include the indefatigable Enrique Encinosa, Antonio de la Cova, Louis A. Perez Jr., and Juan Antonio Blanco.

This book originated with stories that Michael Sallah pursued as a reporter at the *Toledo Blade* beginning in 2002. To that end, we offer our heartfelt thanks to the publisher and editors at the *Blade* for their support of that coverage and allowing us to reprint several photographs of Morgan for this book.

Toledo attorney Gerardo "Opie" Rollison provided us with critical support and wise counsel. In addition, we offer our gratitude to attorney Jon Richardson, who worked behind the scenes to ensure that Olga's story would be told.

Others, as friends or colleagues, provided tremendous spiritual and journalistic advice during crucial stages in the writing of this book, including Johnnie Harmeling; the Reverend Ricardo Mullen, OSA; David Nickell; Kevin Maurer; and Ronnie Greene.

A number of other journalists pursued stories about Morgan over the years. David Grann's elegant piece in the *New Yorker* in 2012 provided rich details about Morgan's life in Cuba. *Miami Herald* stalwarts Alfonso Chardy, Amy Driscoll, and Manny Garcia, who is now executive editor of the *Naples Daily News*, provided continued coverage that eventually led to the posthumous restoration of Morgan's citizenship and renewed efforts to return his remains to America for reburial.

Adrian College professor of Spanish Don Cellini, *National Journal* reporter Alexia Fernandez Campbell, and Roger Redondo Ramos (son of Roger Redondo) translated interviews and documents indispensable in telling this story.

We stand indebted to the work of former *Palm Beach Post* editorial director Randy Schultz, whose illuminating 1979 series on Morgan provided important insights into his character.

We are grateful to our book editor, James Jayo, for recognizing the importance of this work and Morgan's critical role in one of the most significant revolutions of the twentieth century. We also give thanks to our literary agent, Scott Miller of Trident Media Group.

Lastly, but most importantly, we are forever indebted to our wives, Judi Sallah and Suzyn Weiss, and children, who spent many long nights and weekends without us as we pursued the story. Without their love and patience, this book would not have been possible.

Notes on Sources

The events depicted in the book come from extensive interviews with Olga Goodwin (Morgan), dozens of members of the Second Front of the National Escambray, as well as William Alexander Morgan's family and friends, historians, and Cubans who fought in the revolution. We spent a decade researching the story, reviewing thousands of pages of documents from private collections and the National Archives and Records Administration. In addition, we examined hundreds of news stories from the *New York Times*, *Miami Herald*, Associated Press, *Toledo Blade*, and other media outlets. An important source was Olga's memoir, an unpublished 150-page manuscript stored in her basement for years. Her writings provide deeply personal material as well as extensive details of the couple's relationship during one of the most important revolutions of the twentieth century. We also relied on nearly fifteen hours of tape-recorded interviews with key members of the Second Front from the collection of author and former journalist Lee Roderick.

Introduction

We talked at length with numerous members of the Second Front of the National Escambray, including Roger Redondo, Armando Fleites, Domingo Ortega, and Ramiro Lorenzo. We interviewed Hiram Gonzalez, Rino Puig, and others incarcerated with Morgan in La Cabaña. We pulled from transcripts of interviews with Pedro Ossorio, Edmundo Amado Consuegra, and others. We interviewed Olga Goodwin (Morgan) and pulled from historical documents.

Chapter 1

We interviewed dozens of family members and friends of William Morgan. They included Art Ryan, Donnie Van Gunten, Stan Sturgill, Marshall Isenberg, James Tafelski, and others. We drew on transcripts of interviews with Loretta Morgan, Carroll Costain, and her husband, Edric Costain, as well as Charlie Zissan and Edmundo Amado Consuegra. We reviewed Morgan's military records, including transcripts of his court-martial and his army psychiatric evaluation. We talked at length with key members of the Second National Front of the Escambray.

CHAPTER 2

We conducted extensive interviews with family and friends of Olga Goodwin. We interviewed Olga more than a dozen times during the last decade and pulled from her memoir, which included details of her bus trip to take supplies to rebels in the mountains. We also drew from historical documents as well as news stories during military dictator Fulgencio Batista y Zaldívar's rule in the 1950s.

CHAPTER 3

We talked at length with members of the Second National Front of the Escambray, including Roger Redondo and Armando Fleites. We pulled from transcripts of interviews with Edmundo Amado Consuegra. We drew on documents and archival material related to the history of relations between the United States and Cuba.

CHAPTER 4

We pulled from transcripts of interviews with Roger Rodriguez, Isabelle Rodriguez, and others who helped Morgan on his journey to the mountains. We conducted extensive interviews with members of the Second National Front of the Escambray and pulled from historical documents and published material.

CHAPTER 5

We conducted numerous interviews with Morgan's fellow soldiers in the Escambray, including Eloy Gutiérrez Menoyo, the leader of the Second National Front of the Escambray. The men described Morgan's first days in the rugged terrain as well as harsh conditions in the camps. We also drew on interviews with Olga Goodwin, who recounted stories her husband had told her about his early days with the guerrillas. We used military maps and historical documents to pinpoint rebel movements.

Chapter 6

We talked at length with members of the Second National Front of the Escambray, who described skirmishes with government soldiers in early 1958. They also provided military maps and other key documents to help us understand the campaign and strategy. Roger Redondo recounted hiding a cache of weapons critical to the rebels' survival. Menoyo's biography, including his ideological differences with Faure Chomón, was pulled from our interviews, as well as documents and published material.

Chapter 7

We conducted interviews with members of the Second National Front of the Escambray. They described the grueling march to flee Batista's soldiers and recounted how Menoyo pushed Morgan to keep moving after he spotted the American on the ground in pain.

Chapter 8

Our account of Morgan's rise in the rebel unit came from numerous interviews with members of the Second National Front of the Escambray. They recounted Morgan's skills as a soldier and how he trained the rebels in self-defense and to handle weapons. The men also talked about Morgan's altercation with Regino Camacho Santos and described Morgan's courage during an ambush by Batista's soldiers at Charco Azul.

"In the confusion Morgan didn't understand the orders to charge," Roger Redondo told the authors. "William was trapped and fighting for his life." For our account of Morgan's inner thoughts during the battle, we relied on interviews with Second Front members as well as Olga Goodwin. They said Morgan told them what he was thinking when he stood up during the firefight.

We incorporated details of Morgan's letter to *New York Times* correspondent Herbert Matthews to show how the Second Front was emerging as a fighting unit in the mountains. The letter was the first sign to the outside world of Morgan's involvement in the conflict. In it, Morgan articulated why he was fighting.

Excerpt: "Why do I fight in this land so foreign from my own? Why did I come here far from my home and family? Why do I worry about these men here in the mountains with me? Is it because they were all close friends of mine? No! When I came here they were strangers to me. I could not speak their language or understand their problems. Is it because I seek adventure? No. Here there is no adventure only the ever existent problems of survive. So why am I here? I am here because I believe that the most important thing for free men to do is to protect the freedom of others. I am here so that my son when he is grown will not have to fight or die in a land not his own, because one man or group of men try to take his liberty from him."

CHAPTER 9

We talked to Olga Goodwin at length about her journey from Santa Clara to the Escambray. At the time, she was wanted by the secret police for antigovernment activities. We also drew on her memoir, interviews with friends and family members, and historical documents, including news stories, for our account of life in Santa Clara and Las Villas Province in 1958. "I would rather die on the street than go into exile," she told the authors about why she fled to the mountains instead of seeking asylum at a foreign embassy in Havana. Former soldiers of the Second National Front of the Escambray provided details of the base camps, including call signs and signals used to warn sentries of approaching danger.

CHAPTER 10

Our account of Olga's first two encounters with Morgan comes from interviews and her memoir:

"He said he felt very pleased to meet me. . . . I felt so thrilled that words could not come out of my lips. I only looked at him in astonishment and awe. He was so big and different from the others, that I could only look at him," she wrote.

Later that night, Olga recalled Morgan galloping toward her on a white horse, whistling a song she would later know as the theme from the movie *The Bridge on the River Kwai*.

"How are you doing, Olgo?" he asked.

"I am fine, Commander," she said. "But my name is not Olgo. It's Olga—feminine."

Morgan laughed. He was still trying to learn Spanish. "OK," he said. "But to me, you're still going to be Olgo."

CHAPTER 11

We talked at length with members of the Second National Front of the Escambray, including Eloy Gutiérrez Menoyo, Roger Redondo, Armando Fleites, and others. They provided us with critical details about how small groups of soldiers communicated with each other in the field and shared information, as well as how they planned and carried out attacks.

CHAPTER 12

We conducted extensive interviews with Olga Goodwin and used details from her memoir, including how she administered first aid to injured rebels. Members of the Second National Front of the Escambray provided information about the network of messengers and safe houses in the mountains.

CHAPTER 13

For our account of skirmishes in the mountains, we drew on interviews with Second National Front of the Escambray soldiers, including Eloy Gutiérrez Menoyo, Roger Redondo, Armando Fleites, and others. We also used historical documents, including maps, and news stories. Our account of the Rural Guard torturing villagers comes from eyewitness accounts. Morgan included some details in a letter to his mother:

"The other day the Soldiers came to the mountains 1,200 in our zone and burned 14 homes of families who were neither rebels or opposed— the Government killed a 60-year-old woman—who ran from one house to protect her grandchild—And they cut out the tongue, pulled out the fingernails and hung a 72-year-old man who was senile and refused to let them enter his home—these things I have seen and much more."

CHAPTER 14

The chapter comes in part from letters that Morgan wrote to his mother and two children. In the letters, Morgan explains why he's fighting in the revolution and offers future advice for his son and daughter: "Dear Mom:

This will be the first letter I have written to you since I left in December. I know that you neither approve nor understand why I am here—even though you are the one person in the world—that I believe—understands me. I have been many places in my life and done many things which you did not approve—or understand, nor did I understand myself."

He told his mother he left Toledo in December "because I believed it was the wisest thing to do."

Then he described his fellow soldiers and their commitment to the cause: "My men have walked—20 miles in a night to attack these same Soldiers—much of the time we have little food—and we sleep on the ground. But slowly but surely we are driving the Soldiers from the mountains and all over Cuba—men like us are doing the same in the city or the hills."

He ended by saying he hoped his mother now understood why he was in Cuba: "The whole point of this letter is to let you know why I fight here. I do not expect you to approve but I believe you will understand—And if it should happen that I am killed here—you will know it was not for foolish fancy—or as dad would say a pipe dream. As for Terri and Billy and Ann, it is hard to understand but I love them very deeply and think of them often."

Chapter 15

We used Olga Goodwin's memoir to help tell the story of the Batista's indiscriminate bombing in the mountains to try to break the will of the guerrillas. It was during one of the air attacks that Morgan broached the subject of their future. But Olga told him she couldn't think about their future while they were in the middle of a war.

"I don't know you. I don't know anything about you. We must talk calmly, since I don't know anything about your life and, you don't know anything about mine," Olga wrote in her memoir.

Chapter 16

We interviewed Olga Goodwin, and drew on extensive passages in her memoir for details of her leaving camp after her parrot died.

CHAPTER 17

For our account of Jesús Carreras's meeting with Ernesto "Che" Guevara, we drew on extensive interviews with the members of the Second National Front of the Escambray. We also relied on documents and historical accounts of Che's journey to the Escambray and the rift between the Second Front and the 26th of July Movement.

CHAPTER 18

We talked at length to Olga Goodwin and pulled from her memoir. Part of the chapter comes from extensive interviews with members of Second National Front of the Escambray, including Eloy Gutiérrez Menoyo, Roger Redondo, Armando Fleites, Ramiro Lorenzo, Jorge Castellon, and others. While Menoyo was under pressure to make peace with Che, he also had to deal with the increased presence of Batista's troops in the mountains.

CHAPTER 19

Our account of Morgan and Olga's wedding comes from interviews with Olga Goodwin, her family and friends, and members of the Second National Front of the Escambray. We also drew from Olga's memoir: "The month of October arrived and the political situation in Cuba was worse all the time. Several towns were being attacked and, at the end of October, 1958, he told me: 'Olga, we better get married. Nobody knows what's going to happen and I know that I love you very much and that you love me too.' I said: 'It's all right, let's get married as soon as we can.'"

We drew on our interviews with members of the Second Front, including Roger Redondo and Armando Fleites, and military maps, news stories, and archival material for our account of the battle of Trinidad. Redondo recalled urging Menoyo to postpone the mission. As a scout, Redondo discovered the military had sent two companies to Trinidad in anticipation of a rebel attack. Despite the risk, Menoyo moved forward with the plans.

CHAPTER 20

Our account of Menoyo's meeting with Che Guevara was pulled from numerous interviews with members of the Second National Front of the

Escambray, including Eloy Gutiérrez Menoyo, Roger Redondo, Armando Fleites, and others. Documents show that Castro had sent Che to the Escambray to bring all the rebel fighting units under the umbrella of the 26th of July Movement.

CHAPTER 21

We talked at length to Olga Goodwin and pulled information from her memoir. She recounted details of Morgan's uniform and his ritual—how he dressed before heading into the field. Our account of the final push—including the skirmish at Topes de Collantes and Che's attempt to undermine the Second National Front of the Escambray's role in the campaign—was drawn from extensive interviews with members of the fighting unit, including Roger Redondo, Armando Fleites, and others.

CHAPTER 22

We interviewed a number of people who fought with the Second National Front of the Escambray, among them Eloy Gutiérrez Menoyo, Roger Redondo, Armando Fleites, Ramiro Lorenzo, and others. They described critical details about the battles and provided maps and other documents. Our account of the final days of Batista's government comes from historical papers, books, and news stories.

CHAPTER 23

Our account of the Second National Front of the Escambray's campaign to take cities and towns is drawn from numerous interviews with members of the fighting unit, including Roger Redondo, Armando Fleites, and others.

CHAPTER 24

We based most of the narrative of Morgan's time in Cienfuegos on extensive interviews with Olga Goodwin and members of the Second National Front of the Escambray, including Roger Redondo, Armando Fleites, Rafael Huguet, and others. We also incorporated details from Olga's memoir and transcripts of interviews with Morgan's family, as well as news stories about Morgan's role in Cienfuegos and the revolution. We also used documents from the Federal Bureau of Investigation, which had started looking into Morgan's activities in Cuba.

CHAPTER 25

We based the chapter on extensive interviews with Olga Goodwin and her friends and family members. In her memoir, she included details of the challenges facing her husband and the rebels in the wake of Batista's sudden departure. We drew on news stories to help document Morgan's popularity among the Cuban people, who affectionately called him the Americano.

CHAPTER 26

For Morgan and Olga's time together in Cienfuegos, we used material from Olga Goodwin's memoir. Along with interviewing Olga, we also talked to her friends and family, as well as members of the Second National Front of the Escambray. Our account of Fidel Castro's visit and meal in a Cienfuegos restaurant comes from interviews with Olga and others, along with news stories.

"Castro was wearing his fatigues, high boots; his hair was curly and very black, his eyes shined (something that struck my attention highly) and his eyes seemed to laugh when he spoke," Olga recalled in her memoir.

But she said she quickly became disillusioned.

"In reality, I did not see Castro pay much attention to William nor the group under the latter's command. This annoyed and disappointed since I saw that Castro only paid attention and gave importance to his group. I thought that that was not fair and, because of that, I asked my friend (Rosita) to leave, and I did not even want to eat. I only got close to William and told him: am not feeling very well and I am leaving, because there is too many people here and I need a little fresh air. So I left."

CHAPTER 27

The narrative for this chapter comes from extensive interviews with Olga Goodwin and members of the Second National Front of the Escambray, among them Eloy Gutiérrez Menoyo, Rafael Huguet, Roger Redondo, Armando Fleites, Ramiro Lorenzo, and Jorge Castellon. We also reviewed Olga's memoir, news stories, and documents.

Chapter 28

We talked at length with members of the Second National Front of the Escambray, including Eloy Gutiérrez Menoyo, Roger Redondo, Armando Fleites, and others. We drew from extensive interviews with Olga Goodwin as well as from her memoir. We also used historical papers and news stories to help depict the chaotic situation in Havana in the early days of Fidel Castro's government. Fleites recalled details of Menoyo's argument with Che that almost turned into a bloodbath. "It was very tense in the room," Fleites said. "We didn't know what would happen."

Chapter 29

We conducted extensive interviews with Olga Goodwin and her family and friends, including Isabelle Rodriguez, and pulled details from Olga's memoir. During the interviews, Olga recounted her personal conversations with Morgan. We interviewed a number of people from the Second National Front of the Escambray, among them Roger Redondo and Armando Fleites. We used transcripts of interviews with Morgan's family, including Loretta Morgan and Carroll Costain.

Chapter 30

We talked at length with Olga Goodwin and members of the Second National Front of the Escambray. For our account of Morgan's meeting with Dominick Bartone, we drew on those interviews, which included details of private conversations they had with Morgan. In addition, we reviewed National Archives and Records Administration documents that included Federal Bureau of Investigation, State Department, and Central Intelligence Agency files related to William Morgan and the mob. During one of our interviews, Fleites recalled a private meeting with Castro in which the Cuban leader expressed concerns about Morgan because he was an American. Our account of the meeting with Frank Nelson comes in part from Morgan's conversations with Olga and key members of the Second Front, as well as from FBI and other documents.

Chapter 31

Our account of the meeting in which Morgan and Eloy Gutiérrez Menoyo decided to tell Castro about the Trujillo conspiracy was pulled from numerous interviews with members of the Second National Front of the Escambray and Olga Goodwin. We also used her memoir and FBI documents. For the section on Pedro Ossorio's arrival at Morgan's home, we reviewed transcripts from an earlier interview.

Chapter 32

We conducted numerous interviews with key members of the Second National Front of the Escambray, among them Eloy Gutiérrez Menoyo, Roger Redondo, and Armando Fleites. During interviews, Olga Goodwin provided insight into how Morgan juggled details of the plot and meetings with the Trujillo conspirators. Some meetings took place in her Havana home. We also found critical details of the meetings in FBI documents; the agency had a number of informants who called in with regular updates. Our interviews with Olga—as well as her memoir—provided key details of the meeting between Morgan and Fidel Castro to discuss the Trujillo plot.

Chapter 33

To document the Trujillo conspiracy, we interviewed numerous members of the Second National Front of the Escambray, including Eloy Gutiérrez Menoyo, Roger Redondo, and Armando Fleites. In addition, we interviewed Olga Goodwin and reviewed her memoir, which provided insight into problems facing the couple caught in the middle of an international conspiracy. She described in vivid details the characters who regularly showed up unannounced at her door, including the Reverend Ricardo Velazco Ordóñez, a Trujillo confidant. Trujillo had sent Ordóñez to Cuba to check up on Morgan. We also used transcripts of earlier interviews with Pedro Ossorio and FBI and other documents to show that Morgan was under surveillance by federal agents who worked feverishly to try to unravel the plot. Details about the meetings between Morgan and FBI agent Leman Stafford Jr. came from various sources, including FBI documents and Olga's memoir. In our interviews, Olga provided additional information about the FBI's investigation.

Chapter 34

We conducted extensive interviews with numerous members of the Second National Front of the Escambray, including Roger Redondo, Armando Fleites, and others. They provided critical details of how the plot unfolded. They also were in the room when Morgan contacted Trujillo via radio. During the plot, Morgan confided in Olga and several close friends, including Redondo and Fleites. In interviews with the authors, they recounted their conversations with Morgan.

Chapter 35

The narrative for the chapter comes from extensive interviews with Olga Goodwin. We also used details from Olga's memoir and talked to members of the Second National Front of the Escambray about the plot. We reviewed FBI and State Department documents along with news stories. Our account of Morgan's voyage to Cuba with the weapons was drawn in part from FBI documents, which included details of an August 20, 1959, phone call between Morgan and Leman Stafford Jr. It came one week after Morgan's role as a double agent was revealed to the world.

"He apologized for what he claimed was his inability to furnish the true details regarding the purpose of his previous visits to Miami, Florida. He felt that he had not violated any United States laws by his previous actions, although he did feel he may have 'bent' some of them," Stafford wrote.

Chapter 36

We interviewed a number of people who participated in the Trujillo conspiracy, including Eloy Gutiérrez Menoyo, Roger Redondo, Armando Fleites, and others. We talked at length with members of the Second National Front of the Escambray who were in a Havana house when Fidel Castro and Camilo Cienfuegos confronted several adversaries involved in the plot to overthrow the Cuban government. We reviewed documents, news stories, and FBI and State Department documents, including cables and memos.

Chapter 37

The chapter's details were culled from extensive interviews with Olga Goodwin. She also described in her memoir how the Trujillo conspiracy elevated Morgan's profile in Cuba. In the aftermath, Morgan had become a celebrity.

"After the 'Trujillo Conspiracy,' there was much change in our lives, because way before this problem, he had a lot of followers. But when it happened, their sympathy toward him increased. I mean there was a lot of movement around his person, not only within Cuba, but in the Cuban radio, television. Many American journalists called him constantly and asked him for interviews. So my place was constantly full with American journalists," Olga wrote in her memoir.

Chapter 38

Our account of Morgan losing his US citizenship comes from extensive interviews with Olga Goodwin and Morgan's family members and friends. We also reviewed State Department, Central Intelligence Agency, and other documents. We interviewed numerous members of the Second National Front of the Escambray about protecting Morgan in the wake of the Trujillo conspiracy. We pulled the transcripts of broadcast journalist Clete Roberts's interview with Morgan. During the session, Roberts asked him about the revolution, Morgan's relationship with Fidel Castro, and Morgan's loss of American citizenship. He also touched on Morgan's marriage.

Roberts: "You know, Bill, what you've just told me—the meeting with Mrs. Morgan, the romance, the kind of a life you live—sounds to me like all of the movie scripts that were ever dreamt about in Hollywood. How has it happened that you haven't offered a diary for sale?"

Morgan: "I don't believe you should cash in on your ideals. I don't believe I was an idealist when I went up into the mountains, but I feel that I am an idealist now. At least I have an awful strong faith in an awful lot of people and what they want to do."

Chapter 39

We talked at length with leaders of the Second National Front of the Escambray about how Fidel Castro's secret police began watching

Morgan. In a series of interviews, Olga Goodwin said her life with Morgan during this period was difficult. She had a newborn. They had just moved into a new apartment—her fourth home since the revolution ended. She told us she dreamed about moving to the United States to raise their family. But after Morgan lost his US citizenship, she knew that was out of the question. We drew from Olga's interviews and memoir for our account of Morgan confronting Fidel Castro in front of a live television audience. At the time, Castro was beckoning a crowd to join him in denouncing America. Her memoir was a valuable resource for Morgan's decision to create a farm for fish and frogs.

CHAPTER 40

Our account of Morgan's push to get the fish and frog farm up and running comes from interviews with Olga Goodwin, Morgan's friends, and members of the Second National Front of the Escambray, including Roger Redondo. We used transcripts of interviews with Edmundo Amado Consuegra and Pedro Ossorio. During this period, Olga recalled that Morgan took Antonio Chao Flores under his wing, trying to keep him from getting in trouble.

"Describing this young man is for me, in a certain way, a reason for pride, since I deemed him an extraordinary young man," Olga wrote in her memoir. "William and I thought of him as our son. He had a fair skin, was very amiable, affectionate and fluent in his conversation, and had extraordinary political ideals. He had a soft, penetrating and pure look in his eyes, a short height, blond hair and quick movements upon walking, never fearful and courageous to a maximum, ready to face any danger and even look for it at any time. I looked at him at times and told him: 'I fear for you, because at times you are a little impulsive and I think that something could happen to you.' He smiled and told me: 'Don't worry; nothing will happen to me.'"

CHAPTER 41

We talked to Olga Goodwin at length and had access to her memoir, providing critical details about the couple's family life. Our account of the *La Coubre* disaster comes from numerous interviews with Olga and members of the Second National Front of the Escambray, among them Eloy Gutiérrez Menoyo, Roger Redondo, Armando Fleites, and others, as well as from historical documents and news stories.

CHAPTER 42

We interviewed key members of the Second National Front of the Escambray, who provided critical information about their struggle to find a way to counter Fidel Castro's tilt toward the Soviet Union. In a series of extensive interviews, Roger Redondo and others told us that no military unit was more opposed to Communism than the Second Front. They had publicly proclaimed this position. They had even expressed their views to Castro. Our account of Morgan's decision to run guns to the Escambray comes from interviews with Olga Goodwin, Second Front members, and Cuban historians, among them Enrique Encinosa. We also drew on historical documents and transcripts of interviews with key players, including Frank Emmick. Olga's memoir provided information on Morgan's fight to free Jesús Carreras from jail.

CHAPTER 43

The chapter derives from extensive interviews with Olga Goodwin and members of the Second National Front of the Escambray, among them Rafael Huguet, Roger Redondo, and Armando Fleites. We also drew from historical documents—especially for the section on the emerging Soviet presence in the Escambray. We also reviewed news stories and numerous books on the Cuban revolution. For the birth of Olga's second daughter, we pulled information from Olga's memoir.

CHAPTER 44

Many of the critical details of Morgan's and Olga Goodwin's arrests come from Olga's memoir and from our extensive interviews with her during the last decade. We also pulled material from our lengthy interviews with members of the Second National Front of the Escambray, Morgan's friends and family, Cuban historians, State Department documents, and news stories.

CHAPTER 45

We based much of the narrative of Morgan's incarceration in La Cabaña and his wife's house arrest and subsequent escape on interviews with Olga Goodwin and members of the Second National Front of the Escambray, among them Roger Redondo and Armando Fleites, as well as transcripts of interviews with Pedro Ossorio Franco and Edmundo Amado Consuegra. We used Olga's memoir to provide critical details about her meeting with Morgan in La Cabaña and about how she escaped house arrest with her two young children by drugging Cuban guards.

CHAPTER 46

We conducted extensive interviews with members of the Second National Front of the Escambray, among them Roger Redondo, Armando Fleites, Eloy Gutiérrez Menoyo, Domingo Ortega, and others. Redondo and Fleites talked at length about their decision to flee Cuba. Our interviews with Olga Goodwin provided details of her journey to the Brazilian embassy, where she was granted asylum. We also pulled information from her memoir. During interviews with Cuban historian Enrique Encinosa, he revealed that his father provided a safe house for Olga and her children as they eluded the secret police.

CHAPTER 47

Our account of Morgan's incarceration in La Cabaña and his March 1961 trial comes from numerous sources, including transcripts of interviews with Pedro Ossorio and Edmundo Amado Consuegra. We also interviewed journalist Henry Raymont, who covered the trial for United Press International. We reviewed Morgan's last letters to his mother and Olga, and we examined historical documents, including the trial transcripts (translated by Donald Cellini, former Spanish professor, Adrian College). In addition, we drew from news stories and Olga's memoir, which described her escape from the Brazilian embassy in a desperate attempt to reach Morgan in Camagüey. Our account of Loretta Morgan's frantic attempt to save her son's life came from a number of sources, including the transcript of an interview with her in the 1980s, as well as documents and letters revealing her appeals to congressional and religious leaders on her son's behalf.

Chapter 48

We drew from a number of interviews with people who were in La Cabaña the night Morgan was executed, among them Hiram Gonzalez and Pedro Ossorio (tape-recorded in 1983). We also reviewed historical documents and an account written by the Reverend John Joseph McKniff, the priest who heard Morgan's last confession and then escorted him to the execution wall. McKniff described Morgan's death by firing squad. Among the documents were Morgan's letters to his mother.

"I have made my peace with God," he wrote from his cell. "I can accept whatever happens with my mind clear and my spirit strong."

Our account of Olga's arrest was drawn from our extensive interviews with her as well as her memoir written in 1982.

BIBLIOGRAPHY

Books

Anderson, John Lee. *Che Guevara: A Revolutionary Life*. New York: Grove Press, 1997.

Bethel, Paul D. *The Losers*. New Rochelle, NY: Arlington House, 1969.

Bonachea, Ramón L., and Marta San Martin. *The Cuban Insurrection 1952–1959*. New Brunswick, NJ: Transaction Books, 1974.

Castañeda, Jorge G. *Companero: The Life and Death of Che Guevara*. New York: Alfred A. Knopf, 1997.

Castro, Fidel. *Che: A Memoir*. New York: Ocean Press, 2005.

de la Cova, Antonio Rafael. *The Moncada Attack: Birth of the Cuban Revolution*. Columbia: University of South Carolina Press, 2007.

Dorschner, John, and Roberto Fabricio. *The Winds of December*. New York: Coward, McCann & Geoghegan, 1980.

English, T. J. *Havana Nocturne: How the Mob Owned Cuba . . . and Then Lost It to the Revolution*. New York: William Morrow, 2008.

Escalante, Fabián: *The Secret War: CIA Covert Operations Against Cuba 1959–1962*. New York: Ocean Press, 1995.

Guevara, Ernesto Che. *Guerrilla Warfare*. 3rd ed. Wilmington, DE: Scholarly Resources, Inc., 1997.

Kelly, John J. *Father John Joseph McKniff, O.S.A.* Rome, Postulator General's Office, Order of St. Augustine, 1999.

Mallin, Jay, and Robert K Brown. *MERC: American Soldiers of Fortune*. New York: MacMillan Publishing Co., 1979.

Matthews, Herbert L. *The Cuban Story*. New York: George Braziller, 1961.

Paterson, Thomas G. *Contesting Castro: The United States and the Triumph of the Cuban Revolution*. New York: Oxford University Press, 1994.

Ryan, Henry Butterfield. *The Fall of Che Guevara: A Story of Soldiers, Spies, and Diplomats*. New York: Oxford University Press, 1998.

Shetterly, Aran. *The Americano: Fighting with Castro for Cuba's Freedom.* Chapel Hill, NC: Algonquin Books, 2007.

Verdeja, Sam, and Guillermo Martinez. *Cubans: An Epic Journey, the Struggle of Exiles for Truth and Freedom.* St. Louis: Reedy Press, 2011.

Von Tunzelmann, Alex. *Red Heat: Conspiracy, Murder, and the Cold War in the Caribbean.* New York: Henry Holt and Company, 2011.

Weiss, Mitch, and Kevin Maurer. *Hunting Che: How a US Special Forces Team Helped Capture the World's Most Famous Revolutionary.* New York: Penguin Group, 2013.

Archives and Documents

Cemetery records, Colón Cemetery, Havana, William Alexander Morgan, Jesús Carreras, 1961–1971.

CIA, Confidential, Summary of Counter-Revolutionary Plot. August 8–17, 1959.

———, Invasion of Cuba, September 1, 1959.

Escuela Normal para Maestros de Las Villas, República de Cuba Ministerio de Educación, Olga Maria Rodriguez Farinas, Titulo de Maestro Normal, March 16, 1959.

FBI, Miami, Confidential, Internal Security, Background Investigation, Neutrality Matter, May 21, 1959–March 14, 1960, Leman Stafford.

———, report to FBI Director J. Edgar Hoover, Cuban Rebel Activity in Cuba, 30th of November Movement, April 10, 1961.

FBI, New York, SAC to FBI Director J. Edgar Hoover, Dominican Republic, Trujillo bounty on Morgan, February 3, 1961.

Goodwin, Olga (Morgan), 150 pages of handwritten and typed notes (Spanish and English), describing her background, the revolution, and her life with William Alexander Morgan, 1981–84.

Iglesia Parroquial del Vedado, Havana, baptismal certificate, Loretta de la Caridad, May 9, 1960.

Morgan, William Alexander, letters to Loretta Morgan (1958, 1961), William Morgan Jr. (1958), Ann Morgan (1958), and Olga Morgan (1961).

National Archives and Records Administration, Washington, DC. This archive includes Central Intelligence Agency, US Army, and

Defense Department documents and military intelligence files related to William Morgan, Fidel Castro, and Ernesto "Che" Guevara's guerrilla war in Cuba and the US government's response.

Ohio Department of Health, Division of Vital Statistics, original birth certificate, William Alexander Morgan, St. John's Hospital, Cleveland, April 19, 1928.

Trial Records of William Alexander Morgan, La Cabaña, Regular Council of War, Captain Jorge Robreño Marieges, president of tribunal, March 10, 1961.

US Army Intelligence, report to FBI Director, US Citizens in Cuban Government Positions, March 11, 1960.

US Immigration and Naturalization Service, report to FBI Director J. Edgar Hoover, Loss of Citizenship (CO-1085-C), March 14, 1960.

US State Department, *Foreign Relations of the United States, 1958–1960*, Volume IV, Cuba, Document 469.

US State Department, Foreign Service, telegram from Ambassador Philip Bonsal to State Department in Washington, DC, warning of conspiracy to overthrow Castro by Dominican leader Rafael Trujillo, with "William Alexander Morgan reportedly key factor" in the plot, July 31, 1959.

———, letter from US Ambassador Philip Bonsal to Assistant Secretary of State for Inter-American Affairs Richard Rubottom, about deteriorating relations between Cuba and United States, December 2, 1959.

———, Memorandum of a Conversation, William A. Wieland, US Rep. Adam Clayton Powell, March 12, 1959.

———, telegram from US Ambassador Philip Bonsal to State Department in Washington, DC, about strained relations between Cuba and United States, October 6, 1959.

———, telegram from US embassy in Chile to US embassy in Cuba, confusion over US disclosure to Fidel Castro on Trujillo conspiracy, August 12, 1959.

Periodicals

Albarelli, H. P., Jr. "William Morgan: Patriot or Traitor?" WorldNet Daily.com (2002).

Branson, Robert. "Frogs in New Command of Toledo Major in Cuba." *Toledo Blade,* April 11, 1960. http://www.latinamericanstudies.org/morgan/Morgan-04-11-60.htm.

Driscoll, Amy. "US Reclaims Citizen Who Led Cuban Rebel Fighters." *Miami Herald*, April 13, 2007.

Eaton, Tracey, "Widow Pushes for Remains of Yankee Commander." *Dallas Morning News*, March 31, 2002.

Flick, Jim. "The Ordeal of Frank Emmick." *Toledo Blade Sunday Magazine*, February 3, 1980.

Grann, David. "The Yankee Comandante: A Story of Love, Revolution, and Betrayal." *New Yorker*, May 28, 2012.

Havana Post. "US Turns Down Morgan Citizenship Request." February 5, 1959.

Matthews, Herbert L. "Cuban War Aided by Second Front." *New York Times*, April 3, 1958.

Miami Herald. "Dockworker Set Ship Blast in Havana, American Claims." March 7, 1960.

———. "Once Cuban Hero, Buried as 'Traitor.'" March 11, 1961.

Revolución. "Comerciaremos con el Mundo Entero. Roa." July 26, 1959.

Sallah, Michael. "Cuba's Yankee Comandante." *Toledo Blade*, March 3–5, 2002.

Schultz, Randy. "In Pursuit of Dreams." *Palm Beach Post*, November 4–8, 1979.

Toledo Blade. "Castro Names Toledoan to Military Post." January 5, 1959.

———. "Cuba Cancels US Tour by Morgan." March 4, 1959.

———. "Cuban Army Discloses Arrest of Major Morgan, Ex-Toledoan." October 22, 1960.

———. "Ex-Toledoan Reported in Cuban Prison." November 16, 1960.

———. "Ex-Toledoan to Tell Cuba Story in City." February 27, 1959.

———. "Leader of Castro's Jungle Fighters Wants to Return Home to Toledo." January 5, 1959.

———. "Morgan Buried in Cuban Crypt, Fugitive Wife Stays in Hiding." March 13, 1961.

———. "Morgan of Toledo Fights to Retain His Citizenship." September 6, 1959.

———. "Morgan's Widow Seized in Cuba." March 18, 1961.

———. "Toledoan's Death in Cuba Detailed." August 2, 1963.

———. "William Morgan." June 20, 1963.

Toledo Times. "Toledoan Held in Solitary, Havana Hears." November 17, 1960.

———. "Morgan Killed As Anti-Red, His Note Says." March 17, 1961.

———. "Quitting US Rights, Toledo Man Confirms." September 25, 1959.

Velazquez, Jose Sergio. "Llevado W. Morgan a Juicio." *El Mundo*, March 10, 1961.

INDEX